BALANCING ON THE EDGE

Resilience Without Burnout

Marina Bezuglova

While books are designed for general use, please consider the following safety precautions: Ensure that the content of this book is appropriate for the intended age group. Keep this product out of reach of young children unless specifically designed for their age group. Supervision is recommended for children under 3 years of age due to potential risks such as small detachable elements, sharp corners, or the possibility of paper cuts. Avoid exposure to fire, heat sources, or water to maintain product integrity and prevent hazards.

EU Conformity Declaration
This product complies with the following safety regulations and standards to ensure consumer safety and product quality: Regulation (EU) 2023/988 of the European Parliament and of the Council on General Product Safety (GPSR): The Consumer Product Safety Improvement Act (CPSIA), Section 101. The Californian Safe drinking water and toxic enforcement act. (Proposition 65) EN71-Part 1: Mechanical and Physical Properties EN71-Part 2: Flammability EN71-Part 3 Migration of certain elements.

Published and Manufactured by Softwood Books
EU Responsible person: Maddy Glenn
Office 2, Wharfside House, Prentice Road, Stowmarket, Suffolk, IP14 1RD
www.softwoodbooks.com
hello@softwoodbooks.com

EU Rep:
Authorised Rep Compliance Ltd., Ground Floor, 71 Lower Baggot Street, Dublin, D02 P593, Ireland
www.arccompliance.com
info@arccompliance.com

Text © Marina Bezuglova, 2025

All rights reserved.

Without limiting the rights under copyright reserved above, no part of this publication may be reproduced, stored, or introduced into a retrieval system, or transmitted, in any form or by any means (electronic, mechanical, photocopying, recording or otherwise) without the prior written permission of both the copyright owners and the publisher of this book. This book was created without the use of artificial intelligence tools. The author does not grant permission for this manuscript to be used for training AI models or other machine learning purposes.

Paperback ISBN: 978-989-33-7462-7

CONTENTS

Foreword — 5
The Mental Trauma of the 20s.... — 7

Part 1. The Many Faces of Stress — 10
Stress and Burnout vs. Balance and Well-being — 10
Reward System — 18
Stress is Wonderful and Terrible ... — 24
    The Positive Effects of Stress — 26
    The Damaging Effects of Stress — 35
Is it a Lot of Stress or is it Just Right? — 42
    Life Upheavals Lead to Illness ... But Not Always — 43
    How to Support Yourself In an Era of Change and Stress... — 47
Watch Out! Work! — 49
    All Mixed Up: New Challenges and Traditional Stressors — 52
    Stress in entrepreneurs — 57
Why Aren't We Equal Before Stress? — 64
    Individual Stressors — 65
    Strategies to Protect Against Stress — 71

Part 2. Professional Burnout — 84
Why Do We Burn Out? — 86
Six Reasons to Burnout at Work and Six Strategies to Prevent Burnout — 95
The Neurophysiology of Burnout — 113
Burnout as a process — 117
    Stages of Burnout — 119
How Do You Get Out of Burnout? — 127
    Change What We Can — the Situation, the Interpretation, and Even Ourselves... — 127
    It All Depends on the Stage of Burnout — 140
How Can Employers Take Care of Employees? — 147
    Programmes to Prevent and Address Burnout — 152
Stress Management Algorithm — 155

Part 3. Mastering Balance: The Path to a Burnout-Free Life   158

Neuroplasticity and Epigenetics — the Key to Health and Happiness   160

Mindfulness as the Foundation of Wellbeing   165

Empathy and Social Connections   177

Goals, Values and Meanings   183

What Truly Matters   194

List of references   196

FOREWORD

The idea to write this book was born after the new pandemic reality changed our lives, and everyone around us started talking about burnout. We found ourselves defenseless not only against the coronavirus infection, but also against major changes — in lifestyle, in work, and in home life. Then it turned out that the challenges of the 20s were not just limited to the pandemic, and we faced geopolitical tensions, economic hardship, and the number of crises in our lives did not diminish. There is too much anxiety, novelty, and uncertainty, and already we call the 20s of our century the 'nervous 20s'. Experts report a serious deterioration of mental health, people complain about stress and burnout, and employers are thinking about how to keep their teams working under difficult conditions.

The topic of mental health has suddenly become of interest to everyone far beyond professional medical circles, and I have to speak on this topic more and more often, including at business conferences. Because it has become clear that one must first learn to manage stress and acquire resistance to external shocks, and then talk about successful business, self-realisation, and a prosperous life.

The topic has become personally close to me, as in recent years at work I had to face cases of employee burnout, provide psychological help, and come up with programmes that would prevent burnout. More and more conscious effort has to be made to maintain internal resources, and not fall apart from negative news and dramatic changes in life.

After my speeches I often receive questions: is it possible to get out of burnout, and cope with this condition without the help of a doctor or a psychotherapist? Less often they ask: how can I learn not to burn out?

And since there are no simple answers to these questions, I decided to write a book to tell the whole truth about stress and burnout on the basis of available research, as well as to think about what to do at the first signs of burnout, how to pull ourselves out of this state, and how to learn to live without burnout at all — no matter how difficult the context we have to face. Whether it is realistic, you will be able to conclude after reading this book. And who knows? Maybe you will learn to think a little differently about yourself and the world around you, and it will lead you to greater resilience and inner balance.

The knowledge I will share is based on research in medicine, social psychology, mindfulness practice, and coaching work with people who were at a dead end, experiencing burnout, and yet found their way to happiness and wellbeing.

To whom would I not recommend this book? It is definitely not for those who know how to balance in the most difficult circumstances, never falling into anxiety, worry, or apathy; who know how to rest, and do it effectively for their health and productivity; and who know how to support their loved ones or employees facing burnout. In general, this book is not for those who already know everything, and know how to use this knowledge for their own benefit and for the wellbeing of others.

If you have fallen into a state where you feel physically and psychologically exhausted; if you feel stressed out and can't even rest; if you want to quit your job because everything is annoying and boring; if you have a feeling of deadlock and feel that your 'battery is at zero'; or maybe you are concerned about this state of your employees or your loved ones — if any of these things are familiar to you, then you should read this book. It has a lot of information that you can relate to your internal situation, and chart a path for change.

I believe that information is useful if it becomes a signal for action and behavioural change. There are no magic pills, and you are unlikely to find them in this book. But there is a chance that while reading, suddenly there will be an inner insight; something will resonate and become an incentive to change. And if you take the first step, you will definitely want to take the second step, and then a chain reaction of changes in the direction of your own needs and wellbeing will start. And if that happens, then the purpose of this book will be fulfilled!

The Mental Trauma of the 20s....

Actually, we are used to living in an era of change, because change is everywhere — crises, job changes, changes in personal life, and simply daily news that no one expected. A great metaphor to help you feel afloat in a world of raging events is the surfer. You're in the ocean, you're just about to be thrown off by a wave, but it all depends on your skills. If you have learnt to stand well on a board, learning on some calm body of water, then later, in the stormy ocean, you will stand on a board and surf quite confidently. So, we all learnt to ride in the familiar ocean of everyday life. But it turns out that we were not ready for big storms.

The COVID-19 pandemic was extraordinary for the challenges it brought: first, we learned of a new virus that is terribly contagious, causes severe complications, is highly lethal, and requires hospitalisation for a significant proportion of those infected.

Fear and worry about health — our own and our loved ones' — was the number one challenge faced. As time went on, it became clear that these worries were not unfounded — many had experienced severe illness personally or with loved ones, and subsequently experienced a long recovery, which medical professionals now refer to as 'Post-covid'. And almost everyone knew people who had died from covid.

A few weeks after we learnt about the insidiousness of the virus, the whole world was already quarantined. And that was challenge number two, as we had to dramatically change our way of life, and learn to do everything from the comfort of our own homes. We had to get reliable internet for work at home, organise workplaces for the adult members of the family, provide computers for everyone, and spread them out in different spaces inside the house.

In a short period of time, the world had changed and new orders had been established: social distancing, closed borders, shuttered public institutions, and prohibition of travelling without urgent need. We had to significantly change our behaviour and urgently acquire new habits — from strict hygiene rules, to building a full cycle of all activities inside our own homes, including not only work but also social and leisure activities. Our minds were completely unprepared for this. And according to the evolutionary habit of reacting to everything new as a threat, the brain habitually deployed the stress response. What else could it be? Our beautiful world — with open borders, plans for holidays, and flights to any part of the world when you wanted it — was collapsing. It seemed that our conquered world, of open communication and intensive travelling, would always be with us. But no: it turns out that any opportunities can disappear at a moment's notice, and you have to plan a holiday somewhere in your backyard — and it's good if your backyard is close to nature, which is known to be healing and fulfilling.

But once we were at home, working remotely, we realised that we were not particularly good at regulating our workload; all the contexts got mixed up, and it began to seem as if we were at home all the time — and at the same time, at work. That's why no one slammed the lid of the laptop at five or six in the evening, but turned to it until late at night, while there were still unanswered questions, requests in the mail, unresolved cases. And there was no end to the questions, because things had changed at work too: business processes had to be transferred online, all employees had to be provided with everything they needed to perform their work functions from home, virtual communication had to be established, and somehow the business must be maintained — which for some had fallen dramatically, and for others was experiencing an unprecedented rise due to the sharp demand for online services — but both of these scenarios created tension and additional stress. On a subconscious level, this endless work was a little distracting from anxious thoughts and uncertainty, from questions of, "What's next?", but in fact it was a drain of energy without replenishment — and even without understanding. And where could we get our energy, when we couldn't even leave the house to go for a walk in the park, or to meet our loved ones?

In addition to the mixing of home and work contexts, many were experiencing fears and concerns about maintaining their jobs and incomes, as changes in consumer demand quickly affected many industries.

Numerous sociological studies from 2020-2021 show the magnitude of the pandemic's impact on people's health and wellbeing. A Gallup international survey (Gallup, 2021) shows that 45% of people reported that the pandemic had seriously affected their lives, 32% reported losing their job or business, and stress levels and negative emotions hit record highs in the last decade.

The Ipsos international study in December 2020 confirmed the fact that the majority of working adults experienced stress in the pandemic; due to personal reasons, family circumstances, feelings of isolation, worries about keeping their jobs, and earning (Ipsos, 2020). Such a powerful set of stressors, that hit people in different countries at the same time, is a major psychological crisis on a planetary scale.

During the 2020 quarantine period, Qualtrix surveyed 2,000 employees in seven countries (Qualtrix, 2020) and concluded that mental disruption affected all groups — entrepreneurs, company employees, executives — with an average of 42% reporting negative changes. No one managed to sit back in the bunker; everyone needed to adapt. An interesting fact was noted by the researchers: the quarantine was better tolerated by those employees who were actively communicated with by managers who showed concern for their health, and were interested in their wellbeing and problems. The loss of social ties at work, including our regular small talks in the kitchen or office corridors, contributed to the growing feelings of loneliness, anxiety, and depression, and they had to be compensated somehow. It turned out that managers, supervisors, and group leaders can seriously influence the psychological mood of the team. Previously, being a 'good guy' was not a profession, but in the new reality this quality has become critical for a professional manager.

Yet we have to admit that mental health has become another casualty of the pandemic, along with economic losses and physical health impairment. Nearly one in three experienced anxiety and depression — 32% and 34%, respectively (Nader Salari et al, 2020). And the decline in mental health was greater in groups that had more mental health problems before the pandemic — women, young people, and low-income groups (World Happiness Report, 2021). Thus, existing inequalities in mental wellbeing have increased, and the topics of equal rights and inclusive societies have become even more relevant.

The pandemic has affected the mental health of so many people on the planet, that it has become a hot topic for every individual, employer, and society as a whole. There is an undoubted benefit to this: we have become more vocal about the problem of mental disorders, unravelling the tangle of contradictions, and finding solutions to the issue. This is the right time to reflect on the value of life, the importance of empathy and support for each other, the need to take care of ourselves, and to become resilient.

The challenges of the pandemic proved to be a kind of inoculation of resilience, as the following years brought geopolitical risks, new challenges, new uncertainty, and anxiety.

We are not immune to surprises, to shocks, to the fact that life turns out to be much more complicated than we expect. But we can become more flexible and open to change, and thus more resilient and sustainable in an unstable and poorly predictable world. Life is not getting any easier, and it is clear that we need to be prepared for the variety of challenges that lie ahead.

PART 1. THE MANY FACES OF STRESS

Stress and Burnout vs. Balance and Well-being

The term 'stress' was first introduced by Walter Cannon in his works where he described the universal stress response of 'Fight-or-Flight'.

Hans Selye formalised the biological model of stress by publishing his first work on the general adaptation syndrome in 1936. He discovered that organisms react in a similar way to a variety of unfavourable factors, which disturb the constancy of the internal environment of the organism. Later, the scientist called adaptation syndrome the 'stress response' of the organism and defined stress as "The organism's non-specific response to any demand placed upon it" (Selye H., 1974).

Selye distinguished three stages of adaptation syndrome:

1. Anxiety reaction, when the body's adaptive capabilities are mobilised.
2. The resistance stage, when the organism engages all of its adaptive responses to return to a new state of balance.
3. The stage of exhaustion, when the organism exhausts adaptation resources and the stressor continues to act. At this stage, the damaging effect of stress is manifested, which is expressed in the disruption of the work of various organs and systems.

The three-phase model of stress has led to some important conclusions — firstly, the stress response is not a bad thing, it helps the organism to adapt to new conditions, i.e. it helps it to survive, and secondly that adaptive energy is not endless, and its depletion can lead to serious health problems, including death.

As a result, Selye introduced the concept of 'eustress', or good stress, and 'distress', or bad stress. The idea of the positive aspect of stress was related to the fact that the body responds in a universal way to any stimulus that leads to the mobilisation of the organism — both positive and negative. If the organism has sufficient resources to cope with the challenges and the stressors themselves are of limited duration, then such stress does not lead to exhaustion and damage to the organism, but has a very useful adaptive value.

Let's imagine an extremely joyful event — for example, a wedding or the birth of a child. The events themselves bring positive emotions, sometimes quite strong, which move the organism to a higher energy level. If you add to this the change of lifestyle, habits, and expansion of responsibilities, it is clear that for the body it will be a challenge, and will take some time to adapt to a new way of life, to create a new balance. Such stress will only be beneficial, as it will lead to the expansion of the boundaries of life, the creation of new skills, the development of family ties, and personal development.

Or, for example, when the organism fights adverse environmental conditions — extreme cold or heat. These challenges also trigger a stress response, but if the exposure is short-term and the intensity remains within the organism's adaptive capacity, it can be considered 'positive' stress. This type of stress trains the body, enhancing its resilience and ability to withstand various external factors.

Damaging effects of stress come if stressogenic factors continue and continue to act, depleting the adaptive capabilities of the body. In this case we will speak about 'distress' — chronic stress — as well as burnout syndrome, which is a consequence of chronic stress.

In general, it is quite difficult for us to live without stress at all. When nothing happens, there is no incentive to change. In this case, boredom sets in; we cannot use internal resources or skills, and we do not develop — and this also leads to burn out. 'Bored out' is in fact no better than burn out.

Here are a couple of sketches from real life:

1. A young specialist decides to leave the company. This decision was preceded by many months of extreme pressure at work, combined with additional serious stress outside of work — education and exams. As a result, everything came to a head, when it was no longer possible to continue working at the same pace, and a holiday did not lead to a reset. After the short holiday, a clear desire to quit work was formed, so as not to return to the excessive workload — the mere thought of which caused a feeling of nausea. In addition, there was an intention to take care of health, which began to demand attention. It should be noted that the initial stage of work in the company was assessed very positively by the employee — the work brought pleasure — but the excessive workload for a long period of time wiped out all the benefits and happy moments.

2. A manager with excellent expertise and experience gets a job in a large corporation, where she hopes to further develop her professional skills, do interesting and large-scale projects, and grow and develop, realising her potential and benefiting people. But, as sometimes happens, it is not possible to immediately land a big project, and for the time being she has to get involved in one project or another. Time goes by but nothing changes. The manager feels bad because of lack of demand, gets upset because of deceived expectations, and inside begins the process of self-assessment; doubts about her abilities, and lacks understanding of what to do next. The state of uncertainty and lack of real challenge, multiplied by natural boiling energy and ambition, gradually leads to a deterioration of health, including reduced immunity and frequent colds. The manager decides to quit the company to stop destroying herself.

Two different situations; in one case, burnout and the need to change something in one's life, was caused by the workload exceeding the psychological and physical resources of a person. And in the other case, boredom, lack of demand, and an inability to realise one's abilities led to a severe psychological crisis with lowered self-esteem, and then to physical health disorders. The reasons are different — in one case external, the other internal — but the body experiences the same stress, and responds with diseases when this state lasts for a long time. It seems a bit strange when they say that illnesses are the body's defense response to help us cope with challenges and stresses, but they really are — if the body doesn't hear and listen to itself, more obvious symptoms of ill-health appear, which often become the main trigger for change. Any illness is always a reason to ask yourself, "Why am I having this? What is it signalling? What do I need to change to regain my health?"

The two cases described above, incidentally, have different endings with regards to the decision to leave. In the first case, after negotiations within the company, the young employee remained in the team but his working conditions and workload were revised. Everything was resolved in a conversation with the manager, which took place after the resignation letter was written. The case was happily resolved, which implied both real changes in work and improvement of psychological state; a return to inspiration and pleasure from work. As practice shows, whether we reach the stage of burnout or not depends, among other things, on social resources — the ability to seek help, to discuss our problems with significant people on whom the solution of the issue may depend, as well as the ability to speak frankly about our needs and feelings.

In the second case, the manager did leave the company to start a new chapter in life. But even in this case, the way back to a sense of flow and inspiration was not cut off. Obviously, if the corporation had managed to interest an experienced employee in an interesting and large-scale project, this would have been a powerful motivation to continue work with engagement and high productivity.

Sometimes it seems to us that some unpleasant situation is a dead end. However, practice shows that it is not. It is enough to turn your gaze in another direction, to stop leaning against the wall, and a new solution will be found, and with it comes motivation, inspiration, and a sense of flow. Of course, this is only feasible if burnout has not reached the point when cognitive functions decrease — which sometimes even requires a long sanatorium rehabilitation, after which it will be possible to gradually return to normal life.

But that's why we are given the awareness to react to the first signals of burnout without bringing ourselves to illness; at the first alarm bells to change our lives, and return ourselves to the state of motivation and vitality.

To feel happy, we need a state of flow in which we utilise our best abilities, meet challenges, and achieve results that are satisfying and empowering. Here, it is appropriate to mention Mihai Csikszentmihalyi's flow model (Csikszentmihalyi M., 2002), which complements Hans Selye's biological model of stress and justifies that we need some level of stress to cope with challenges and obstacles, to become more resilient to changes and open our potential.

According to this concept, we achieve happiness when our skills are sufficient to cope with the challenges we have to overcome. If the number of challenges is too high, internal resources are not enough to cope with these challenges and anxiety sets in; if this state is experienced for a long time, we get chronic stress, accompanied by a feeling of burnout. For example; you have been working for six months without days off, to cope with the workload that has been formed at a new workplace. Even if you like your work very much, in such a rhythm, someday you will inevitably face the fact that your organism will revolt, go into survival mode, and will shut down different organs and systems step-by-step in order to save the rest of your energy, telling you to rest. Even if it turns out to be your dream job, if the demands are excessive and exceed your capabilities, you will inevitably hit a limit — loss of motivation and energy, anxiety, loss, and further along the downward spiral of chronic stress — if you don't change the situation.

On the other hand, lack of challenges and interesting tasks make us bored, feel unclaimed, as if we are losing our accumulated potential — and this dissatisfaction creates another kind of internal conflict. The result is still stress, tension, and burnout from the lack of external stimuli, but with off-the-scale internal tension. The peculiarity of a human being is that we develop a stress response not only to external stimuli, but also to internal ones — like negative and disturbing thoughts that trigger destructive emotions. We may react to an unpleasant thought as if we are in a cage with a predator and expect imminent doom. Threats to health and life are not so common in the modern context, but self-doubt and sadness over unfulfilled expectations are aplenty.

As we can see, our tunnel of flow state is not so wide; where it is possible to feel happy, prosperous, and fulfilled when our resources and skills are balanced by challenges. And pay attention — if there are few skills and not enough inner resource, then the scope of challenges you can handle will be limited. By training and adaptation, step-by-step, we gradually develop our skills — professional, social, and psychological — and become ready to meet larger challenges that stimulate further growth and development. The state of flow can also be explained from the neurobiological point of view: adrenaline and noradrenaline help us to overcome difficulties, learn, and reach new heights, because any achievement requires energy and activity; on the other hand, we experience the anticipation of pleasure, and positive emotions from achievements — and this feeling of happiness is given to us by the dopamine and serotonin systems of the brain. The result is a sense of flow, a feeling of ease despite the effort involved.

So, what to draw on to catch the flow of positive developmental 'stress' without burning out or getting bored? It will be appropriate here to cite the definition of wellbeing as 'a balance between the challenges one faces and the resources one has to cope with those demands' (Dodge R., et al., 2012).

It turns out that for wellbeing it is important to learn how to balance challenges and resources. Is this possible in principle?

By recognising that our wellbeing, like a scale, depends on a balance of challenges and inner resources, we can adjust both scales. By increasing or decreasing the number of challenges — which, let's be honest, we often create for ourselves — we can choose the level of stress we can handle. But we can also work on increasing our internal resources, which is much more promising in a world where we are often faced with crises that no one expected.

Internal resources include physical, social, and psychological resources. They are essentially our personal potential, social capital, and psychological maturity. Internal resources determine our ability to make the most of opportunities and minimise the harm caused by adverse circumstances. It turns out that we ourselves can influence wellbeing to a very large extent.

Internal resources depend on individual talents and experience, but these resources can be consciously developed. Our behaviour and ways of reacting to circumstances depend on habits, and habitual reactions are based on sustainable neural connections. If we habitually get upset at the slightest setback, or if we flare up with indignation at a remark someone has made, we will be afraid to try new things so as not to cause additional pain, and we will close ourselves off from new connections for fear of being misunderstood. As a result, over time we will consistently try to reduce the number of challenges in our lives, shrinking back into a small, confined world where nothing seems to threaten us; our lack of coping ability causes us to avoid anything that requires overcoming. But life is not without challenges — it still throws up surprises and sometimes stuns us with shocking news. And if there's no training in coping, inevitably any stress turns into distress and health problems. Fortunately, at any age, we have the ability to change habits, build new neural networks, and gain resilience and inner strength.

Look at some outstanding people — Richard Branson, Steve Jobs, and many other extraordinary people of our time. What, first of all, defines the scale of their personality? It is the challenges they create for themselves, their conquering of new heights, and not stopping because of failures. Through daring, they expand their lives and contribute to changing the lives of humanity.

Reading Richard Branson's book Losing My Virginity, where the author talks frankly about his path in business — ups and downs, risky hobbies, and fantastic plans — you begin to understand the formula of successful entrepreneurship: without bold dreams, daring intentions, risk appetite, and tolerance for failure, it is difficult to get a great result. He was already the owner of the unique Virgin brand — which combines disparate successful businesses — when he conceived the idea of creating Virgin Galactic, a company aimed at tourist suborbital space flights and launching artificial satellites. Frankly speaking, it seemed to me that this idea was quite a fantastical one and, besides, a number of failures did not favour the rapid development of the project. But in 2021 there was a suborbital space flight, in which the founder of the project himself participated. It is possible to discuss for a long time why it is necessary and to whom it is useful, but one thing is obvious: there are people who push the boundaries of the possible, and thus show the way to future achievements and breakthroughs.

Not everyone is able to achieve the dreams that large-scale personalities realise, but it is not required. Remember the rule of correlation between challenges and internal resources: there is no point in inventing challenges that you cannot cope with. But step-by-step, millimetre by millimetre, changing yourself, changing your ways of reacting, expanding the boundaries of what is possible — this is the way to manage your wellbeing.

What the pandemic and other current challenges have taught us a little is to stop focusing on what we cannot change. Experience has shown that the quickest to adapt to constraints and uncertainty, are those who accept the new conditions and focus on managing those areas that are within their control. For example: you cannot leave the house because of a quarantine, but you can influence how your life at home will be organised and how you will perceive the new living conditions.

Internal locus of control means the willingness to take responsibility for what is happening and to make one's own efforts for change. But to do this, you have to dare not to complain about circumstances, but to start creating those circumstances yourself.

"Men are disturbed not by things, but by the views which they take of them." — these words belong to Epictetus. The freedom to perceive events belongs to us under any circumstances. Recently, I have noticed that the philosophy of the Stoics is gaining popularity (the most famous representatives are Marcus Aurelius, Epictetus, and Seneca). For them, the ideal is a person who courageously and with dignity accepts external circumstances, while having the inner freedom to manage his own perception of the situation and to develop his personality in every possible way, despite the circumstances. This philosophy has proved to be very useful in modern circumstances; helping you to manage your life, even when you do not know what will happen tomorrow or in a month.

There are also many studies which show that a sense of control has a positive impact on life satisfaction, job satisfaction, and psycho-emotional status, and also contributes to faster adaptation to unpleasant circumstances, whether they be personal, changes at work, or economic losses. It is hardest to find control points in situations of chronic stress and burnout. In this state, people most often do not see any way out, or a possibility to influence anything at all. Sometimes they simply lack the energy and flexibility to look around and find a new solution — though there always is a solution. You can change many things in your life, including your country of residence and place of work, not to mention the freedom to perceive and interpret circumstances in a more positive way. Often, coaching or self-coaching can significantly help to push the limits of what is within the zone of personal control. And then the traditional question arises: "Is it possible?"

I like the motto: change what you can change in life, accept what you cannot change, and learn to distinguish the former from the latter. Learning to distinguish the first from the second is not easy, but it is very important. Perhaps we learn it all our lives. And this is the main wisdom of life: to learn to react correctly to circumstances, to change oneself, to change circumstances — or to accept them, if it is impossible to do otherwise. Such a skill is not formed overnight; it involves developing awareness, critical thinking, the ability to manage emotions, and cultivating a positive attitude towards oneself and others.

Key Takeaways:

- Stress is a useful reaction of the body, which allows us to adapt to life's changing conditions, and promotes personal development and growth through overcoming difficulties. The damaging effect of stress occurs when the scale of challenges exceeds the stock of internal resources. In this case, 'distress' or chronic stress occurs, as well as burnout syndrome as a consequence.
- Internal resources (physical, social, and psychological) depend on individual inclinations and acquired experience, but these resources can also be trained as a skill.
- The most resilient and adaptable people are those who focus on areas that are within their control. They are willing to take responsibility and make efforts to change.
- The formula for wisdom is to change what you can change in life, be able to accept what you can't change, and learn to distinguish the former from the latter.

Reward System

Feelings of inspiration and motivation have a lot to do with the production of neurotransmitters and the reward system. It makes sense to learn a little more about this system.

Imagine a gloomy autumn morning. Saturday. You are tired from the working week, you feel that you need a rest — a reboot — so you want to spend the day quietly, switch off your head, and indulge in some quiet relaxation. You are already planning how you will quietly and calmly recuperate after an intense week. And suddenly you get a call that today someone very significant to you is coming to visit, and spending time with this person always feels like a holiday; a friend, a relative — someone with whom you always feel good. Straight away, your level of mood rises and from nowhere there is energy which was not there 15 minutes ago, and you immediately want to prepare for the arrival of this important person in your life. The guest has not yet arrived, but energy and joy have already arisen in your soul — this is the reward system that is activated by the expectation of pleasure.

Behaviour and wellbeing are linked to the production of neurotransmitters, so understanding brain chemistry is in some ways the key to managing wellbeing. The neurotransmitter dopamine and the reward system are most associated with this area of behaviour and wellbeing.

The reward system is a set of brain structures that are involved in regulating behaviour through positive emotional responses. A major role in this system is played by dopaminergic neurons, which ensure the transmission of neural impulses using the neurotransmitter dopamine. Given the central role of dopamine in the reward system, it is sometimes referred to as the dopaminergic or dopamine system.

The activation of the reward system will occur universally, regardless of the type of stimulus — whether it is a chocolate bar, a date with a loved one, or the realisation of an important professional project. Dopamine will be synthesised in anticipation of pleasure, in any case. Surely you have noticed that when you fail to achieve what you have planned — a project does not progress, or the desired relationship does not develop — you want to sweeten the bitter pill of failure with something. In this case, everything that will predictably lead to the activation of the reward system comes into play: someone will eat a chocolate bar, someone will want to drink a glass of wine, and someone else will be distracted by an interesting film or a favourite hobby. There are many different ways, simple or complex, to energise yourself with dopamine. That said, it's a good idea to consciously choose the most rewarding ways for yourself.

There is such a concept in product development, of 'jobs to be done', when a product is created for a 'job to be done' — namely, to fulfil some need. And when we realise what need this thing fulfils, we can find a substitute for it, i.e. another thing that does the same job. For example, a cigarette may well fulfil the function of socialisation — it is important for you to go out for a break and socialise with your colleagues. Or perhaps you just need to relax and take regular breaks. That's why some smokers, having overcome nicotine cravings, return to the habit again, because they haven't found a substitute that fulfils the job that the cigarette was 'hired' to do. So it is with the dopamine boost; if you hang on to soap operas, or fixate on food every time you want to reward yourself, think about what else can create a sense of pleasure and reward. 'Jobs to be done' can be realised in many different ways, among which there are clearly those that are beneficial without the risk of harm.

Now let's take a closer look at how everything is organised in the rewards system. The main components are the ventral tegmentum and the nucleus accumbens (NAc). The ventral tegmentum is located in the midbrain, and is represented by a cluster of dopaminergic neurons. The outgrowths of these neurons penetrate all floors of the brain, from the ancient brain to the new cortical structures (neocortex). The main dopamine pathways of the brain start from the ventral tegmentum.

NAc is a group of neurons in the ventral part of the striatum. NAc receives information from the dopamine neurons of tegmentum, as well as from neurons in the prefrontal cortex, amygdala, and hippocampus. It receives information from these different structures and compares the result — how much the expectation of reward coincided with the pleasure received. Learning, and the formation of reinforcing signals of success, are associated with the work of the nucleus accumbens — if a behaviour resulted in a reward, this behaviour pattern will be approved for future reproduction.

The Brain's Major Dopamine Pathways.

1. The covering region (tegmentum) is connected to the limbic system: neuronal outgrowths go to the amygdala and hippocampus, as well as to the NAc. These connections form the mesolimbic dopamine pathway. This pathway is associated with feelings of desire, pleasure, and addiction.

2. The tegmentum extends neurons to the prefrontal cortex (PFC), and these connections form the mesocortical dopamine pathway, which is associated with learning and motivation. This pathway is involved in the formation of action plans.
3. Dopamine neurons also send outgrowths to brain regions associated with movement. The nigrostriatal pathway, which includes substantia nigra neurons, is associated with motor stimulation. It links the substantia nigra neurons to the dorsal striatum, which is involved in learning and habit formation. It is the dorsal striatum that helps us to create useful habits, for which later we no longer spend our will and energy but habitually perform a sequence of actions — for example, immediately after waking up we do exercises (if such a habit has been formed).

The dopamine system is a reward system that works mainly on the anticipation of pleasure. This anticipation activates the tegmentum neurons; they respond by releasing dopamine and sending impulses to other parts of the reward system, where the information is processed, a response is formed, and a behavioural act takes place. However, we do not always make a decision in favour of the expected reward. When we make decisions, we weigh the benefits against the possible losses. And while the NAc is responsible for evaluating rewards, the amygdala is responsible for evaluating losses. The amygdala scans the world around us for threats; the more active the amygdala is, the more negative situations it will predict, reducing the likelihood of deciding in favour of a reward.

From the amygdala and tegmentum, neural outgrowths also go in the opposite direction — to the nucleus accumbens and tegmentum. In this way, feedback is used to confirm the result obtained, in response to the expectation of reward. This is how the brain learns and shapes future expectations.

Robert Sapolsky, in his book Behave: The Biology of Humans at Our Best and Worst, describes a series of studies that examined how the dopamine response was shaped by comparing expectation and consequence. Monkeys were trained to receive either two or twenty units of reward, depending on the circumstances. If they received four or forty reward units in situations where the usual two or twenty were expected, in both cases dopamine levels jumped in response to the excessive outcome. And if they were given one or ten units of reward, it decreased accordingly. That is, the value of dopamine changed in a similar way for multiples of the gain. Thus, the response of the dopamine system increases if the outcome exceeds expectations, and decreases if the outcome is worse than what the brain has prepared for. And when the outcome meets expectations, the dopamine system stays where it is.

Now let's apply this biological law to real life and think about why perfectionists are always dissatisfied, and don't like to take risks or start something new. Their image of the result, their expectations, always exceed reality, and this does not provide positive reinforcement for the future — because the reward system is set up anticipating more than it can get. As a result, motivation decreases and the desire to do something disappears — because the result does not meet expectations. The reward system does not kick in if negative feedback has occurred too often in the repertoire of life experience.

Knowing how the reward system works, it becomes clear why dividing a big result into small tasks, and confirming the result of these small steps, helps us to move forward so well. The motivation system is constantly fuelled by small achievements, and as a result we keep trying to get this boost again and again. That's why it's so important to say to ourselves, "I'm doing great!" when we achieve any positive result, no matter how small.

Given the biological mechanism of positive reinforcement, it is clear that we need to be very careful about setting our own expectations. If your goals are very rigid and defined, the result will not always hit the target. When inconsistencies occur frequently, this is the path to disappointment, apathy, and the desire to give up, because a positive result does not happen. The broader the image of a good outcome, the more likely it is to receive positive reinforcement and continue on the path of achievement.

Motivation to fulfil goals is closely linked to the workings of the reward system and training. When there is a mismatch, and expectations are not reinforced by results, psychological problems begin — on the one hand, dissatisfaction, and on the other hand, bad habits can form as a substitute for rewards. It is known that alcohol and some drugs have a strong influence on the dopamine system, stimulating dopamine receptors as if replacing the natural ways of obtaining neurotransmitters of happiness. This artificial blow to the receptors leads to significant breakdowns in the system, and the result is a loss of sensitivity to natural pleasure stimuli.

However, in general, the pleasure habituation effect is a fairly universal response to repeated positive stimuli. We quickly get used to good things, and it takes more and more rewards to get pleasure. There's even a term called 'hedonic adaptation' or 'hedonic treadmill'; no matter what a person desires, however much, once they get what they want, they quickly lose interest in what they have achieved, and more and more new stimuli are required. You have dreamed of a beautiful, new car, and your dream has come true — but soon this car will become something ordinary, and not an object of constant joy. You dreamed of a new house, and now you have finally moved into it. After a while, this house will seem ordinary to you, and you will think of a new object for anticipation. And if you orientate to external stimuli of pleasure, this is a treadmill that will lead nowhere but to a thirst for more and more pleasures. Orientation to inner values, a sense of meaning, a sense of purpose, create a more complex structure of motivation, and bring more joy every day. And this level of pleasure can be maintained for a long time by orienting your life in the direction of some important goal. And here, we can't do without the involvement of the prefrontal cortex and its connection to the reward system.

The formation of intention for a purposeful activity is the result of an interaction between the prefrontal cortex (PFC), which is responsible for planning, and the reward system, which gives the dopamine. The PFC plans goals and objectives based on the benefit to the individual, and creates an intention. Next, the NAc and ventral tegmentum area need to be activated. But in order for the dopamine neurons to become excited, it is necessary to prove to the lower floor of the brain that the intentions of the prefrontal cortex are not only useful, but also pleasant. After all, only then will the reward and motivation system begin to work. This is why coaches so often ask their mentees: Why do you want this result? What good will it bring you? How will you feel when you get this result? By thinking through all the benefits, we make promises to the reward system that we are planning not only efforts and pain, but expect something pleasant as a result. Otherwise, it is unlikely that the ventral tegmentum will get excited about such plans and give you valuable dopamine for accomplishing them.

What happens in the case of chronic stress? When adaptation mechanisms are depleted, energy becomes scarce and, in this case, the upper floors of the brain responsible for planning and goals are switched off; the mesocortical pathway is damaged. In this case, one does not want to achieve anything; there is not enough energy to desire something. The brain saves energy and does not use it to fulfil long-term goals.

As burnout and chronic stress develop, the damaging effect of stress hormones on the dopamine system becomes more and more pronounced: dopamine becomes less and less available, the sensitivity of dopaminergic neurons to stimuli decreases.

As a result, anhedonia can develop, when the organism not only does not react to long-term goals, but is also unable to enjoy simple things that have always brought pleasure in the past, e.g. tasty food or good music. This is the next stage of burnout and a deep damage to the reward system, which affects both mesocortical and mesolimbic dopamine pathways.

It is important to be aware of your needs and intentions; to work to fulfil them but be sure to give yourself a break, not to get caught up in plans and tasks. You can reflect a little on where your energy is, what you want, why you need the result you are striving for. If you put your thoughts in order, you will have clarity and energy to move.

Key Takeaways:

- The reward system is a set of brain structures that are involved in regulating behaviour through positive emotional responses. Dopaminergic neurons and the neurotransmitter dopamine play a major role in this system.
- To keep you motivated, it is helpful to divide a long journey or large task into small steps and celebrate small victories. It is best to avoid setting rigid goals to avoid disappointment and loss of inspiration. The broader the image of a positive result, the more likely you are to receive positive reinforcement and continue on the path of achievement.
- Chronic stress has a damaging effect on the reward system; firstly, the brain saves energy for planning and goals and does not want to achieve anything. As chronic stress worsens, the joy from simple things that were pleasurable in the past may also disappear.
- Awareness and clarity about one's needs, goals, and intentions is a prerequisite for maintaining motivation and realising aims.

Stress is Wonderful and Terrible ...

Thanks to the work of twentieth-century physiologist Walter Kennon, the metaphorical definition of the stress response 'fight-or-flight' has entered common usage. The scientist showed the connection between the emotional and bodily reactions of the organism, in response to stressful stimuli. When the body feels threatened, there is an increased release of adrenaline; the emotional sphere reacts by experiencing feelings of fear or anger, which eventually forms a behavioural response in the form of fight or flight. Due to the stress response, the body mobilises energy, blood glucose levels rise, blood circulation increases, and as a result the muscular system is able to develop much greater strength than normal, thus increasing the chance of surviving the threat. In his book The Wisdom of the Body, Walter Cannon views the body's ability to cope with the effects of stressors as a positive adaptive response, which helps to maintain the constancy of the internal environment (or homeostasis) in response to changing conditions. Such a defense reaction of the organism is a manifestation of the body's wisdom.

As mentioned earlier, the biological model of stress was formulated by Hans Selye, who can rightly be called the godfather of stress theory. The basis for his discovery was laboratory experiments with rats, into which he injected crude and toxic extracts from the gland secretions of animals, and subsequently subjected the unfortunate rats to tests. To the scientist's surprise, regardless of the type of stressor, the exposure resulted in a stereotypical set of changes in the rats' bodies. He invariably noted increased activity of the adrenal cortex, atrophy of the thymus gland and lymph nodes, and the appearance of ulcers in the gastrointestinal tract. The poor rats suffered as a result of the experiments, but not in vain: as a result of such experiments, Selye discovered that the organisms had a universal response to any presented challenges — the stress response, which was originally called the adaptation syndrome by Selye.

As you might remember, the Selye model of stress starts with a phase of anxiety, when the organism alters its characteristics to cope with changes, followed by a phase of resistance, which corresponds to the phase of adaptation to new conditions. Then comes the exhaustion phase — this occurs if the stressor is prolonged and the adaptive capacity of the organism is depleted; then comes disease.

Selye associated the last stage with the depletion of the so-called 'adaptation energy'. In essence, it turns out that organs spend too much energy on defence, neglecting the support of other organs and systems that are not directly involved in the stress response. To escape from a predator, energy, activation of the cardiovascular system, endurance, and muscle strength are needed, while the digestive, reproductive, and immune systems can wait until the moment of escape. But what happens in the modern world, when we experience more often not acute, but chronic stress? And not from escaping from predators, but by painfully reacting to social interactions, suffering small but frequent stressors — traffic jams, overload at work, problems with a child at school, conflicting relationships with family, and so on and so forth? As a result, the organs and systems whose activity would be inhibited under stress suffer chronically, and the constant activation of the cardiovascular system leads to serious overloading of the heart and blood vessels.

Let's take a look at the basic links in the body's stress response.

A stressful stimulus, whether external or internal (we can successfully develop a stress reaction in response to a disturbing thought), reaches the amygdala, our radar that monitors threats. Recognising a signal as threatening, the amygdala urgently triggers a reaction before the stressful stimulus has even reached the top floor of the brain — the neocortex. This is why we are able to react by stopping abruptly or jumping back when we see a stick in the grass — just in case it is a snake. It takes a fraction of a second to immediately react, then the body will continue to unfold the stress response if the alarm is not false and the stressor is still active.

The amygdala transmits a signal to the hypothalamus, which connects several links of the stress response. The very first echelon of the defense reaction, acting from the first seconds, is the activation of the sympathetic nervous system. Branches of sympathetic nerves release the neurotransmitter **norepinephrine**, which affects internal organs; heart rate increases, respiratory rate increases, blood pressure rises, blood is filled with oxygen, and the body prepares to flee or fight. Next, the sympathoadrenal system is switched on to maintain the body's combat readiness, and the brain layer of the adrenal glands begins to produce adrenaline to help norepinephrine. The hormones enter the bloodstream and prolong the action of the sympathetic nervous system. Noradrenaline and adrenaline are responsible for maintaining increased cardiac output, blood pressure, glucose levels, and heart rate during the action of a stressor.

If the stressor persists, the hypothalamic-pituitary-adrenal system (HPA) will be activated to further unfold the stress response. This mechanism will provide metabolic reorganisation to adapt to the ongoing threat. It is understandable — if the threat was not just a snake in the grass, but a predator that can pursue for several hours, it will take a lot of energy to run away and save your life. In today's realities, we don't run away from predators, but we can get stuck in stress reactions damaging to our social wellbeing not for hours, but for months and years. HPA is precisely what will maintain long-term stress. This chain works very coherently through the consistent production of several hormones. The activated hypothalamus produces a specific hormone (corticotropin-releasing hormone) that signals the pituitary gland to produce adrenocorticotropic hormone (ACTH) into the blood. In turn, under the influence of ACTH, the cortical layer of the adrenal glands begins to produce the glucocorticoid hormone cortisol. The role of cortisol is extremely important in the body — it affects metabolic processes, stimulating the synthesis of glucose molecules on the one hand, and on the other hand contributing to the replenishment of glucose in the form of glycogen in the liver. In general, this hormone helps to replenish and preserve the body's energy resource.

Noradrenaline, adrenaline, and cortisol can be called the main humoral trio of the stress response, whose actions provide both positive effects for adaptation to new conditions and damaging effects under severe or ongoing stress.

But these hormones are not the only ones responsible for the stress response and its inherent effects on the body: the pancreas begins to produce glucagon, which breaks down liver glycogen into glucose molecules to provide energy to cope with difficulties, and the pituitary gland begins to produce thyroid-stimulating hormone, which affects the thyroid gland. And this is by no means a complete list of hormones activated by the stress response.

In addition, in response to stress endorphins will be produced, which provide pain relief in the event of injury, or increase mood and euphoria when no pain relief is needed. Endorphins provide the high spirits that we may occasionally experience after a heavy workout, a dangerous situation, or a risky decision.

The Positive Effects of Stress

Given the body's vivid hormonal response in response to stressors, we can assume that we even need a certain level of stress that we can control — through adrenaline, noradrenaline, and endorphins we get a burst of energy, our body tone increases, a sense of novelty is created, and our mood increases. Therefore, we tend to seek some dose of danger or fear through play, adventure, rides, scary films, sports and competitions, risky business decisions, and overcoming difficulties on the way to a goal.

Norepinephrine and adrenaline are responsible for the overall activation of the brain; we experience a feeling of alertness, motor activity is stimulated, we learn to overcome difficulties, and we have the energy to do so thanks to the stimulating role of stress hormones. As a result, we learn successful coping strategies and feel positive emotions when we achieve victory.

It is almost impossible to develop and learn new skills without activating the stress response. Think of yourself when you are just starting to develop a new skill — learning to ride a bike, drive a car, or surf. At first, each action requires maximum concentration and energy expenditure; we practice the skill over and over again, and get frustrated when we fail. The moment of overcoming becomes a moment of triumph and happiness! At once, the usefulness of this behaviour is recorded in the experience bank, the brain remembers that regular training leads to victory. And then, after mastering the skill, we can perform the necessary activities in a semi-automatic mode, expending minimum energy and without putting the body out of balance. In this case, we no longer need increased levels of adrenaline — the body feels in a comfort zone and is in balance.

As soon as you come up with a new challenge, the system will be out of balance again; the stress response will again provide the energy needed to cope with new challenges, and we will once again go through this journey of coping and learning from stress to reaching a new equilibrium. And how the period of stress will be emotionally coloured depends on how you view life — as a struggle or as an adventure. You can reduce the drama, add humour, irony, and play, so that difficult situations become a fun game of level-playing rather than a life-or-death struggle. Switch on your imagination, add game excitement, and your life will become an exciting adventure!

A huge role in the stress response is played by endorphins, a group of chemical compounds that are chemically similar to opiates (morphine-like substances from which a number of drugs are derived). It is known that opiates provide analgesic effects, as well as a feeling of euphoria. It is for the sake of these effects that endorphins are released during stress. They help to tolerate pain (which occurs in the muscles during prolonged exercise, for example), and also increase the body's adaptation to physical stress. The effects of endorphins during prolonged exercise can be seen in marathon runners. There is even such a concept as runner's euphoria — an elevated mood that occurs during prolonged physical activity. In this state, the body is more resistant to pain and fatigue, and it also makes you feel happier and calmer. This mood can last for quite a long time after training or competition. So in addition to the hard, physical test, marathon runners get a dose of happiness from the body for overcoming pain and fatigue, and reaching the finish line. It is important to remember that marathon races require long pre-training, and you should not try to reproduce the euphoric state of a runner just because you want to be in a good mood. The release of endorphins colours the emotional response to stress, improves mood, and stimulates further efforts to cope with difficulties. It is no coincidence that being under stress can push us beyond the normal limits of our capabilities.

Moderate stress leads to improved memory, alertness, and even pleasure. It has been observed that cortisol in moderate doses promotes the release of dopamine (while prolonged elevated levels of cortisol will, conversely, damage dopamine production). Cortisol acts in the same way on cognitive function: in the case of short-term stress, cortisol stimulates memory, while in the case of prolonged stress, it inhibits it. The hippocampus, which is involved in memory processes, has a lot of receptors for cortisol, so in a crisis situation we can remember or retrieve more important information. But in a situation of chronic stress, there are fewer synapses in the hippocampus, which has a negative effect on memory. You can probably think of situations where stress has helped you think more effectively — if you went into an exam feeling alert and well-rested, the short-term stress of answering a question will only stimulate clarity of thought, and you will retrieve all the information you need from memory. Conversely, if you have not slept for a week and your body is exhausted, it is quite difficult to hope for clarity of thought at the exam. Therefore, folk wisdom says that on the eve of the exam it is better to get a good night's sleep than to cram all night.

We need moderate stress to develop, to overcome obstacles, to feel invigorated and energised. When you live in a comfort zone for a long time, you sometimes want to challenge yourself in order to feel alive and invigorated. However, to tickle your nerves a little, you don't even need to invent anything; the whole entertainment industry serves this purpose — from nerve-jangling rides and extreme sports, to virtual computer games and horror films. Alternatively, positive stress can be experienced by starting new projects or learning new skills. Everyone makes up their own game and adventures to feel the colours of life, and cheer themselves up.

The desire to experience stress varies greatly from individual to individual, particularly the noradrenergic system — the body's regulator of activity. There is a cluster of neurons in the brainstem called the locus caeruleus ('blue spot'), which is one of the main sources of the neurotransmitter noradrenaline. The locus caeruleus is part of the reticular formation, which is largely responsible for activating the cerebral cortex, maintaining wakefulness and attention, and selecting behaviour in response to the environment. The triggering of the stress response is directly related to the excitation of the locus coeruleus and a few other noradrenergic structures. The system of projections of the locus coeruleus is quite extensive: neuronal outgrowths ascend to different parts of the brain (cortex, amygdala, hippocampus, striatum), and descending projections go to the spinal cord, releasing in all these areas the neurotransmitter norepinephrine, which causes a feeling of alertness, causes a surge of energy, reduces fear, and increases aggression. If there is reduced activity of the noradrenergic system, this can be manifested in lethargy and apathy. Good activity of the blue spot will be associated with an interest in all things new; a willingness to throw oneself into new projects, overcome difficulties, and learn new skills. But as with everything, moderation is key; it is important not to overdo the activity of norepinephrine, otherwise mental problems and behavioural disorders are not far away. We are rather strongly conditioned by our brains, and if you have an active blue spot, chances are that you will be constantly inventing new challenges, burning at work, having a considerable arsenal of hobbies, and, most likely, a passionate personality — rushing into projects, and forgetting about sleep and rest. And all of that can be fine, except for the danger of inadvertently burning out. Therefore, I recommend that all passionate people learn to periodically slow down their fast train, to stop and rest. Biological preconditions undoubtedly mean a lot, but do not forget that you are the driver of the fast train, and awareness is your decision-making tool.

Whether we are harmed by stress or benefit from it depends largely on how we perceive the difficulties we have to endure.

In 1998, a study of 30,000 adults was conducted in the USA. They were asked how much stress they had experienced in the last year. They were also asked if they thought stress was bad for their health. Eight years later, scientists looked at mortality data from this group and compared it to the answers to the stress questions. It turned out that high levels of stress increased the risk of premature death by 43% — but this only related to people who were convinced that stress was bad for their health. Meanwhile, high stress in the absence of a belief that it was bad for health, did not increase the risk of premature death in any way (Keller A. et al., 2012).

I've been thinking about different attitudes towards stress — what influences how a person perceives stress? It may well be related to the scale and duration of the stress, which also influences beliefs. If the stress is not chronic and we have the resource to cope with it, we don't feel that it is harmful; on the contrary, such acute stress hardens us. And if it is severe and prolonged stress, then it is no longer a matter of belief but of the consequences themselves, and the real loss of health. This is the dilemma of the multiplicity of stress, and its impact on a person.

But it is also possible that attitude towards stress is a manifestation of optimism or pessimism. For some people the glass is half full all the time and for others it is half empty. This is manifested in the optimists' "everything that happens is for the best" life attitude and the pessimists' "there is nothing good and there never will be" attitude. Plus, it has been proven in many other studies that optimists live longer and happier lives. Anyway, good stress toughens us up, and an optimistic outlook on life helps even more.

Together with stressful situations, we gain experiences that enrich us, and life becomes more multifaceted, colourful, and interesting. It is known that manageable stress neighbours with positive emotions. Life in the flow is impossible without positive stress, because in this state we develop our best talents through overcoming and enjoy not only the achievement, but also the process itself, when you forget about everything in the world and dissolve in your favourite activity.

Strange as it may seem, sources of stress are often also sources of meaning. For example, for parents, raising children, their growing up is a constant stress. Parents worry endlessly about their children's health, behaviour, environment, education, their destiny — and these are all sources of anxiety, worry, sleepless nights. But how much pleasure we also get from parenthood — the joy of interacting with our children, pride in their achievements, love and support in all situations. Of course, it makes us happy.

Imagine that you have an interesting, exciting job and three children in your life. Would there be a lot of stress? Absolutely — there can't help but be — since both of these areas of life are important to you and they don't easily fit together. But there will also be more happiness when you are able to juggle different aspects of your life, manoeuvre through the turbulent flow of events, and enjoy everything — risk, speed, love, support, a sense of stability in an unstable environment, and living in accordance with what is important to you.

A meaningful and interesting life is impossible without overcoming stress, and the more we try to avoid life's challenges, the less depth, meaning, and joy we get as a result. This is the price we pay for the safety and constancy of our environment. By shielding ourselves from pain, suffering and threats, we shield ourselves from life itself. And sometimes fate gives us a kick, to give our psyche a little shakeup.

So, should we consider such shocks in a negative aspect? Sometimes you have to tell yourself it's long overdue and hit the road. "No matter how big or soft or warm your bed is, you still have to get out of it." — this quote is attributed to American performer Grace Slick, and it perfectly captures the need for changes that will either happen consciously, at our will, or invade our lives when we didn't call for them at all. We just have to get up and go!

Nowadays, it is difficult to find a person who has not experienced life's various twists and turns associated with the need to change jobs or even professions. It has become part of our life: companies are often transformed, mergers and acquisitions take place, and mass layoffs are accompanied by mass dismissals; technologies change, automation and robotisation of production release human resources engaged in manual processes. Obviously, reality requires us to be more flexible, but human nature is such that it is not easy to accept the loss of a job when you are comfortable and life is running smoothly. I, myself, was a participant in the process of two companies merging due to a global deal, and observed the stress level of employees who have no place in the new structure. And people who are facing professional deadlock, or the need to change jobs, are coming to coaching more and more often.

Case Study Story:

Elena, a middle manager, had worked for the company for about 10 years and lost her job due to business restructuring. She had a very successful career with many achievements under her belt, and always received the highest performance evaluations from her bosses. It is especially hard to take the blow of being fired when it seems that thanks to your good work you are in control of the situation, you do everything possible to remain successful and prosperous, and you've acquired a mortgage and pleasant habits that a high position in a big company gives you. This is what happened to Elena. She came to the session in pain and in denial about the situation. "Why? Why me? Everything was so good, what did I do wrong?" all these questions came out, along with emotions of anger, rage, grief, fear. What to do next when you can't afford a long period of unemployment? Family responsibilities and a mortgage force you to act, rather than go on a long search for yourself. But a long search wasn't needed. During an hour and a half of dialogue, answering questions like, "If this layoff was a valuable gift, what might it be?", Elena came to the epiphany that in fact in the last couple of years in the company was no longer development; prospects were unforthcoming and, it turns out, there were periodic thoughts to change the sphere of activity, to expand the scope of responsibilities. But these weak internal voices were quickly extinguished by the advantages of the job: everything is well-established, excellent relations in the team, good compensation. After all, the best is the enemy of the good. After thinking about what would happen if she experienced another five years at the same company, in the same position, my coachee concluded that it would be stagnation, a loss of valuable development time. As a result of the session, the employee who had suffered in a real and psychological sense turned into a creator of her own destiny, with a clear plan of further steps, and the energy of anger was turned into the energy of creation. The story ended in a very positive way; within two months a new job was found (and at no financial cost, as corporations often pay generous severance packages to employees to negotiate such a separation). With the new job came new goals and objectives, and life was given a new impetus.

When I mentioned that the story was over, that wasn't quite right. The story never ends for as long as we live. It's just a stressful episode that knocked us out of the saddle for a while, threw us out of our comfort zone, but that's just to step up a notch, and gain experience in passing difficult lessons. And there will be other lessons and new experiences to come.

If we analyse our own lives or the lives of others, we will realise that growth and development often occur thanks to crises, dramatic changes that are accompanied by leaving the comfort zone. Of course, it is pleasant to be in a comfortable environment — the organism saves energy and maintains the constancy of the environment, internal and external. And we want to keep this beautiful balance, to prolong it. But in this state, we reproduce habitual patterns of behaviour and exploit the skills we acquired years ago. The brain does not develop, because it has no reason to create new neural networks. The unchanging comfort zone is stagnation and reduced mental flexibility.

Only by stepping out of our comfort zone do we have a chance to discover something else about ourselves, to gain new experience, to learn useful skills. And this gives us a wealth of sensations, the brain develops and transforms, and the number of neural connections increases. Therefore, when we are thrown out of the comfort zone, it means that we are in the zone of growth and we can congratulate ourselves with new opportunities, even if they are not yet visible on the horizon. But it is also important to allow yourself to grieve about the past. It's normal to experience ambivalent emotions — we can allow ourselves to feel sad about loss and welcome change at the same time. Surely everyone has experienced such a complex set of feelings in their lives. Let the feelings come, stay, and go, and we will gradually moor ourselves to a new comfort zone, which, however, will also not last forever.

As practice shows, the lessons of life reward us with greater resilience and greater satisfaction with life. And trust in life gradually grows — everything that happens to us is for a reason, in addition to difficult and painful experiences it is valuable to us, and if these difficulties happened, it means that we can cope with it. Stress in this case is the source of energy we need to achieve. We can do well to learn how to melt the energy of anger and anxiety into the energy of action. But to do so, we have to rethink the meaning of stress in life and accept as a fact that the whole strategy of growth is based on overcoming difficulties, gaining experience for future victories.

Very interesting research was conducted by Mark Siri regarding the impact of stress on a person's mental health. In his article, published in 2010, he questioned the prevailing belief that the experience of traumatic situations always increases the risk of mental disorders and other illnesses. As a multi-year study found, adverse life events can also promote resilience, resulting in positive effects on mental health and wellbeing.

During the study, participants were asked if they had experienced any of the negative events on the list, such as serious illness or loss of a loved one, financial difficulties, divorce, life-threatening or other traumatic situations. Then, over a period of four years, the researchers observed whether the number of traumatic events experienced would affect a person's wellbeing. The expected linear relationship between the number of negative events and wellbeing was not found. What was found, however, was a U-shaped distribution curve, which indicated that a moderate number of life experiences predicted relatively lower overall stress, fewer symptoms of post-traumatic stress disorder, and higher life satisfaction over time. Participants with the most or least stress, on the other hand, were less satisfied with life and showed more health impairment. These results show that everything is good in moderation, and anything that doesn't kill us can actually make us stronger (Seery M.D. et al., 2010).

On the other hand, we cannot idealise the role of hardship; we need to recognise the pros and cons. Realisation of the benefits of difficult lessons cannot lead to denial of all the disadvantages of trauma — pain, experiences, losses. Only a realistic view of the situation with all its costs makes it possible to experience later stressful growth, to be less afraid of life and to accept challenges. The ambivalence of emotions, the recognition of both positive and negative experiences, is the recognition of life in all its diversity. It's normal to be both bitter about the loss of something meaningful, and yet ready for new adventures. It shows that everything is valuable — both what has happened to you and what awaits you next. The only thing left to do is to live all these experiences without closing yourself off to bitterness, and by opening yourself up to new things. Is that possible? This is the only way possible when we change jobs or say goodbye to relationships, and many other different passages in life, giving an incredible variety of emotions with different signs. We accept, live, let go, and move on.

Humanity in 2020 experienced an exceptional stressful event in its scale; the world faced a new, unknown virus. Stress levels increased for everyone, without exception — social isolation, lifestyle changes, some people lost their jobs or businesses, some people lost loved ones or their health, and some people had many stressors triggered at once. This virus has hit the whole planet hard, and anxieties and fears have grown immensely.

But we must recognise that in addition to all those experiences, many of us have also gained advantages in the new reality. Remote working has allowed people in megacities to significantly improve their quality of life by saving money and time on transport, which used to take up a large part of the lives of city dwellers. The place of residence no longer determines the place of work, and this offers much more flexibility for both employees and companies that can hire staff from different cities and countries. The development of online services over the quarantine period has enabled a leap in the provision of digital services five years ahead of the pre-quarantine trend. The pandemic has also ensured a great advancement in online education and its accessibility; educational programmes and courses from the most eminent universities in the world have become accessible, without the need to be physically present. Our world, physically closed within national boundaries, has become much more open and borderless in virtual reality.

This combination of pros and cons has led to the fact that the overall level of happiness and life satisfaction on the planet did not decrease in 2020, as evidenced by two international studies — the World Happiness Survey (2021) and the Gallup State of the Global Workplace (2021). Stress levels and negative experiences have increased, mental health has deteriorated, but wellbeing has not declined, proving that we have the strength to endure hardship and appreciate life even more.

And it seems that the inoculation of resilience gained in the pandemic, and the skill to work from anywhere on the planet, has been very useful to us in preparing for the future. The world has become even more fragile and unsettling, but humans have also become more adaptable and mobile, able to choose where to live regardless of where they work. We are gradually becoming digital nomads, pushing the horizons of our lives and gaining new experiences.

Stress not only helps us survive, but also helps us develop, learn, and realise the value of life and its beauty. What remains to be understood is how to use stress to our advantage, while minimising the negative effects.

The Damaging Effects of Stress

But not everything is so great with the body's stress response — it happens that stress leads to serious damage and illness. Unfortunately, we don't always manage to catch and keep stress in the zone of wellbeing, without burning out — but also without getting bored. Sometimes it begins to rule our lives, and the magnitude of our own reaction can be more devastating than the stressor. Sometimes the main factor of stress is a psychological reaction in response to uncertainty, or changes in life that are neither good nor bad until we give them the appropriate colouring.

If we live in constant anxiety or in a series of small, endlessly shifting unpleasant situations, stress develops into chronic stress, and the stress response begins to damage organs and systems in the body. Sometimes chronic stress is the result of our response to micro-stressors, each of which is minimal, but when combined on an ongoing basis, they can create endless discomfort and reduce quality of life. Think about how you react to stimuli such as traffic jams, broken appliances, criticism from others, children's behaviour, unrealised expectations, uncertainty, slow progress in a desired direction, your own imperfections, an unpleasant conversation, a messy room — if most of these events make you anxious, annoyed, or very upset, you have a good chance of living in a state of chronic stress, as these stressors are constantly present in our lives. It all depends on how much importance we assign to each event.

Prolonged stress is very likely to lead to mental health disorders, causing anxiety disorder or depression. How does this mechanism work? Constant stimulation of the amygdala, our threat controller, as well as the locus coeruleus, a supplier of norepinephrine, an activator of the sympathetic nervous system, will lead to chronic activation of these systems and constant anxiety. In extreme situations, this can lead to generalised anxiety disorder or panic attacks. Prolonged elevation of cortisol levels leads to a breakdown of the reward system and impaired dopamine production. Essentially, chronic stress affects the same links that are involved in the mechanism of depression. Does stress necessarily lead to depression? Not at all, but it can trigger depression in a person, especially if there are genes that predispose to the condition. After all, hereditary traits rarely work with a 100% guarantee, they are more likely to be realised in an environment conducive to the disease.

Indeed, mental health problems and stress have a serious impact on the health of the working population. The CIPD (The Chartered Institute of Personnel and Development in the UK) report on the UK Employee Health Survey shows that mental health disorders are on the rise, most notably depression and anxiety disorders. Together with stress, mental health problems are among the leading causes of long-term absence from work, along with physical injuries and acute conditions. And the World Health Organisation (WHO) estimates that depression is one of the leading causes of disability worldwide.

Stress not only leads to an increase in mental illnesses, but also generally reduces the quality of life. Chronically elevated cortisol activates the amygdala, and as a result its synapses become more excitable; the number of connections between neurons increases. What does this mean on a domestic level? We become extremely sensitive to threats even where there are none. We are afraid of everything, everywhere, and just in case — what if something happens? Surely you have met such anxious individuals who worry all the time and cannot enjoy life because they cannot let go of anxiety; they are fixated on negative scenarios and not only cannot relax themselves, but also suffocate others with their hyper-parenting.

Chronic stress also reduces the effectiveness of the prefrontal cortex (PFC), which regulates the amygdala, is responsible for self-control, assesses risks, and suggests solutions. This means that we are less able to control ourselves with sound reasoning, and rely more and more on automatic reactions. This condition often occurs in burnout, when a person gets worse and worse, but he or she sees no way out, has no perspective and keeps hitting the same point. To change behaviour, to think of a way out, you need to switch on creative thinking, and there is no resource for that — the brain works in survival mode.

Chronic stress can also impair memory: studies have found a decrease in the size of the hippocampus, atrophy of dendrites (outgrowths of neurons), and a reduction in the number of synapses in the hippocampus (Gianaros et al., 2007; Magariños et al., 1997). The hippocampus is crucial for the perception of new information and learning, and weakening its function inhibits the search for new solutions, making it difficult to break deadlocks. Sometimes it is surprising to see a person who clearly does not like his work, is burnt out, and negatively disposed; why does he not think about how to change the situation, to make life easier, to look for a new job after all? But for these changes, sometimes there is a lack of energy or ideas.

Stress, which is difficult to control, leads to a feeling of helplessness and a loss of joy in life. If you are always anxious, looking for threats and defending yourself against them, the body obligingly supplies glucose to the blood, increased amounts of adrenaline and cortisol circulate in the blood, while other hormones are imbalanced. Such a condition is a serious risk of developing not only mental health disorders, but also the basis for the formation of various somatic pathologies. There is no doubt that the basis of many diseases is a psychological component, which is most often associated with chronic stress. The target organs of chronic stress can be the cardiovascular system, gastrointestinal tract, immune system, reproductive system, skin, and systems involved in metabolism.

When stress is constantly aimed at mobilising energy, this also translates into increased production of glucagon, a hormone that releases glucose from glycogen stored in the liver. Add to this impaired insulin production, and we can expect blood glucose levels to be elevated — which increases the risk of developing diabetes.

The immune system is very sensitive to the action of glucocorticoids (which, if you remember, include the stress hormone cortisol). These hormones are used in medicine to inhibit the actions of the immune system when it starts attacking everything around it, unable to discern who is friend and who is foe. This is why glucocorticoids are an important component of therapy for autoimmune diseases, severe allergic reactions like Quincke's oedema, or the cytokine storm of a new coronavirus infection.

One can imagine what happens to the normal immune system when it is attacked by elevated levels of cortisol as a result of prolonged stress. Of course, elevated levels of naturally produced cortisol are not comparable to medical doses of hormones that virtually shut down the immune system, but still cortisol causes a decrease in immune function. Stress suppresses the formation of lymphocytes, shortens the time lymphocytes are in the blood, and depresses the production of new antibodies. As a result, the body's defense response to viruses and bacteria is reduced.

It is known that latent viruses, such as herpes, become active during or after a stressful situation. Surely many people can remember that their student days, during the exams period; when the body is exhausted from lack of sleep, heavy mental load, and anxiety about passing exams, it is often at this time that herpes infection is activated and rashes appear on the lips. This is just a dormant virus which noticed a gap in the defence system and took the opportunity to come out of hibernation and start actively multiplying, until the immune system came to its senses and tamed the rebel.

The immune system is simply unable to perform its functions well because the body limits its actions, due to the need to conserve energy: "All for the front, all for victory"; minor inflammatory reactions or infections will wait until the body has dealt with the main threat for which all this mobilisation has been undertaken. And the immune system not only protects against viruses, but also tracks cancer cells to protect against a far more dangerous disease than the common cold. Although now with the emergence of a new respiratory virus, there is nothing trivial in respiratory infections — Covid-19 has a considerable striking potential. The outcome of an encounter with the virus will also depend on the level of stress and the state of the immune system.

By the way, it should be noted that lack of sleep and, in general, violation of the sleep and wakefulness regime are themselves quite strong stressors that can lead the organism into a state of chronic stress without any additional external stimuli. And then the whole cascade of damaging effects of stress unfolds along the chain.

During stress, the reproductive system also slows down. In animal studies, it has been shown that stress reduces sex drive in both sexes, females ovulate less frequently, and males have problems with erections and produce less testosterone. The same is true for humans. Many observations show that more than half of the visits of men to doctors with complaints of reproductive dysfunction are associated with psychogenic impotence, and not with an organic disorder. In addition, the role of stress can be traced in an increased likelihood of miscarriage or preterm labour. And Robert Sapolsky in his book *Why Zebras Don't Get Ulcers* mentions the study of Theresienstadt concentration camp inmates that showed that 54% of women of reproductive age stopped menstruating.

The threats to the cardiovascular system under chronic stress are obvious, as it will be constantly aroused by the stressor response. And to activate the cardiovascular system, a modern person does not necessarily have to face a threat to life — often routine interactions spur the stress response: a conversation with a boss, a quarrel with a partner, trouble at school with a child. As a result, according to WHO statistics, the main causes of death in the world are cardiovascular diseases — ischaemic heart disease and stroke. And the role of stress in the development of pathologies of the cardiovascular system nowadays is beyond doubt.

Stress will not always lead to disease in all organs that are affected by stress hormones. Disease often occurs where there is an additional risk due to genetics or environmental factors; for example, if there are many people in the family who suffer from cardiovascular disease. In this case, the chances are that stress will hit this system first, as a family history of the disease will indicate the likelihood of hereditary predisposition (although family history may be related not only to genes, but also to psychological mechanisms for responding to external stimuli). Or if you are constantly breaking your diet, in addition to being a carrier of the bacterium Helicobacter pylori, whose role has been proven to cause peptic ulcers. In this case, the action of a stressor may be the final trigger for gastric and duodenal ulcers.

But we are quite capable of regulating our response to stressors and turning off the 'start' button of the response system. Unfortunately, the drama of modern man is that most of the time we misuse our protective stress response — we don't often have to defend our lives against threats, but we can invent our own stressors and imaginary threats. It is possible to constantly exploit the system that evolution has created to adapt to threats, just by mentally going over and over in your mind the troubles at work, unfulfilled expectations, recalling an endless list of tasks and replaying problematic stories and dialogues in your head. In order to experience a very strong emotion we sometimes don't even need any external stimuli — just one thought is enough to construct a cascade of threats and visualise the final catastrophe. In doing so, notice that nothing has changed except your way of thinking about an event. Strong emotions through a chain of physiological processes in the body can affect physical health. Just imagine — your thoughts control your emotions, and your emotions control your health. You change your thoughts, and your life and health change. And we complain that we can't control anything in our lives! We can certainly influence our own thoughts — it requires awareness, identifying erroneous judgements and correcting them. If you can't do it yourself, you can go to a psychologist and do similar exercises with him, and it will be easier than treating multiple illnesses as a consequence of chronic stress, which you have driven yourself into through your way of thinking and interpreting events.

A small example.

I was doing a session with a woman who was complaining about a life full of anxiety and stress, because she owes everyone: family duties, work obligations, and so on, every day, and there was no end to it. It started to stress her out and she mentioned that she was a 'hamster in a wheel' all day long. We talked a bit about why she does what she does. It turned out that both aspects of life are very important to her — she loves her job, which also allows her to provide a decent living for her family, and she loves her children, even though they are a significant stress factor in her life. I asked her how she might describe her busy life with a different metaphor: if not a 'hamster in a wheel', what else might her life be like? From the visual images suggested, she chose a surfer on the waves — very similar to how she was constantly looking for balance, carried at speed, but still standing and not falling. Changing her metaphor, and realising why she does all these things on a daily basis, has given her a very different perspective on life — a chance to look at her hectic life in a more positive way.

It is also inherent in humans to be anxious and fearful of the unknown, of uncertainty, of not knowing what will happen tomorrow. It is obvious that evolution has made sure that everything unknown must be labelled 'dangerous' just in case, because the main purpose of all adaptive reactions is to preserve life. Fortunately, humans have a mind that allows them to be aware of their thoughts and reactions. And observations of our reality lead to the conclusion that the world is becoming less predictable, but not that it is becoming more dangerous. And it's high time to rethink uncertainty — it's always an opportunity, not just a threat. But only our conscious mind can turn a threat into an opportunity, thereby changing our thoughts and emotions about it.

Whatever traumatic situations or difficult living conditions may be, it is important to recognise that health impairment in response to prolonged stressors does not occur at 100% probability — much depends on our internal perception of events. And this means that we have the ability to manage our health and wellbeing regardless of events that we cannot influence. We just have to learn to think differently about stress.

Key Takeaways:

- Noradrenaline, adrenaline, and cortisol are the humoral trio of the stress response, whose actions provide both positive effects for adaptation to new environments and damaging effects under severe or ongoing stress.
- We need a certain level of controlled stress to live an active life. Through adrenaline, noradrenaline, and endorphins we are energised, our body tone increases, a sense of novelty is created, and our mood is elevated. When we are under stress, we can exceed the limits of our abilities, which is not achievable in a normal state.
- A meaningful and interesting life is not possible without overcoming and stress. Growth and development often occur through crises, dramatic changes that are accompanied by stepping out of the comfort zone.
- Whether we are harmed or benefited by stress depends largely on how we perceive the difficulties we face. Our attitude to stress will depend on the strength and duration of the stressor, on our inner resilience, and on our optimistic or pessimistic outlook on life.
- Chronic stress reduces the effectiveness of the prefrontal cortex (PFC), which is responsible for self-control, assessing risks, and proposing different solutions. As a result, we are less self-managed and have difficulty finding solutions, due to rigidity of thinking.
- Chronic stress reduces quality of life, and can also lead to somatic diseases and mental health disorders.

Is it a Lot of Stress or is it Just Right?

So, we have learnt that it is best to balance on a wave of positive stress, which can be managed, and to avoid prolonged excessive stress, which can cause such consequences that you will have to go to the doctor later. But how can we manage stress if we have been living in survival mode for a long time, have got used to this state of discomfort, and in general can't imagine we could be better, happier, and healthier?

In everyday life, the word 'stress' is mentioned in different contexts; it is both how we feel and the events that put us in this state. We combine both the body's reaction to stress factors and the stressors themselves (unfavourable events) into one word — 'stress'. It's not very scientifically rigorous, but it's perfectly acceptable for the common usage of the word. I will mostly refer to stress as an adaptive reaction of the organism in response to the impact of stressors, but sometimes, for convenience, I will also use it in a broad, common sense.

It's a good time to break down brick by brick what determines how much stress is in your life. And here I would use the word stress as both a reaction and a stressor, because stressors can be external — for example, objectively traumatic or threatening events, and they can be internal — our way of perceiving reality, interpreting situations as threatening. The individual way of perceiving events can be a much more serious stressor determining our condition than any objective difficulties.

Let's understand what the level of stress depends on. And for this purpose, it is worth answering a number of questions:

> What events are happening in my life, and what are my relationships with the people around me?
> How is my relationship with work?
> How is my relationship with myself?

Life events and relationships — a level of social stress that sets an important context for life, and it is quite possible to evaluate it objectively.

Relationships with work — more often than not, these are the very factors that potentially lead to burnout (if you stick to the scientific view that burnout is workplace stress).

Relationships with ourselves — the stories we tell about ourselves, how we treat ourselves, how we care for ourselves.

By investigating all these aspects, it is possible to recognise many stressors and causes of burnout. And when we recognise the causes of stress, we get the key to managing our inner state.

Life Upheavals Lead to Illness ... But Not Always

The role of stress in disease has long been disputed by scientists. Psychiatrists Thomas Holmes and Richard Rahe made a great contribution to proving the influence of social stress on the development of diseases in the last century. Based on preliminary studies that proved the connection between life shocks and the emergence of somatic diseases, the scientists decided to quantify the degree of stressfulness of each of the potential life events that require adaptation.

In 1967, Thomas Holmes and Richard Rahe conducted a study that allowed them to develop a scale to measure stress levels. In the study, respondents ranked 43 events according to the degree of life change and the length of time needed to adapt. For example, marriage was assigned a score of 500, and all other situations were ranked against marriage in terms of the degree of life change and length of adaptation time required. Respondents assigned a score to each event: the higher the score, the greater the level of adaptation to change required to reach a new equilibrium point.

The result was the SRRS (The Social Readjustment Rating Scale, Holmes & Rahe, 1967), a stress scale or social adaptation scale that reflects the perceived level of stress — or need for adaptation — associated with various life changes. The more events, the more resources will be needed for adaptation. Not only undesirable events require adaptation, but pleasant and planned events such as a wedding or pregnancy also lead to a stress response. After all, every one of these changes forces you to adapt to a new way of life, to give up some habits and acquire others.

The SRRS instrument has become one of the most commonly used tests for measuring stress levels, and the study by Thomas Holmes and Richard Rahe is recognised as one of the most influential in psychology. Thirty years later, other researchers attempted a revision of the SRRS and concluded that the instrument developed still retained validity and was a useful test of stress measurement, although the new study slightly adjusted the weights of events in terms of stressor severity (Judith A. Scully et al., 2000).

So, I propose to estimate what level of stress load you have had to endure over the last year. To do this, you can take a test using the table and calculator.

To find out your stress level, simply tick off those situations and events that have happened to you in the last year, and then add up the total score that all the marked events score.

#	Stress factors	Scores
1	Death of spouse	100
2	Divorce	73
3	Separation/Separation of spouses	65
4	Detention in jail or other institution	63
5	Death of a close family member	63
6	Major personal injury or illness	53
7	Marriage	50
8	Being fired at work	47
9	Marital reconciliation	45
10	Retirement from work	45
11	Major change in the health or behavior of a family member	44
12	Pregnancy	40
13	Sexual difficulties	39
14	Gaining a new family member (birth, adoption, etc.)	39
15	Major business readjustment	39
16	Major change in financial state	38
17	Death of a close friend	37
18	Changing to a different line of work	36
19	Major change in the number of arguments w/spouse	35
20	Taking on a mortgage (for home, business etc.)	31
21	Foreclosure on a mortgage or loan	30
22	Major change in responsibilities at work	29
23	Son or daughter leaving home (marriage, attending college, etc.)	29
24	In-law troubles	29
25	Outstanding personal achievements	28
26	Spouse beginning or ceasing work outside the home	26
27	Beginning or ceasing formal schooling	26
28	Major change in living conditions (new home, remodeling, etc.)	25
29	Revision of personal habits (dress manners, quitting smoking)	24
30	Troubles with the boss	23
31	Major changes in working hours or conditions	20
32	Changes in residence	20
33	Changing to a new school	20
34	Major change in usual type and/or amount of recreation	19
35	Major change in church activity	19
36	Major change in social activities (clubs, movies, etc.)	18
37	Taking on a loan (car, TV, freezer)	17
38	Major change in sleeping habits	16
39	Major change in number of family get-togethers	15
40	Major change in eating habits	15
41	Vacation	13
42	Major holidays	12
43	Minor violations of the law (traffic tickets, disturbing the peace, etc.)	11
	TOTAL	

How can the test results be interpreted?

Up to 150 points — low stress; the probability of getting sick as a result of stress is low.

150-299 points — medium stress; moderate risk of disease.

A score of 300 or more — high stress; the risk of disease in the next two years is high (Peter A Noone, 2017).

But if you score over 300, don't be in a hurry to create more stress about your hectic life! A high level of social stress does not mean definite disease, only an increased risk of becoming ill. The realisation of risk depends very much on the individual characteristics of the person — their ability to take care of themselves and interpret life's upheavals. You may remember the study mentioned earlier that showed that high stress leads to an increased risk of premature death, but only for those who are convinced that stress is detrimental to their lives. So let's look at what can help us weather the storms of life and stay healthy.

In one of the training sessions I conducted, a participant, after calculating her score on the stress scale, exclaimed, "Wow, I just now realised how many changes I've had in the last year: I got married, moved to another country, changed jobs and got pregnant! What am I supposed to do with these points now?" And then a few seconds later she answered herself: "I need to rest more, make myself feel good, and slow down on the renovations in the house."

Once we realise the level of upheaval in our lives and understand that we are experiencing increased stress, the answer for what to do comes naturally. If it is difficult — we should have more rest, gain strength, please ourselves, and mitigate the shocks of life by taking care of ourselves. And if you have had a fruitful year for changes — you should slow down with new projects and events that are within your control. Festina lente (Latin) or 'Hurry slowly' — one of the favourite expressions of Emperor Octavian Augustus, who never started a business unless he was sure that he would gain more when he won than he would lose if unsuccessful. So it makes sense when starting new, big things to check with your internal reserve of energy, which depends on the recent stress load. Sometimes it is better to delay, and choose a good moment to start a big business, when there are resources and no risk of burnout.

I hope that you have been able to breathe calmly if you were surprised by a high score. If you are still not sure how to behave in a situation of high stress, the following chapters of this book will give you hints on how to develop inner resources and cope with difficult periods of life, without losing your health.

How to Support Yourself in an Era of Change and Stress...

Do not be alarmed if you score high on the stress scale — this is another consequence of the pandemic and other challenges of modernity. Almost everyone has faced a lot of changes in recent years: change of job or business transformation, unfamiliar format of remote work, relocation out of town or to another city or country, anxiety about illnesses, uncertainty about job security or earnings, and changes to habitual lifestyle.

Obviously, the number of points scored increased for everyone, so it's only natural that everyone started talking about stress, burnout, and declining health.

What should you do if you happen to live in a time of change? Simply give yourself a rehabilitation period, to recover from the upheaval and take more care of yourself.

When microbiologists grow cell cultures of living organisms, they carefully prepare the nutrient medium and create a constant temperature; if the cell culture begins to develop poorly, it is a sign that it is necessary to improve conditions, change the environment, and create the most comfortable regime. And then the cells will survive. Our organism is an extremely complex system of cells, and the law of environment also applies here. It is important to create the most supportive environment for the organism, and it will heal itself.

Our supportive environment is a caring attitude to ourselves and optimal fulfilment of our needs. Consider it a spa treatment; rehabilitation of the organism based on the use of natural factors, rest, sufficient sleep, regular nutrition, unloading the mind from information flows. Think about it, maybe now is the time when the organism needs just such a rest? It is ideal to create such a regime during a holiday, but during working days you can pay a little more attention to your needs, create a gentler regime for yourself; after all, if the level of stress is higher than normal, the level of self-care should be increased.

Try adding anything that is missing for an optimal supportive environment:
- physical activity if you don't move much
- mental relaxation in the form of digital detox and nature walks
- socialising with friends and family if you feel isolated

Or maybe all you need to do is get enough sleep, and you'll have plenty of energy! Then this is your magic anti-stress pill.

The turbulent period we are going through is a lesson in caring for us. We have now realised that the world is fragile, and human beings are vulnerable. That life and health are important. Both the person and the planet need support, and the place to start is, as always, with ourselves. So welcome to the world of caring —

first and foremost, for yourself. And this is not selfishness, but the first step to caring for others!

Key Takeaways:

- The level of stress depends on the magnitude and duration of stressors, which include: social factors — life events and relationships; organisational factors — relationships with work; personal factors — relationships with self, beliefs, self-care. By identifying stressors, we have the key to managing our internal state.
- If you have experienced a lot of life shocks recently, it makes sense to pay attention to yourself: take more rest and soften the blows of life by taking care of yourself. And you can also temporarily slow down with new projects and events in your area of control. This will allow you to restore your energy level and not lose your health in the struggle with life's difficulties.

Watch Out! Work!

Work is a place where we can fulfil intentions and plans, do things we love, make friends, receive support and recognition, gain financial independence, and earn valuable life experience. But it is also a place where we can suffer, experience tension, endure injustice, feel conflict with our values, experience stressful Mondays, and generally lose our health.

We must admit that work is a stressful area of life, and as research shows, most people in the world are not satisfied with their jobs. Tom Rath and Jim Harter's book *Wellbeing: The Five Essential Elements* cites the results of a massive international Gallup study that suggests that only one in five of those surveyed like what they do. Just imagine, when asked, "Do you like what you do every day?", only 20% of people can firmly answer, "Yes."

And professional wellbeing is an important component of happiness. We spend most of our time at work, and how we feel at work has a serious impact on our psychological wellbeing and health.

The first thought when you think of the one in five who are happy with their job is how lucky they are! But is it luck? Maybe there is a lot of personal influence in our relationship with work? We do have the power to influence — we can change both the work itself and the conditions in the organisation, or we can transform our inner state. Stressful situations in the work environment cannot be avoided, and managing stress at work is a skill that everyone will need.

I've been lucky in my life; more often than not, my romance with work has been mutual and happy. But even in such marvelous stories it is difficult to avoid dramatic events.

I have several careers under my belt, including academic medical research, but I have worked in marketing and social research for the longest time. For more than 15 years I worked as a top manager in an international company, where I enjoyed doing applied research. And, you know, gradually I got used to the managerial role; when the company takes care of you, you take care of it, and you have a love marriage for many years.

When everything is good and stable, there is an illusory feeling of control over circumstances. But life turns out to be much more creative than we are, with our habits and stereotypes. It shows us a path that we don't like at all and insists that we take it. And you stand at the crossroads with a sense of inner resistance, and at the same time with the understanding of the need to make a step forward. And so the company where I had worked for many years underwent a process of transformation, as a result of which we experienced first-hand what mergers and acquisitions are all about. The controlling interest was taken over by an investment finance corporation, which decided to restructure the company by selling some of the business. We had several directors in our branch, including me, and it was the part of the company that I was in charge of that was decided to be sold. It was like a thunderclap. It turned out that, with our illusion of control, we had no defence against such surprises.

For a year with the team, we lived without knowing where we would end up. I was flooded with emotions from my employees — psychological support became an important part of my work during that time. I had to somehow motivate people, reassure clients, and also maintain my own resources. It was a difficult and emotional period. But it also became very fruitful for me: I did not waste time, I acquired additional psychological education and became a coach. The circumstances were difficult, but I managed to stabilise emotionally quite quickly. By that time, I was already seriously engaged in meditation and yoga practices, had mastered psychological tools, and learnt how to return myself to a resourceful state in different circumstances.

As it turned out, it was easier to survive a long period of uncertainty than to get information about a global deal a year later. The company was selling its businesses to a major global competitor. The acquirer had its own similar businesses, and to duplicate them meant removing a competitor from the market. It was strange, the fate of my team looked even more uncertain, and of course it caused a storm of emotions that was difficult to handle even for me, hardened in the practice of stress management and meditation. I was facing difficult negotiations with a new company about the future of the business they were acquiring. Under the terms of the deal, all employees were hired under their current employment contracts, although in practice it was more complicated due to the disparate structures of the two companies. My team was not in the best emotional state, with some considering leaving to avoid going to a major competitor with an unclear future. I had a very difficult thought process about whether to go or quit. I didn't really want to go to a competitor, and in case of dismissal I would have received a good compensation according to the contract. But I had a whole team behind me, about 100 people, and I was their boss, and it was a business that I had spent 15 years building from scratch. I cared about the business — and the people who were under stress and uncertainty.

We had a long negotiation process in which we moved step by step from the position of competitors to that of partners. There were many inconsistencies in structure and duplicate positions, but we managed to find compromise and many solutions. As a result, both sides made concessions to reach an acceptable agreement. I did not have to sacrifice anyone or anything, and that was my main internal condition for the transition. This case was an affirmation that one must accept the world as it is and still be comfortable with one's values. This is what a sense of inner control is all about — consciously following one's values. Another important conclusion was that if you don't expand your comfort zone, then life will make sure that you get out of your zone of wellbeing and go on a journey to develop your skills, and find a new zone of balance.

My management style seriously changed during that period — I became closer to a supportive type of leadership. Now I realise that real leadership is not about learning to "do as I do", but about discovering everyone's individuality. Then, both people and business develop, and a wonderful, authentic environment is formed in which it is pleasant and natural for everyone to exist. And in this environment of like-minded people, it is easier to survive external storms, which we have no shortage of and, it seems, never will. And the discovery of inner potential and individuality in each person still fascinates me — it is more interesting than playing the business game.

The crisis period turned out to be very productive for me; I wrote a book, became a wellbeing coach and expert, did a course on wellbeing skills, and started running a pro-wellbeing blog. My world expanded beyond my corporate job and time became scarce. So I started working for the corporation only four days a week to make time for other projects. Before I would never have thought that a top manager could work less than a full week, but it turns out that anything is possible if it is important and valuable to you. And multi-employment is a new trend today — it's worth everyone taking a closer look.

Now I think about how my life would have turned out without a serious career shakeup, and I realise that this crisis would have had to be invented anyway, in order to expand the boundaries of my world. It seems that I need to learn to create new challenges without a 'magic kick', and expand the territory of my manifestation in life.

There are significant benefits to be gained from a stressful period, although many dramatic stories are known. Sometimes people lose their health, lose faith in themselves, or go into depression when faced with a serious professional crisis.

Whatever the circumstances of life, it is important to direct your energy to what you can control, and then a solution will be found, and after a while it will become clear why you needed this crisis.

All Mixed Up: New Challenges and Traditional Stressors

We already knew that work is a source of stress, but with the beginning of the pandemic a real epidemic of burnout started. Having learnt a little about stress factors, now you can understand the reason: the adaptation energy reserve was depleted by an incredible number of changes. Not all of them were work-related, but all of them required energy for adaptation. And there were a lot of changes at work, like remote working, new business processes, and increased or decreased workload (which is equally stressful). And the traditional annoying factors didn't disappear, either — difficult clients, demanding bosses, insufficient remuneration, and other routine annoyances. It's all become too much to keep in balance. Add to this the lack of communication, and informal contacts on a remote basis, and here is the result: the level of discomfort increased, anxiety became stronger, fatigue accumulated, signs of burnout appeared, and, as a result, staff turnover increased. Some people changed jobs in the hope of getting new inspiration and dopamine, some went freelance, and some went on extended leave (sabbatical) to rehabilitate and/or find meaning.

After the first lockdown of 2020, when many people complained about stress, fatigue, and burnout, I was approached by the founder of the agency RODNYA Creative PR Studio with a proposal to conduct a study on the mental health of employees in the advertising industry. The communications industry has always been considered quite stressful to work in: tight deadlines, extremely demanding clients, competition of creative ideas within the company, irregular working hours, and many other stressors awaiting employees who have devoted themselves to this challenging and yet interesting career. In the pandemic the situation has worsened, and the topic of mental health has become very visible to businesses, as stress in the workplace leads to significant problems — from increased staff turnover to dissatisfied customers.

As a result, with the support of professional communications associations, we conducted a survey of about 500 employees in the industry. With the help of this survey, we tried to understand where the levers are that can be used to influence the psychological wellbeing of employees.

What did we see in the survey results? Almost half of employees do not feel psychologically safe at work (44%), almost one in four feels anxious (24%), 38%

have depressive moods, and more than 60% of employees work overtime. I think that similar figures would be found in a study of working people in general, because in one of the European reports I saw a figure that 42% of employees do not feel psychologically safe at work.

Work as a source of psychosocial risks is beyond doubt but, as a rule, these risks are also superimposed on the personal circumstances and individual characteristics of a person. As a result of the study, we found that the state of psychological wellbeing is influenced by a complex of individual and organisational factors. It turned out that employees who know how to take care of themselves — nutrition, sleep, physical activity, communication, self-acceptance, and respect for personal boundaries — are much less likely to develop symptoms of stress and have a higher level of life satisfaction. It turns out that a lot depends on you and me, no matter where we work. On the one hand, taking care of yourself increases your inner resource and expands your comfort zone, and on the other hand, taking care of yourself prevents you from staying in a toxic environment for long.

The work environment, of course, also contributes to mental health with positives and negatives. For example:

- A corporate culture that encourages workaholism provokes psychological dysfunction: employees do not feel safe, are often stressed, feel drained at the end of the day, and most work overtime
- Unfavourable management style also has a negative impact on wellbeing: employees often report symptoms of burnout, they lack days off for rest, most are dissatisfied and are thinking of changing jobs.
- Caring for employees and introducing wellbeing programmes has a very positive contribution: most feel safe, complain less about burnout symptoms and job dissatisfaction, and are less likely to consider leaving their employer.

Interestingly, some demographic differences also showed up. Women turned out to be more sensitive to stress factors, and more often reported symptoms of burnout. And the most critical group in terms of mental health was young people, which is also confirmed by international studies.

Social research often becomes a call to action. As a result, a company can influence those stressors that are within its sphere of influence: for example, by improving corporate culture, developing managers' empathy, and introducing wellbeing programmes. But the company can also educate and encourage employees to adopt healthy lifestyles. And in turn, employees can take responsibility, take care of their health and personal boundaries, and make decisions about where to work and when to consider changing employers.

But where was the impact of the pandemic on the mental health of employees? The pandemic caused a lot of changes that had to be adapted to. Probably the main symbol of the changes in the work environment was remote working. It was unfamiliar and strange but unavoidable, so everyone had to learn new skills to work from home. In our study, the factor 'remote work' was far from first place among stress factors: only one in five mentioned the impact of remote work on mental health. Although it's worth noting that this factor proved to be more important for new employees who had worked with the company for less than three years. Remotely, we continued to exploit the relationships we had built offline, so it was particularly difficult for new employees to settle in without close ties to the team.

However, remote work has also brought advantages: we have learnt to do everything without going to the office. It must be admitted that for residents of megacities, who spend several hours a day travelling, the possibility of not having to go into the office has become more of an advantage than a disadvantage. And now many people are asking about the possibility of working remotely when looking for a job.

So, what has been the negative impact of remote working? The first thing we've all encountered is the lack of boundaries between work and home, and the resulting imbalance of work and leisure. Many people have noticed that they work longer hours when working remotely and the work calendar gets tighter. But this is the part of the problem that is well manageable, because it involves learning new rules, creating new habits and rituals. That's why many companies have conducted training on how to 'come to work' and how to 'leave work' when at home, how to build boundaries between work and home without leaving the room, how to stop replying to messages after the end of the working day, and how to plan breaks between endless online meetings. Now our life is gradually building rules of not writing emails outside of working hours and, if you must write, to turn on the function of delayed mail delivery so as not to interrupt a colleague from personal business, or to put an alert for non-urgent messages. Or shift the time of meetings by 5-10 minutes — not at 13.00, but at 13.05, assuming that the previous meeting may end at 13.00 and everyone needs at least a short break. Maybe such actions cannot radically solve the problem of work/rest balance, but they carry an important message — personal time is valuable, a break during the working day is very important. It becomes a call to action to structure your day with self-care and, in fact, productivity in mind.

I have a secret dream and even hope that most companies will overcome the unhealthy tendency towards workaholism, and work-life balance will be a socially approved behaviour. Taking care of ourselves, our employees, and the company's bottom line are links in the same chain. Maybe that's what the pandemic was given to us for — to finally pay attention to the individual and address long-standing problems that were previously overlooked.

The second problem of remote work, which did not immediately become apparent, was the deterioration of mental health due to the reduction in informal communication. It was not difficult to restore work processes in remote mode — a huge number of services were at our disposal. When we plunged into the virtual reality, we realised that the work processes were working as they should, but people were clearly missing something. What they lacked was warm human communication, conversations when meeting in the corridor, going to lunch together, interaction with other colleagues who were not connected in the projects. An invisible community bond was broken, which is not critical for solving work tasks, but is very important for good psychological wellbeing. People are eager to socialise, and often those who need a social circle and friendship with colleagues are employed. This is what we were suddenly deprived of, and it was one of the reasons for burnout.

How do you regain social connections even in virtual communication? Here, too, we are not without novelties. We started to plan informal communication in the same way as we plan business meetings. Some teams came up with the idea of drinking coffee together on Monday mornings — everyone pours coffee in their own kitchen, but you can use the screentime to convey the emotions of a great weekend, share the latest news, and at the same time get in the mood for the working week by checking plans and tasks. And someone has established a ritual to gather the team on Friday evenings, when you can exhale, remember what good or not-so-good things happened during the week, share plans for the weekend, and come up with some activities that can be carried out together. Very simple rituals that add warmth to the formal atmosphere of business communication.

The third reason for burnout in remote conditions is that managers stopped seeing their employees, and therefore did not notice the first signs of burnout. Conversations with subordinates only on work, distribution of tasks by mail, and lack of personal contact sometimes led to the fact that the employee did not reveal his personal problems. As a result, they took their work beyond their limits, tried not to let down the team, lasted as long as they had enough strength, and then wrote a resignation letter, leaving with the words that the work was destroying his life. The manager is perplexed and wants to help, to relieve him, but in neglected cases, delayed action does not help any more — the employee has decided to run away, no matter where, as long as it's away from this job.

It is the very sad when people who could have done a lot more — both for their own development and for the success of the company — leave because they could not cope with the tension, and no one helped them in time to figure out how to solve their problem. As a result, the company loses valuable staff, and the person acquires an avoidance strategy when facing difficulties. It's a lot of damage all round. And there is no other solution here but to train the emotional intelligence of managers of all levels — from top management to group leader. Knowledge about burnout and its stages, how to notice the first signs of burnout, how to talk to employees who are remote working — this is a sample list of questions that we discussed with managers in our company. It was important to learn how to give support and talk about feelings with employees. And the positive feedback I received from managers on the results of the training convinces me that emotional intelligence skills, and elementary knowledge about human mental health, make a huge contribution to the prevention of burnout at work.

Managers are often the best in the profession, not people specialists, so it doesn't even occur to many people that an employee should be given regular feedback — and especially positive feedback, not just negative. Not all managers realise that some people take on more tasks than they can handle because they don't want to fail, or they want to be irreplaceable — there are so many different motivations for working to the limit. And yes, the manager has to keep an eye on the workload, prevent unfair distribution of tasks, and sometimes even encourage the employee to go on holiday or take time off if he or she has worked over the weekend. I can see from experience that managers respond very well to new knowledge and literally become more caring towards their employees. The next step is to practise empathy and caring skills, thus building a corporate culture of wellbeing.

Remote working has indeed exacerbated the problem of burnout, but it has also raised the issue. And if the pandemic gives us a good boost towards embedding a culture of wellbeing, just as it has given a boost to all online services, then the lessons of recent years do make sense.

Stress in entrepreneurs

Once I wrote a post in my blog, where I stated that the best cure for employee burnout is the development of emotional intelligence of managers. I shared information that caring managers have less burnout among their employees because they talk to their subordinates, take interest in their problems, notice changes in behaviour in time, and try to alleviate the plight of their people. My old friend Olga, with whom I once worked in a corporate job, responded, though she has been out of the labour force for several years and is now an entrepreneur, having founded a company. She has a small team which provides consulting work for international clients. Olga wrote in the comments of the post that small business owners sometimes wish there was a manager too, who would take an interest in health and problems. But entrepreneurs have a hard time with support.

For me, this comment was a reason to think about the stress factors of entrepreneurs and freelancers. I noticed that social psychologists and counsellors who study stress at work do research and make recommendations mainly for the corporate sector. "That's not fair!" I thought. The economy is changing, the digitalisation of everything is increasing, the whole world has learnt to work remotely during the pandemic, and all of this gives a massive boost to entrepreneurship and self-employment in various forms. But it also brings new challenges, new stressors that don't exist in the corporate environment. Leaving employment gives you a breath of freedom — there is no supervisor above you anymore, you can shape your own workload, you are free to do what you want — but at the same time there are many other stressors.

I decided to research this topic, and conducted interviews with entrepreneurs and freelancers. As a result, I have a whole list of stressors — as well as possible ways of coping with stress — for people who are self-employed.

1. The line between work and personal life is virtually disappearing. This factor has been noted by employees in remote work, but for the self-employed the problem is exacerbated by the absence of corporate rules and any other guidelines that make it clear when to start work and when to finish it. Moreover, thoughts revolve around work all the time, and everything else becomes less important. As a result, you can dive into work with your head, neglecting all other spheres of life, including family, children, leisure, sports, and socialising. The outcome of such immersion is obvious — neglecting rest and energising activities leads to gradual burnout and poor health. At a certain stage, one has to realise that a job which consumes the rest of one's life brings more problems than benefits.

One consultant who travelled tirelessly to meet with clients created difficulties in his personal life. His family did not see him for months at a time, which of course affected his relationship with his wife and children. Fortunately, when his wife rebelled, our consultant listened and changed his work rules. He now only travelled on a case-by-case basis, charged extra money for this service, and worked remotely most of the time. He also began to schedule Fridays as family and children's time in his calendar, in addition to weekends. And what was the result? It turned out that these rules had a very positive impact on the business as well. Having established a clear schedule without excessive travelling, he began to manage more work, business began to go even better, and time with his family became emotionally nourishing and rewarding. Every person needs a work-life balance, and people who work for themselves need to think about it specifically, creating their own code of work and rest.

It's mindfulness that helps entrepreneurs and freelancers build boundaries, make personal rules, and exercise discipline. And now more and more people are moving into self-employment to free up time for hobbies and self-development, reducing the number of days a week they are busy working. Apparently, disciplined and organised people manage to do this quite well, as proper organisation of work allows them to maintain both their earnings and an optimal rhythm of life. So, the factor of blurred boundaries is not a judgement for conscious entrepreneurs.

Additional pressure can be created by the idea that how much you work is how much you earn. It seems that you rest more and earn less. But it's not all linear! You need to take a broader view — you can think about improving the operational component of your work, learn to delegate routine operations, and introduce technologies. And in the consulting business, a sought-after expert forms a network of consultants around him, who he attaches to projects if there is too much work. It seems that the whole world is becoming an ecosystem: it is no longer necessary to hire people, you can unite partners around you and bring them into your business as needed.

2. To be responsible for everything — the motto of an entrepreneur. As my friend Olga says: "Entrepreneurs are those who like to control everything and take responsibility. And if you don't have the skill to control and take responsibility, you will burn out immediately. An entrepreneur is a 'jack of all trades', and if you resist these multiple roles, you will break down at the first stage."

So first of all, you have to acknowledge that you are fully responsible for yourself. This requires being prepared to seek new orders when work runs out, learning marketing, and developing your personal brand. Today, numerous channels exist to promote both yourself and your products — not only through advertising, but also through social media and public speaking.

I remember when a colleague of mine decided to start his own business. He left the company, and for some time he was under stress because he realised that he had to do, himself, everything that was done in the company by various departments — he was responsible for accounting, IT, marketing, sales, and operations. If you accept this situation as a necessary condition for entrepreneurship, then you build everything up over time — you have to learn some things yourself, and for others you hire external performers. In any case, you have to recognise that the number of tasks in your head is growing, and this can be a source of anxiety.

There is also the problem of delegation — when a personal brand has been created, there is a high risk of missing something and destroying the ideal image. In this case, it seems dangerous to involve outsiders in the work — especially in consulting or creative work. There's a fear of dropping the high bar, ruining your reputation, and then your business is over. But as your workload grows, there's no way to cope without clever delegation and expanding the number of assistants. It's better to think about building a reliable team as soon as business expansion looms on the horizon.

3. Lack of support is a serious challenge to working outside a team. As a rule, we have friendships at work, we are ready to rely on colleagues when something goes wrong, or we can ask for help from a manager and work together to solve the problem. And HR is often busy coming up with teambuilding initiatives and satisfaction surveys. In collective work, a circle is formed that supports us in different situations, even if we are not always aware that we have this support. But when people go into self-employment, they lose this social circle. What happens then? As a rule, family members take on the role of support; who else is there to discuss business or share concerns with?

I know of a case where a woman who was a self-employed counsellor returned to working for a company, after her spouse fell ill. She had lost the usual support from her spouse, and her husband's illness also required involvement. All of this together exceeded the size of her internal resources. It became impossible to take care of the business and support her husband on her own, which led to the decision to return to employment — where there is work to be done but the corporation takes care of the rest.

My friend Olga shared with me how she made up for the lack of support when she set up her consulting agency after moving to Georgia from the UK, where she had worked for a corporation for 10 years. Of course, it was not without the support of her spouse, but she found a great solution by joining a professional community. It is not only a support group in difficult cases, but also a creative resource. We need collective brainstorming to get beyond our own limited thinking, and when you work alone, all you have going on is your own thoughts, which are difficult to develop further. So a community of peer advisors becomes a kind of mastermind group, bringing people together through regular meetings, to help each other achieve their goals and jointly solving the challenges everyone faces. In my opinion, for the community of entrepreneurs and the self-employed, mastermind groups are a very promising area for support and professional help. And if you don't know of such a community in your area, it can start with you.

My former colleague Anastasia, who left a job for freelance employment, confirms that as soon as you change your office job for 'free floating', the intensity of your social life decreases, and the number of contacts drops. Often this has a positive effect — there is no need for formal socialising, there are more opportunities to choose those with whom you will keep in touch. But for some people, the drastic reduction in social interactions is a major stressor. In addition to other significant changes, it may well cause anxiety and frustration. At this point, it is important to join a community, to find a club of interest, whether professional or hobby. That is why Anastasia has become a member of several clubs that reflect her interests, such as coaching, which so far brings in less income than her main freelance activity, but has the potential to become the main source of income over time.

4. Instability is one of the main entrepreneurial fears. There is little stability in the world in general, and this is especially felt by people who are deprived of corporate guarantees. For example, a company might experience a business downturn yet still not lay off employees as they are a valuable resource; if staff reductions do begin, you can expect several months' salary as compensation, which is also a help in difficult times. The self-employed have no one to rely on but themselves, and the only way for them to reduce anxiety and fears about unstable income is to create their own financial safety cushion, to help in case of fluctuations in demand,

and unforeseen crises or 'black swans' (a term coined by Taleb in 2010). Consider the fact that in case of illness, there is no pay for sick leave, and it is necessary to earn for their own social security fund. All this should be taken into account early on, and then there will be less anxiety.

Entrepreneurs contributing to their own stress resilience is not unreasonable, either. Learning to cope with setbacks, failures, or unexpected circumstances, learning strategies for managing one's condition through sport, an optimistic attitude, the ability to see the future through negative events — all these are skills that are quite developable.

There are many cases when a difficult period results in positive changes in life, if the resource that remains in your control is properly managed. Olga, now an international counsellor from Georgia, also had a difficult period when the pandemic started. Since the lockdown, many clients were at a loss, not knowing whether they should do the projects they had planned. As a result, there was no work for six months. Of course there was anxiety about the future, uncertainty, and confusion about how long it would all last. But it was also an opportunity to take a fresh look at the situation, and use the time that had been freed up to do things that had been out of reach in times of high project loads. She started to develop social networks and participated in many conferences; as a result, her number of contacts grew, and she formed a circle of people who later became partners or clients. By the time commercial activity resumed, Olga was already in a different capacity as an expert — she had strengthened her personal brand, and her professional connections had become stronger and more diverse. Truly, in every difficult period lies a valuable gift that can be utilised to great advantage.

5. The pursuit of perfection is a strong stressor for entrepreneurs. Entrepreneurs are often people who are constrained by corporate boundaries. They strive for more, imagine a different future, make plans, set goals. But if you set goals too rigidly, you can experience great stress from the fact that the result is different from what was planned. The result will always be somewhat different: life makes its adjustments, there are new factors that were not taken into account when planning, the straight road turns into a winding path. If you don't take it for granted that life is wiser than our plans, if you don't learn to turn failures into experience and wisdom, you will inevitably burn out from unmet expectations.

Entrepreneurs tend to compare their results not only with their own goals, but also with the results of others in their niche. Nowadays, it is common to share your successes on social media. And when you read what others have achieved, you immediately get an inferiority complex mixed with envy. There is nothing wrong with envy, it all depends on how you dispose of this feeling — if it motivates to do something differently and develop, that is a positive, but if it brings despondency and depressive thoughts, there is nothing good in it. How you dispose of the information you get from social networks, how you work with your feelings, depends on you, on your cognitive evaluation. It's always good to think about the fact that everyone has their own path, their own pros and cons. Everyone has unique value, and speed is just one characteristic of the path — and not necessarily the most important. As one entrepreneur told me, "You look at social networks and realise that you have no time for anything, everyone has already run far ahead. Then it is important to accept yourself, your pace, and say to yourself, 'I am a snail, I take a long time to work through everything, I take a long time to harness, but I do get there." It is important to learn to recognise and not devalue your personal results, even if they seem insignificant.

But I've heard a different attitude towards social media and its perfunctory nature. As another businesswoman says, "Social media is just for showing off. It's like a catwalk — mannequins don't walk around in gowns and curlers. It is good to use them for this very purpose — a facade of oneself, showing the best side of oneself. Among other things, it boosts self-esteem. If you write something clever, or how successful you are, you'll like it yourself. Then you get more likes, and generally your mood is lifted."

I guess if you look at social networks with irony or use them as a channel for advertising, that is also a way to go. The main thing is to treat yourself in a friendly way, with care, in some places with self-irony and humour, but necessarily with an understanding of your inner value, and awareness of the facade of everything that is flaunted on social networks. Book a photo shoot and your best photo will be as good as a famous blogger's — if that's what you're after. The main thing is awareness, peace of mind, and a friendly attitude towards yourself and your achievements.

Key Takeaways:

- Work is a source of increased psychosocial risks. But we have the opportunity to control our working relationships by changing the place of work, changing the work environment, or transforming our perception of the situation. A crisis at work has the potential to lead to personal and professional growth, if we respond appropriately to challenges and learn valuable lessons from difficulties.

- The pandemic has provoked many changes in the working environment, increasing the risks of employee burnout. But on the other hand, employers have started to pay more attention to staff health and building a corporate culture of wellbeing.
- Entrepreneurial stress is another problem of our time. Entrepreneurs, freelancers, and self-employed people experience increased anxiety due to high vulnerability to crises. In addition, they lack the social support from colleagues and managers that employees in employment have. Professional communities and mastermind groups could replace the lack of support and communication in the working environment.

Why Aren't We Equal Before Stress?

According to Hans Selye, "Stress is not what happens to us, but how we feel about it", and we can see this by observing the stress reactions of different people. You've probably noticed that some people deal with difficulties and stressful situations quite easily, while for others any little thing causes a lot of tension and anxiety. Why are we not equal before stress?

In reality, the reaction to stress will depend on many reasons: life experience, personality, and accumulated external and internal resources to cope with difficulties. All of these together will determine both individual reactions and the choice of coping strategies. As a result, some people turn out to be quite resistant to life adversities, while some find it difficult to tolerate even small stimuli.

Stevan E. Hobfoll, one of the world's leading stress researchers, has made significant contributions to the study of the psychological effects of natural disasters, war, and terrorism. He developed the Resource Conservation Theory, which is used in the study of the effects of acute stress. The theory proposes that stress should be viewed in terms of the loss — or threat of loss — of resources. From Stevan E. Hobfoll's perspective, life circumstances in themselves, such as a change in social status, relocation, divorce, or job loss are not stressful unless they are followed by a loss of resource stores, which is a key factor leading to stress (Hobfoll et al., 2006).

Resources are those values that a person possesses and endeavours to preserve and enhance. They include material values that a person possesses (income, house, objects of material wellbeing), as well as non-material categories, which include social resources (social status, relationships, social support), and internal, personal ones (physical and mental wellbeing, system of life values, optimism, resilience, sense of inner control). According to Hobfoll, it is personal resources that are the main components of stress resilience and adaptability.

Stressful events are not only a threat, but also an opportunity for development. And the more accumulated resources we have — physical, psychological, and social — the more resilience we possess, and the better we are able to turn stress into growth. Under the pressure of stressful circumstances, resources are mobilised and further developed. Then we talk about the phenomenon of post-traumatic or stressful growth, when people do not just cope with stress, but achieve more by increasing their inner resources.

If wellbeing is a balance between challenges and internal resources, then imbalance and stress arise if we lack internal resources. And the greater the gap between resources and challenges, the greater the stress and its effects on the body.

When faced with stress, it is important to make the best use of your accumulated arsenal of resources and to continue investing in your development. And we have to face stressful events and uncertainty surprisingly often. What is left in these conditions? Simply to live, developing our tolerance for uncertainty; not forgetting to rejoice in every day and moment of happiness; experiencing the joy of communicating with close and beloved people; doing what we like, what is important and valuable.

The level of wellbeing depends much more on the individual, rather than being something random like a fortunate coincidence. You probably know of people who live happily with themselves and the world without great wealth or fame; they have simply caught their 'ikigai' — a Japanese word for the meaning of life, or the reason for happiness. It can be said that this is the reason why a person rises from bed in the morning — to approach the day's tasks with a sense of pleasure. This inner joy provides resilience in the face of difficulties, and they skillfully balance the level of challenges with their resources. And they are as happy as they can be. And there are contrasting examples: rich and famous people who have many ambitions and many challenges, but lack the resources to cope optimally with circumstances. As a result, immature strategies of stress management are used, such as alcohol, drugs, and eating disorders. It is difficult to talk about personal wellbeing in the presence of addictions and health problems.

Everything we can control is within. By managing our resources, we can control stress and achieve psychological wellbeing. And our inner wellbeing determines the quality of our decisions and choices that shape our lives. So, through managing our resources, we manage our lives.

Individual Stressors

Now let's look at how we ourselves, without much external challenge, can create our own stress by depleting our own reserves of resources.

Physical health is the basis for life activities. Our behaviour is directly related to our overall health. We behave actively or passively depending on the energy available. Using the example of a coronavirus infection, we can consider how the body responds to the intervention of the virus: a healthy body, with a good level of immunity and no co-morbidities, will quickly cope with the disease and recover;

while a depleted body and co-morbidities can lead to a severe outcome, including death. In the same way, the state of health will also affect the ability to cope with other stressors — at work or in one's personal life. And the effects on the body can vary too. A higher level of physical resources means a higher resistance to stressors.

One of my clients, Alexander, came to coaching to deal with a set of personal and professional problems that were progressively growing. It was difficult to make decisions: whether to quit his job or not, whether to break up with his partner or not. Along the way, it turned out that Alexander was sleeping rather little — an average of five hours a night. Lack of sufficient sleep for one to two weeks is a sufficient reason for chronic stress with all its consequences, including loss of energy and rigidity of thinking. I had to explain to my client that with such lack of sleep, it would be difficult to make effective decisions and restore psychological balance. It would be a good idea to get a good night's sleep first. As a rule, such ideas are not accepted at first — you don't want to change your usual way of life, and in general, you don't come to a coach for advice on getting a good night's sleep. Although Alexander was aware that insufficient sleep is bad, at first he could not find an extra two hours of sleep in his day. Fortunately, having later created a serious intention to improve his sleep, he was able to adjust his regime to sleep at least seven hours every day. And the results didn't take long to show up. Just a few days later, Alexander reported that he felt surprisingly well; he had more energy, more enthusiasm, and the sessions started to be fruitful — his rested brain started working at full capacity. Six months later, everything in his life got better — the necessary decisions were made and he started a new career, which he had not dared to do before, and his relationship with his partner got better. He had big plans ahead of him, and a calm confidence in his soul that everything was going as it should. And the first trigger for change was a simple step — getting a good night's sleep, and restoring physical resources.

So if you suddenly find yourself stuck in a dead end and the solution is not forthcoming, you should first check what state your body is in: how much you sleep, how you eat, move, rest, balance your work and personal life. Lack of sleep and rest are stressors that can lead to burnout. But daily routines are within our control, and if you balance work and rest, you'll be more resilient and more productive. Sometimes working less means getting more done.

I classify work on improving physical health as 'quick wins' — it is the replenishment of physical resources that gives an immediate contribution to increasing energy levels; the desire to act arises, stress tolerance increases, and solutions are found to the most difficult situations. When it is not clear what to do, you should start with your body, with contribution to your physical state. Energy will increase, cognitive processes will improve, and gradually new solutions and a new outlook on circumstances will come.

My journey into mindfulness and wellbeing practices started with yoga, mindful living, and taking care of my health. When you pump the channel of physical energy, it gradually starts to arrive, then there is enough energy for the next step — you start to think about awareness of yourself and your needs, you want to put your mind in order. That is why it is no coincidence that after body practices I came to meditation and mindfulness practices, and got a psychological education. Changing yourself also leads to changes in your external life — you start to express yourself outwardly, make connections, try new projects. The idea to write my first book also came in the process of realising my needs, and a desire to share my thoughts with the world. This journey of listening to yourself and building your life trajectory never ends, but to stay on track, it's important to take care of your energy. Otherwise, you will have to live in survival mode rather than on a creative vibration.

Psychological resources are another line of protection on which the outcome of any stressor depends. If we are able to withstand stress, if we are able to handle our feelings with care and accept them, if we are able to live our emotions in an ecological way without destroying our lives or the lives of others, then we have a good resilience. This means that failures are not able to knock us out of our rut for a long time, because we are able to accept unpleasant experiences and react to them adequately.

On the other hand, we can create our own stress by simply thinking catastrophic thoughts in response to any threat, even imaginary ones. We can get stuck in a mental replay of real or potential failures, feeling shame, guilt, fear, or anxiety. It is human nature to spend large amounts of energy worrying about things that will never happen. If we let this habit blossom into a lush flower, constantly fertilising the soil of anxiety, this will be our internal preconditions for chronic stress, burnout, and illness. Of course, when the external background is unstable, changing, or uncertain, and lately it has often been just that, we experience a whole bunch of emotions that create a sense of inner anxiety. And at the same time, it's a good opportunity to learn to experience emotions and accept change in an ecological way.

We often try to change our feelings and experiences, to overcome unpleasant feelings, to get rid of them. Sometimes it is more helpful to just look at the emotion, to surrender, to accept, to acknowledge that, yes, this is an unpleasant experience that I don't like. But I can be with it. And then the difficult emotion loses its power; it becomes just an experience that we can experience without struggle or displacement. It turns out that the lesson of experiencing difficult emotions is there, and there is less resistance and suffering. And this seems to be the only way we can learn to live in peace with this fragile, anxious world.

We provide ourselves with stress through automatic thoughts and beliefs that sound in our heads like a radio. It seems to us that we all perceive the same reality but, no, everyone's reality is different, and radio antennas are different — some people play Radio Relaxation (but it is necessary to tune in to this wave on purpose), and others have Radio Anxiety or Hopelessness FM switched on by default.

The fact is that reality is given to us in sensations and in no other way. If we imagine that our mind is a mirror, then reality is just an image in the mirror. And mirrors are different — exaggerating reality or diminishing it, clean or polluted, or with a system of filters and impossibility to perceive some colours. What's my point? To the fact that we ourselves can choose which mirror we use to look at the world. And the more friendly a mirror we have, the better we feel in this world, and the less tension we feel.

Cognitive-behavioural therapy offers the skills to critically analyse one's own thoughts, through which to identify and change harmful thoughts that interfere with one's life. For example, many people have a habit of making a big deal out of things, i.e. looking at an event through a magnifying glass and imagining horrible consequences. Think of how we react when a teenage child comes home late or is out of reach for hours. Do you remember what comes to mind in those instances? I don't know about you, but I have often had the worst assumptions in my head in these situations. If you do not work with such thoughts, you exhaust yourself, then exhaust the child, and create an atmosphere of fear in the family; what follows is the strategy of hyper-parenting to somehow cope with anxiety, and as a result, the relationship with the child will spoil — it can even slow down the normal process of growing up. And after all, the fault is just the habit of catastrophising any event. What helped me in these cases was an observer's perspective. I realised that I have a very active amygdala, which is always worried about everything, so I tried to calm it down with the help of alternative thoughts. Firstly, I remembered that it was not the first time I was worried, that usually everything ends well, and that my thoughts were just a product of the active amygdala, which sees everything as a threat. I made sure to thank my active amygdala for doing this work, and seeing the risks, and then I counter-argued why those risks were probably not significant. I thought about other reasons why the child did not contact me, weighed the risks of different events, remembered what happened last time, and gradually came to a more realistic scenario of the situation.

When the habit of thinking constructively and critically appears, the emotions gradually calm down; they are subordinated to the course of thought. As a Japanese proverb says: "Worry does not eliminate tomorrow's problems, but takes away today's peace". It is the ability to return today's peace that we need to learn in order not to get an anxiety disorder.

Or there is also such a well-known phenomenon as mind reading — knowing what other people are thinking. It seems that someone thinks badly of us or even has negative intentions. Most often these are projections of our own thoughts that have nothing to do with reality. We simply 'read' the thoughts we fear the most — after all, our brains are very sensitive to any kind of threat, explicit or invented. But when we learn to recognise that these are just our thoughts and fears, we can find alternative explanations for people's actions and be critical of our projections. A friend of mine once shared with me that she feels like she is seen as a bad mother. I know she works hard, yet children and family are a big part of her life and she spends great time with her kids, coming up with cool trips with a focus on child development. So, I was surprised by her 'bad mother' thought. I asked her how she knew that's what people around her think, and who specifically thinks that. She replied that she suspects even her kids' nanny thinks that way because, "What else could she be thinking when I get home late?" "Oh, anything," I blurted out. "Maybe she thinks you work hard so you need her services, and that's why she has a job." Seeing the surprise in my eyes, my acquaintance wondered at the justice of her thoughts. She concluded that she was the one who thinks this way about herself when she gets home late, and attributes her own thoughts to others. Before we 'read minds', it is always wise to consider whose thoughts we are reading and where they come from.

If you just observe your thoughts a little bit — practice thinking differently — you get a sense of freedom. After all, we can adjust our mirror of reality ourselves, thereby reducing the influence of internal stressors, which are sometimes more destructive than external events.

These days, anxiety can also arise due to high information load and multitasking. This stress factor haunts many managers, executives, and professionals who work with a lot of information, who are constantly switching between tasks and projects, jumping from meeting to meeting, and communicating with a large number of people. These are often successful people who enjoy what they do, but at the end of the day they experience a feeling of information overload and vague anxiety; there is a feeling that something has not been done in time, or something has been forgotten. Needless to say, against this background sleep problems easily arise — difficulty falling asleep, frequent awakenings, or early rising. The brain does not calm down and it is difficult to go to the phase of relaxation. This type of anxiety is quite natural for a busy person.

It is difficult to stay healthy and happy in our multitasking world, where it seems that you must have several heads to think about different problems. But we still only have one head, even though we now divide it between many different tasks and contexts. And because I like to load myself up with multifaceted tasks, I learnt long ago that it's quite difficult to deal with large information loads and multitasking, without the tools of mindfulness and relaxation. We simply become aware, put the information on the shelves, don't let anything unnecessary into our consciousness, periodically learn to refuse something, practice relaxation techniques before going to bed, and from time to time arrange a mental detox — a day without gadgets, without communication, in contact with ourselves and the present moment. And then the problem of how to calm the mind and replenish your psychological resource will be solved.

Social resources are also our coping capital, or conversely, problematic social relationships themselves can be a stressor.

When faced with difficulties, asking others for help can be very helpful. In this case, we can get real help for what we lack — for example, friends can lend us money, or thanks to connections we can get valuable information about where and who to go to in a difficult situation. And there are many different issues that can be solved thanks to the 'six degrees of separation'. It all depends on whether there is a habit of asking for help, and whether there is a social network around that can respond to requests. I've always been fascinated by people who easily ask for help and quickly find information, contacts, resources when they need it. I still nurture that skill in myself. Having good social connections, I rarely use them for personal use when I am experiencing difficulties, and only in some critical cases can I ask for help — sometimes I don't even remember that someone can help me, although I know that most of the time people willingly respond to requests. Psychologists have long ago proved that to do pleasant things to others is to give yourself joy and pleasure. So, it's good to give your social circle this opportunity more often.

An important help from our social circle is emotional support through empathy and sympathy. Such support is even more effective than actual deeds. We are very social beings and it is important for us to be understood. That's why it's so important to ask for help and share your feelings when the need arises. And, of course, it should work the other way round too — you should be more attentive and empathic to other people's feelings. Then one can feel the real power of social connections. With this strength, we feel more secure from any adversity and difficulties.

On the other hand, if there are issues with building healthy relationships — if you feel lonely, isolated, alienated, or suffer from toxic relationships that take energy — then that distress that needs resolution.

Whatever the circumstances of life, we have internal resources and the capacity to cope with them. But we also have internal stressors that can lead to chronic stress and burnout. The good news is that internal resources and individual stressors can be influenced by ourselves.

Strategies to Protect Against Stress

Each of us in our own way forms a line of defense against stressful influences, and as a result we reap the benefits of our coping strategies. Coping is a strategy for dealing with stress, when we make certain efforts to reduce stress tension.

Stress, as we already know, is a response to changes that require the body to adapt. The brain assesses the situation and if it recognises a threat, it also forms a strategy on how to deal with that threat. If we feel we have enough resources to cope with the situation or the threat is minor, then we won't worry about it too much — we'll relegate the stressor to the category of insignificant and forget about it. For example, in the past, when you've fallen ill with a mild cold, it was generally perceived as a threat, but still minor. The assessment of the disease itself and the body's resources allowed you to calmly endure this unpleasantness without much stress. Our experience of coping with similar situations in the past allows us to remain calm and predict a favorable outcome. It was quite different to experience cold symptoms during the COVID19 epidemic — this had never happened before, the outcomes of coronavirus infection are different, so the anxiety was greater. Although if we were confident in our physical resources, we were likely to adapt quickly to this new threat without much panic. Our inner state and emotional reaction to a stressor always depend on the interpretation of the situation.

Emotions serve as a measure of the good and bad in our lives, thereby telling us how we should act. If something we value is hurt, we experience anger, which gives us the energy to protect our values. If we experience fear, we will take action to reduce the risk of what we fear. And joy will provide positive reinforcement for the actions that caused the joyful state, so we will try to keep repeating the programme. In fact, emotions do not depend on the event itself, but on the evaluation we make of it. To experience anger in response to something, we must first realise what is at stake — the wellbeing of our loved ones, our own health, or perhaps an important goal that we are striving for with all our passion. Depending on the interpretation, an emotional response will arise. The same event can evoke diametrically opposite emotions. For example, a silver medal at the Olympics may be a triumph for someone who has never won a medal before, but for another athlete who has trained to win a gold medal, it will be a bitter failure. The perception of the event will depend on the context and personal history.

So, it's not all that clear-cut with emotions, some people are happy about an event and others are sad in response to the same thing. Evolutionarily, emotions evolved from simpler ways of adaptation, such as reflexes and physiological needs. Simple adaptation mechanisms don't require our interpretation — they clearly cause us to act one way or another. For example, a neurologist tests the knee reflex by tapping the patient's knee with a hammer, and if there is no abnormality, there is no other option — the knee will twitch in response to the hammer stimulus, with no regard for context or our motives. We are also conditioned by physiological needs, although we have some degree of freedom: for example, if we are hungry, we can be patient for another hour, but we are still forced to satisfy this need at the first opportunity. But with emotions we have relative freedom, because different people will have emotions of different character and intensity for the same stimulus. Many factors will determine the individual reaction — past experience, life goals, way of thinking, and the context of the situation. It turns out that our thoughts, values, and motives come between the stimulus and the reaction. In this case, the emotional response is a response not to the stimulus itself, but to the meaning of the stimulus for the individual.

Building on the link between event interpretation and emotion, American psychologist Richard Lazarus created a model of stress based on cognitive appraisal. The evaluation of an event creates a subjective picture — based on which, stress of a particular intensity will arise.

Since each person will assess the situation differently, everyone's stress level will be different. How does the cognitive appraisal process work? The first level of assessment concerns the event itself, and the degree of its impact on the person's life, and the secondary assessment concerns the resources that can be deployed to solve the problem. For example, a person faces a dramatic event, such as losing their job because the company is forced to downsize. From the point of view of primary assessment, this is quite a dramatic event for almost every person — unless you have secretly dreamed about it for a long time, without deciding to take such a step yourself. Still, for most people, losing a job is an extremely unpleasant experience. The secondary assessment (how well I can handle it) becomes the determining factor. For instance, someone who has built a sufficient financial cushion will feel less anxious than a person with no savings and a mortgage. One may calmly look for another job based on their interest, while the other may become depressed, fearing financial ruin is imminent. Or people may differ in their life experiences: one person might have faced such challenges many times before, with positive outcomes. They may also have an in-demand specialty and a strong sense of self-confidence. Such an individual is likely to react more calmly than someone encountering job loss for the first time. In the secondary assessment, we draw on our resources and past experiences, which help us choose the best coping strategies and manage stress more effectively.

As a result of cognitive appraisal (or interpretation) we get an emotional response; it may be a little anxiety or a lot of fear, or perhaps anger and a whole bunch of other emotions that will provoke this or that behaviour. There are two main types of response to a stressful situation: you can change the situation (problem-oriented coping) or you can change your attitude to the situation (emotion-oriented coping). That is, one can change one's state either through transformation of the situation and active actions, or through adaptation by changing one's attitude to what has happened. In the latter case, we accept the circumstances as they are, but look at them from a different angle that does not create emotional tension.

It may seem that a strategy that focuses on actively changing the situation is better than emotional coping, where we learn to explain the situation differently. This is often true, but it is not always possible to change the situation. The choice of strategy therefore depends on the context — the circumstances, the resources available, and the possibility of change in principle. Flexibility and the ability to choose the best way to respond is adaptability and resilience.

Stress is often associated with unfavorable life circumstances, such as losing something valuable. It can also arise from difficult social interactions, whether in the workplace or within the family. The body will try in every possible way to cope with the discomfort and find a new balance. And in each situation, different strategies can be useful. In certain cases, it is better to change the circumstances, but sometimes it is useful to simply change the angle of view and start interpreting the situation in a more positive way. When working as a coach with clients facing professional deadlocks, I recall cases where the best solution was to leave the job — an act that safeguarded health and opened new opportunities. In other situations, the greater value lay in keeping the job but shifting one's perspective on the situation, combined with small adjustments to the nature of the work. Ultimately, only the person facing the decision knows the answer to the question of what is best. It is their unique combination of individual traits and specific context that determines the way out of stress. The key to finding an optimal solution lies in cultivating awareness of one's resources, values, experiences, goals, and motives.

Nowadays, many people are experiencing an existential crisis, pondering questions like "Who am I?" and "Where am I going?". This crisis creates a tension that demands resolution. It is crucial to cultivate resilience to uncertainty, as solutions and answers rarely come immediately. Often, one must search for them, both within oneself and in external circumstances. This process requires developing self-awareness and a deep understanding of one's true needs. From there, a clear decision can emerge — whether to change the situation or to focus on accepting and finding value in what already exists.

Sometimes, in a stressful situation, it is important not to rush to change the circumstances but to work on the inner state. This approach is especially important for preserving family relationships, where problems have accumulated but great value remains.

Whether you aim to change your circumstances or your psychological attitude toward them, it is crucial to rely on yourself and maintain a sense of control:
- *I can change my state of mind*
- *I shape my circumstances rather than merely stating what happens to me*
- *I make conscious choices and take responsibility for what happens in my life*

We can learn to accept what cannot be controlled, and to organise our lives in the best possible way within the limits of what is manageable. Moreover, we always have the freedom to perceive circumstances in a way that is kinder and more supportive to ourselves.

Now let's take a closer look at the eight types of coping strategies proposed by Richard Lazarus. Two of them refer to problem-focused coping and six refer to emotion-focused coping, aimed at changing attitudes. To make the theory of coping strategies more relatable and applicable to real-life situations, I sought to create verbal metaphors for each of them.

Change-focused coping (or problem-focused coping) can involve either confrontation — asserting oneself through conflict and aggression — or rational attempts to change the situation through planning and consistent action.

Confrontive coping, or the 'Fighter' Strategy For instance, if you haven't received the promised pay raise you've been waiting for, you might choose to confront your boss. Open conflict rarely resolves such issues and is more likely to create additional problems, but in some cases, it may result in your demands being met. Confrontation isn't always aimed at changing the situation — it is often an impulsive act meant to reduce emotional tension.

Since confrontation is challenging to classify as a purposeful action with predictable outcomes, it is more commonly seen as a maladaptive strategy. However, this does not mean that conflict cannot be the optimal approach in certain situations. For example, if your child is threatened by bullies, you would immediately rush to their defense without hesitation. In such cases, open confrontation is not only appropriate but also necessary.

Planful problem-solving, or the 'Manager' Strategy When you think about fixing a situation peacefully. In this case, you still aim for action, but only after thinking about and choosing the best steps to take. You analyse the situation and develop a plan, taking into account the prevailing conditions, available resources, and past experience. Using the same example, where you did not receive the promised pay rise, you schedule a meeting with your boss, present your arguments, back them up with facts, and agree on the next steps. Perhaps not now, but with a slight delay, your request will be considered. Having a concrete plan to change the situation helps to reduce emotional reactions even before the problem is resolved.

Planful problem-solving is generally regarded as an adaptive strategy, with substantial evidence supporting this: people who actively address situations and resolve problems peacefully tend to experience higher levels of wellbeing and health. However, this strategy is not always optimal in every situation. Over-reliance on analysis, rational calculation, and planning can come at the expense of spontaneity, intuition, and emotion.

Rationality can effectively address the visible part of a problem, but it risks suppressing emotions — and with them our deeper needs, which often communicate through our emotional sphere. Personally, I am a strong advocate of the strategy of planning solutions, but I always validate my action plan through my emotions. I try to visualise my emotional state after implementing the plan: how will I feel in that scenario? Only if I sense no resistance at the level of my body and emotions do I confirm my choice. If my plan feels more comfortable on paper than in my inner state, I return to the starting point and search for alternative solutions.

The next family of strategies, emotion-focused coping, brings together six rather different ways of coping with stress through changing attitudes towards the stressor.

Distancing, or the 'We Don't Care' Strategy This way of reacting means that we try to devalue what happened. To distance yourself from the problem, you can focus on something positive, reduce the significance through rationalisation, incorporate humour, and reduce the drama of what happened.

Sometimes it really does make sense to ignore certain irritants. For example, a family member didn't wash a cup and left it on the table. Is there any point in getting angry about it? Maybe it's better to tell yourself how good it is that I have a family, each with their own habits; we are all close people and love each other.

I know very resilient and psychologically pumped-up people who have learnt to ignore insults from others. They don't get worked up when they get bullied, realising that it's not their problem — it's the problem of the person trying to shift their anger or their problems onto someone else. This is a pretty wise way of reacting to stimuli that don't make a big difference in your life. But if you artificially try to devalue something important, it will still affect your state of mind — if you experience a troubling symptom and instead of going to the doctor, you simply chase the troubling thoughts away, this strategy can have dramatic consequences.

It is useful to employ the 'We Don't Care' Strategy if you realise that you are producing a strong emotional response to trivial stimuli. For example, a mess in your son's room results in an outburst of anger on your part, and costs you a damaged relationship with your child for several days. In this case, it is appropriate to recognise the level of threat and the level of your reaction, and consciously reduce the significance of the event.

It is important, however, to avoid maladaptive use of this strategy, where you devalue your true experiences, underestimate the significance of the stimulus, and miss the opportunity to change the situation.

Self-controlling, or the 'Man in the Box' Strategy This involves efforts to regulate your feelings and actions. On the one hand, you try not to show your feelings, and on the other hand, you try to control your emotions so that you don't act impulsively. Such a strategy can be very useful in the moment; instead of giving in to the first impulse, you find the strength to sleep on the problem, in order to make an informed decision with a fresh head.

However, keeping your feelings under lock and key all the time is a time bomb. If you don't recognise and process your emotions, they build up inside, exacerbating the stress tension that can explode into a nervous breakdown, burnout, and depression. Unfortunately, the desire to succeed at any cost often makes us hide our weakness, because it spoils the glossy picture of success that mass culture sells us. The value of achievement is so high that it becomes shameful to show one's failure, one's vulnerability. And this teaches us to be good in all circumstances, not to show our problems, not to share our feelings. Everything is hidden deep inside, so that no one guesses. But this strategy leaves you alone with your problems — you can't even ask for help, because then you show weakness.

Self-controlling is useful in terms of preventing impulsive, destructive behaviour, but everything is good in moderation. Sometimes it is good to allow yourself to wallow, express your feelings, get support, gain resilience, adapt to the situation, and move on.

Seeking social support, or the 'We Are Together' Strategy Another way of coping with failure or distress, both asking for help to solve a problem and seeking emotional support to alleviate the inner state can work to one's advantage. Sometimes people share their troubles through social networks and quickly get help — contacts, information, participation, kind words. When hundreds of people write words of support — it becomes a little easier to experience any grief. It is only important not to forget to address your social circle, without fear of appearing weak, incompetent, or unsuccessful. It is believed that extroverted people, who are sociable and easily make contacts, are better able to cope with stress. This is because it is easy for them to share their news and ask for help. This is a quality we should all learn from.

Can such a strategy become maladaptive in some contexts? In some cases, it can; if you rely too much on external connections, become dependent on other people, it inhibits the development of internal resources and self-reliance. Everything is good in moderation!

Accepting responsibility, or the 'Protagonist' Strategy This implies that you recognise your role in the problem, and try to responsibly resolve the situation. After all, if you understand what actions led to the problem, you can find a solution by changing your own behaviour. Awareness of personal responsibility is a good chance to change your situation, because realising you are the main actor and not a puppet in the hands of circumstances, gives motivation and impetus to action. But this strategy is dangerous for excessive self-criticism and self-accusation, which can lead to depression. And depression does not stimulate action at all.

So, recognising yourself as the protagonist of your life is very useful — if you don't slip into self-obsession and thoughts of "I'm not OK."

Escape-Avoidance, or the 'Ostrich' Strategy When someone seeks to simply escape from a difficult situation. This coping mechanism focuses on ignoring the problem like an ostrich burying its head in the sand; a person might hope the issue resolves itself while they distract themselves by sleeping, eating, numbing the pain with alcohol, or relieving tension with pills.

While medication may serve as an acute remedy in a critical moment, it is not a sustainable coping strategy for managing stress. Relying on painkillers or other forms of avoidance is unlikely to foster the development of effective coping skills. However, the experience of actively managing stress is invaluable and can always serve as a resource in the future.

Avoidance strategies should be used very carefully, after observing how this coping plays a role in your life. And if there are eating disorders, problems with alcohol or other substance abuse, it is worth recognising the problem and thinking about using other coping strategies.

Researchers most often refer to this strategy to maladaptive, but in a situation of acute stress or psychological trauma, it can be useful in achieving a short-term effect of reduced emotional tension.

Positive reappraisal, or 'Stress Growth' Strategy This means giving a positive meaning to an event in terms of its benefits for personal development, for gaining life experience. "The pessimist sees every opportunity as a difficulty, and the optimist sees every difficulty as an opportunity." Words often attributed to Winston Churchill, though their authorship is unconfirmed. Regardless of the source, it is hard to disagree with the sentiment. Indeed, many negative events have a positive meaning after time, though in the moment it is quite difficult to assess it.

As Steve Jobs famously said in his legendary commencement speech to Stanford University graduates: "You can't connect the dots looking forward; you can only connect them looking backward." When Apple was already a $2 billion company with 4,000 employees, Steve Jobs was fired from the company he had created. What could be more dramatic? And yet after months of not knowing what to do next, the burden of being a successful man was replaced by the ease of a start-up with nothing to lose — and Steve Jobs entered one of the most fruitful periods of his life. He started two companies, NeXT and Pixar, and importantly, started a family. Apple subsequently bought NeXT and Steve Jobs made a triumphant return to Apple, and Pixar became a very successful animation company. In his opinion, none of this would have happened if he hadn't been fired from Apple.

Now imagine that you have the skill to connect these dots with perspective, and immediately realise that failure is a bitter medicine that will definitely help. If you view failure as a gift of fate, completely different solutions appear, and other goals and opportunities begin to emerge.

I really like to think about the meaning of failures and try to learn something useful from them. The idea for this book you are reading was also born from the proverb "If it were not for luck, misfortune would have helped." The idea for the book was born at a time of some pause in my teaching. I had a number of programmes planned, which were unexpectedly cancelled due to another quarantine lockdown. It was frustrating that plans were being disrupted — that once again, nothing could be planned or predicted. But then there was the free space in the calendar — I found myself completely free for some time. And then I thought I must make good use of this gift of free time, which I never have. So, the idea for the book was formed, the seeds of which were sown thanks to my forced downtime, which freed my head for new projects.

Is the strategy of positive reassessment always beneficial? There are some nuances to keep in mind if you like to see the positive side of everything. The grief acceptance curve typically begins with shock and denial, followed by anger and bargaining, then sadness, and finally, acceptance. It is at the stage of acceptance that one can see the possibilities and benefits and start planning the next steps, seeing a new horizon. But what happens if you jump straight to positive reassessment, skipping all the previous stages? Most likely, the unexpressed emotions that you skillfully pushed away after seeing the beautiful horizons will get stuck in the body and will someday make themselves known by a pang of tension, anxiety, or psychosomatic symptoms. It is these undigested emotions that we work through in psychotherapy. We cannot live our lives limiting our experience to positive emotions; we need all feelings to understand what is important to us, what is valuable. So, a positive reappraisal of the event will be beneficial if we respectfully and recognisably accept all the emotions that understandably arise in difficult circumstances.

To study coping strategies and their impact on wellbeing, Richard Lazarus and colleagues conducted a study of 85 married couples in which both husband and wife were interviewed about stressful events in their lives (Susan Folkman, Richard S. Lazarus, 1986, B). The study lasted six months during which, once a month, respondents were asked to recall the most stressful event of the previous week and to answer questions about their attitudes toward that event. During the interviews, questions were also asked about coping strategies that participants used to cope with stress.

The study revealed no significant differences in the coping strategies of men and women. However, women placed greater emphasis on issues threatening the wellbeing of their loved ones, while men were more concerned with serious circumstances related to their work. Overall, this reflects the traditional focus of men's and women's lives at the time. Notably, the study was conducted in the 1980s, before traditional gender roles underwent the transformations we see today. Therefore, it is difficult to predict what the results might be if the study were conducted in the present day.

Among the important findings is the diversity of coping approaches that people used. In different circumstances, the same person used different coping strategies. Although it was possible to find stability in the use of one of the strategies — positive reappraisal. Some people consistently used positive reappraisal in different circumstances, and viewed life's difficulties as lessons of fate from which they learn and grow. It was concluded that it was likely this strategy was more related to individual personality traits than to context. I thought this was an important finding. It turns out that we can deliberately develop the ability to find something good in a stressful situation, in order to improve our state of mind and experience it, recognising its value.

Lazarus' study showed that the more serious the event, the greater the effort required to adapt, the greater the impact on health and the psychological symptoms experienced. Certain coping strategies have been shown to have a negative impact on health. These include excessive use of psychoactive substances — alcohol, tobacco, and narcotic drugs. Avoidance-related strategies were also not good for health, as they interfered with normal adaptation.

Differences were also found in problem-focused coping: the strategy aimed at solving a problem through planning had a positive effect on psychological status, while confrontational behaviour did not at all. Obviously, coping through a planned solution is a more adaptive strategy than conflict.

As we have already mentioned, the evaluation of an event has quite a big impact on the emotional state and, therefore, on physical health. It is useful to ask yourself, "Is my level of stress response always in line with my level of threat?" Think back to a recent situation where you were nervous. Rate your level of emotional reaction on a 10-point scale, with 10 being the highest reaction and 1 being the lowest. And then think about what was the level of threat to you and your loved ones on a 10-point scale (10 being the highest threat to life and health and 1 being virtually no threat). Now compare the numbers: what was your result?

If your reactivity scale score is higher than your threat scale score, this indicates that you are reacting violently to minimal stimuli and using your adaptive energy inefficiently. Hans Selye said that energy is not infinite, and the more we exhaust ourselves by generating stress energy in response to trivial issues, the less energy we have left to live and enjoy ourselves and adapt to more serious stressors. It is worth thinking about — and perhaps reassessing —your stress reactions, if some events are not worth the high attention and energy expenditure.

Some more thoughts on mature stress management strategies that help to change the interpretation of an event and thus change one's state of mind. Our beliefs can play a positive role at a certain stage of life but later on, they turn from useful to a brake, and we continue to follow them without noticing it. For example, the desire to achieve and compete are helpful at a certain stage of life, but if competition and the desire to be the best are made the main principle of life, we are guaranteed chronic stress. Think about it: can you always be the best at everything? Sometimes it pays to lower the bar and start enjoying normalcy. It often happens that successful people set themselves a vector for victories in childhood, winning Olympiads, getting places in prestigious universities, and they do not turn off the route, even when it is possible to take a break and instead of racing for success, to arrange happiness to live in the moment. But no, many continue to live with the motto I can do better, zeroing in on their achievements, checking off new boxes as an indispensable and mandatory condition for happiness. It is useful to revise your beliefs from time to time, changing rigid principles into new rules. Then life becomes simpler and easier, and the world becomes a much friendlier and more pleasant place.

Perhaps the most important skill for everyone is to learn how to deal with adversity, because there is no avoiding it in life. We can't stay on the bright side of life all the time, circumstances are fluid and changeable, so the healthiest way to deal with your emotions is to accept them. But first, it pays to learn the skill of observing emotions and recognising their right to exist. This is why mindfulness or contemplative practices are so useful — they teach us to be in touch with ourselves, with every experience, to feel emotions without resistance. And when we do not resist, we suffer less.

Optimism is another key to resilience. While some say people are simply born optimistic, this isn't entirely true. Martin Seligman, the founder of positive psychology, introduced the concept of 'learned optimism', where individuals develop the ability to view the world through a positive lens — without resorting to 'rose-coloured glasses' or detachment from reality. A positive perspective helps us respond constructively and effectively to challenges.

For example, in the face of a significant failure, it's unhelpful to internalize the belief that "I am a failure." Instead, it is more constructive to view the setback as a single failed attempt and a valuable life experience. This mindset allows you to analyse the reasons for the failure and identify the next steps. Once the root cause is understood, the tools to address the issue become clearer. And with a solution in sight, motivation naturally follows.

Thinking optimistically and constructively is beneficial in any circumstance. Hopefully, it is becoming clearer how our interpretation of stressful events and our choice of optimal coping strategies can positively influence health and wellbeing.

Key Takeaways:

- **Stress is not a circumstance, but our reaction to it.** Our response to stress depends on many factors, including life experience, personality, and the external and internal resources we have accumulated to face difficulties.

- **Resources are the assets a person possesses and seeks to preserve and enhance.** These include material resources (such as income, housing, and material wellbeing) as well as non-material resources. Non-material resources encompass social assets (social status, relationships, and support networks) and personal resources (physical and mental health, core values, optimism, resilience, and a sense of inner control). Among these, personal resources are the key components of stress resistance and adaptability.
- **Internal resources help us cope with stress, but internal stressors can lead to burnout.** Internal stressors include neglecting basic physiological needs (such as sleep, rest, and proper nutrition), ineffective emotional response patterns, unhelpful beliefs, information overload, and excessive multitasking.

There are two main types of responses to a stressful situation:

o Problem-focused coping: Changing the situation itself.
o Emotion-focused coping: Transforming one's attitude toward the situation.

The choice of strategy depends on the context, including the circumstances, available resources, and the feasibility of change. Flexibility and the ability to choose the most appropriate response demonstrate adaptability and resilience.

PART 2. PROFESSIONAL BURNOUT

Burnout as a phenomenon has historical roots — in particular, many writers described the burnout states of their characters in their works of fiction (e.g. A. P. Chekhov, Thomas Mann, Jack London). However, burnout was first scientifically discussed only in the 1970s. American psychologist Herbert Freudenberger was the first to use the term 'burnout'. In particular, Freudenberger defined burnout as a complex of feelings associated with the experience of failure, a sense of exhaustion as a result of excessive expenditure of energy and resources (Freudenberger H.J., 1974). The scientist used this term to describe the consequences of severe stress in workers of 'helping' professions; doctors and nurses —who chose their profession to help people — often experienced burnout. Freidenberger believed that such a condition often develops in people who tend to be empathetic, idealistic about their work, and prone to daydreaming. Their expectations cannot withstand the harsh reality, and prolonged psychological tension results in burnout.

Nowadays we talk about burnout not only in relation to helping professions; any person in any profession can face this condition. Moreover, burnout can relate not only to work, although this phenomenon has been studied primarily from the point of view of chronic stress in the workplace. But whatever the cause, burnout affects all aspects of a person's life, including health, life satisfaction, sense of meaning, and motivation.

Christina Maslach, an American social psychologist, is the creator of the widely recognised three-factor model of burnout. According to Maslach et al., burnout consists of three core components:

1. Emotional Exhaustion, characterized by feelings of powerlessness, fatigue, and a sense of being drained.
2. Depersonalization (or Cynicism), expressed as detachment, callousness, or a negative, indifferent attitude toward work or others.
3. Reduced Personal Accomplishment, marked by a diminished sense of effectiveness, lower self-esteem, a loss of purpose, and a lack of motivation to exert effort in one's work.
(Maslach C., 1997)

Quite a lot of research is devoted to the study of the connection of burnout to various somatic diseases and mental health disorders. Sometimes it is not easy to differentiate burnout and depression, because quite often burnout is associated with symptoms of anxiety and depression. For example, it has been shown that if a person has been diagnosed with depression or anxiety disorder, it is very likely that he or she also suffers from burnout. In other studies of employees experiencing burnout, it was found that 59% of people diagnosed with burnout also had an anxiety disorder and 58% had depression, with 27% having somatic symptoms (Maske U.E. et al., 2016).

Despite the frequent conflation of burnout with depression and anxiety, they are distinct conditions (Koutsimani P. et al., 2019). Emotional burnout syndrome has now been recognised as a separate phenomenon. The WHO has included burnout in its International Classification of Diseases (2019) as a factor affecting health status.

The WHO defines burnout as "chronic work-related stress", thereby legitimizing the understanding that work can pose health risks. Recognising these risks is crucial for both employers and employees, as it fosters a more informed approach to the work environment and one's role within it. After all, forewarned is forearmed!

Why Do We Burn Out?

Victoria loved her job. She worked as a project manager in a consulting company, where her responsibilities included communicating with people, conducting research, and performing extensive analytics. The results of her projects helped clients not only achieve commercial success but also make their businesses more socially oriented. Everything seemed perfect — creative research, utilizing her talents, and a strong sense of purpose in her work. Feeling that her work was meaningful and valued became an additional source of energy and motivation to continue investing in her career.

However, Victoria had no control over her workload. With multiple urgent projects piling up, working evenings and weekends became routine. Initially, her deep engagement with her work prevented her from noticing the warning signs her body was sending — signals that more energy was being spent than replenished. Over time, she began to feel an inner resistance to overwork, realising that she had less and less time for hobbies, socializing, and other aspects of life. Eventually, it became clear that she was constantly repairing her health just to maintain the energy needed to keep working.

Another draining factor was the sense of injustice she felt regarding the imbalance between the effort and time she invested in her work and the rewards she received—both material and moral. "When you think about not being paid extra, it's also about your merits not being recognised," Victoria reflected. She even discussed her dissatisfaction with her manager, who listened attentively and tried to help but ultimately explained that company policies, such as annual salary reviews and fixed caps, made meaningful change impossible. This only deepened her frustration. While employees were told how important and valuable they were, the reality was that management seemed powerless to challenge established rules and constraints.

The strain of overwork continued for two years, pushing Victoria to her limit. To sustain herself, she spent significant sums each month on a psychologist, spa treatments, massages, and taxis for late evenings at the office. These expenses were her way of coping with the fatigue that never fully disappeared. Weekends no longer provided a real reset, and the benefits of a vacation faded within days. What had once been her dream job no longer brought her joy or a sense of purpose.

When energy levels are depleted, survival becomes the priority, and thoughts of meaning and fulfillment take a backseat.

The breaking point came during a challenging project with international colleagues. The client was demanding, unfair, and relentless in exerting pressure. Management offered no support. One evening, after another round of unjustified criticism from foreign partners, Victoria found herself struggling to breathe. She felt a sharp pain near her heart. "It seems too early for a heart attack," she thought, but an article she had recently read about younger people experiencing strokes and heart attacks surfaced in her mind. Unable to call for help, she sat silently crying, her colleagues — busy with their own tasks — failing to notice her distress.

Later, she would refuse to call an ambulance, reasoning that the episode had passed. She relied on the first-aid kit at work to reduce her elevated blood pressure, took a taxi home, and made the final decision to quit. A cardiologist later diagnosed her with neuralgia and strongly advised her to change her working routine. This time, Victoria listened.

"I didn't know what I would do next, but I knew I had to save myself. When you're burned out, fear of the unknown fades — it's replaced by an instinct for self-preservation," Victoria recalls. She quit without a plan, understanding it was the only right decision at the time.

It took her a year to recover from the burnout she had fallen into. During that year, she worked slowly at her own pace as a freelancer, taking on just one project per month. She gradually rediscovered her love for her profession, and re-engaged with her many creative hobbies.

Today, Victoria is carefully establishing her own rules for how she works as a self-employed professional, striving to find a healthy balance between income and workload. What helps her avoid burnout now? She remains in touch with her emotions, continues working with a psychologist, and relies on a supportive circle of friends and colleagues. This network provides her with the social connection and reassurance that she is not alone, and can always seek help when needed.

If you've ever experienced burnout, some elements of Victoria's story may feel familiar: over-involvement, external pressures, unfair rewards, persistent fatigue, and declining health. Her story is not unique. Under the right conditions, anyone can become a victim of burnout. In today's world, burnout has become an increasingly prevalent issue.

Research from the CIPD (The Chartered Institute of Personnel and Development, UK) highlights that stress is becoming one of the leading causes of both short- and long-term employee absence. In 2021, 79% of employers surveyed reported staff missing workdays due to stress within the past year, a figure that rises to 91% for organisations with more than 250 employees.

The primary causes of workplace stress are linked to high workloads, though the COVID-19 pandemic also featured prominently among the main stressors. Many individuals are experiencing mental health challenges, including anxiety, depression, and post-traumatic stress disorder (PTSD).

In response, employers are increasingly prioritising employee mental health by implementing corporate wellbeing programmes, with a strong focus on mental health support. Notably, organisations that adopt a strategic approach to wellbeing report positive outcomes, benefiting both employees and the organisation as a whole (CIPD, 2021, 2022).

Why does burnout occur?

You're already familiar with how an acute stress reaction develops — a sharp, temporary response that gives the body a quick jolt. Once the threat is gone, the body typically returns to equilibrium. But what happens if you keep pressing the stress response button, constantly stimulating the production of noradrenaline, adrenaline, and cortisol?

In this case, exhaustion inevitably sets in, and the body will begin to plead for relief. It will stop responding to interests, goals, plans, and ideas, shifting into conservation mode to preserve energy for survival. What will you experience then? Most likely, you'll feel fatigue, emotional exhaustion, a lack of motivation to work, and perhaps even an inability to perform tasks you once handled effortlessly. This is nothing less than a defense mechanism — a 'stop' command to a reckless driver.

Some people can't stop themselves because they're wildly passionate about the race, others are driven by external pressures, but the outcome is the same: if you keep your foot on the accelerator while ignoring the brake, burnout becomes inevitable.

Take a moment to reflect on your own life; how much of it is rushed, overworked, filled with looming deadlines, strained relationships, irritations, or anxieties about the future? If these patterns persist day after day, month after month, year after year, you may find yourself caught in a loop of chronic stress without even realising it.

The body, however, will send signals: fatigue, apathy, insomnia, headaches. If these warnings are ignored, the body will escalate to 'heavy artillery' — depression or somatic illnesses — forcing you to stop, seek treatment, and take an involuntary rest.

Is it worth letting it get to that point?

When work is your whole life…

Unfortunately, burnout often affects valuable employees — responsible, engaged employees who will never let anyone down (except themselves) and can always be relied on. The burden of a responsible employee who is committed to work is often a prerequisite for burnout. After all, what is a person who won't let you down to do? He won't sleep at night, but will make a report by the right time; he won't go on holiday, but will work to deliver a project to a client on time. Good employers come up with a lot of employee support initiatives to limit burnout: some offer long sabbaticals with job security, some pay for additional leave, and many companies have started providing psychologists or introducing corporate mindfulness programmes. In general, the list of wellbeing programmes offered by responsible employers is endless. But no matter what companies do, a lot depends on the employee: they need to realise that constantly sacrificing their health for work is a losing strategy.

Burnout is often manifested in those who identify themselves too much with work. In this case the importance of other spheres of life is greatly underestimated. Communication with loved ones takes a back seat — and it is interaction with other people that allows you to look at yourself and your problems from the outside, as well as a little distraction from the fixation on work tasks.

When work consumes all your time, you have to sacrifice walks, trips, and hobbies to stay focused on the big idea or the never-ending list of work tasks. Although it is in a relaxed state that the brain finds creative solutions, if we are to believe the stories of many discoveries that were made while sleeping, walking, or relaxing. But a brain with just one dominant activity — work — has a hard time switching to other activities. And if you're highly fixated on work, your expectations can be quite high too — whether it's recognition, financial interest, career, or idealistic thoughts. There's a huge premise of burnout in inflated expectations, too. And if the idea you were burning for at work fails, it's a total failure, and there's nothing else meaningful left in your life; it's a tragedy and a cause for depression.

Faced with burnout, people whose life was fixated on work have to discover new values and learn to enjoy simple pleasures, such as socialising, nature, walks, and hobbies. But in order to rewrite their attitudes, sometimes it is necessary to work with a psychotherapist. Therapy can help uncover the root causes of an overattachment to work, which often stem from childhood experiences. For instance, the desire to always earn perfect grades, win academic competitions, never be late, or complete schoolwork flawlessly are habits that are generally beneficial. They can lead to a strong education and career success. Yet, life is far too diverse and complex to rely solely on being the best or the perfectionist in every situation. Sometimes, circumstances call for lowering the bar slightly; to prioritise health over achieving another top mark. However, rigid attitudes often prevent such reasonable choices, forcing individuals to uphold an unsustainable standard of perfection.

In these cases, psychotherapy not only helps people recover from burnout but also enables them to rearrange their internal priorities. It fosters the ability to make different choices in challenging situations, and encourages the development of new habits and behaviors to replace the rigid patterns that repeatedly lead to burnout.

Disturbing the balance of effort and reward

The Effort & Reward model, or the imbalance of effort and reward, is a pretty good indication of the cause of burnout.

If one works too hard, whether under the pressure of circumstances or as a result of voluntary dedication, then expectations of reward will be high. And when perceived rewards clearly lag behind the expenditure of energy and effort for a long time, such a conflict will inevitably lead to burnout.

If we work overtime, maintain a relentless pace, endure the pressure of tight deadlines, and constantly adapt to endless changes, sooner or later we begin to question the purpose of such hard work. Without sufficient time to replenish our reserves of strength and energy, our focus inevitably shifts to the other side of the scale — the rewards that should compensate for our valiant efforts.

Obviously, expectations of fair remuneration first of all relate to material rewards — salary, bonuses, benefits — because work should satisfy basic needs and provide the desired standard of living. But it is not only material rewards that we look for in labour; we also look for recognition of merit, the opportunity to develop professionally and personally, to live in harmony with our values and, of course, the opportunity to do what we love. As the saying goes, "Find a job you love, and you'll never work a day in your life."

The fewer benefits we perceive in a job and the more effort we invest, the sharper our sense of injustice becomes. The effort-reward imbalance model is supported by research indicating that such an imbalance significantly increases the risk of chronic stress-related disorders, including depression and coronary heart disease. (Siegrist J, 2017).

At the same time, even significant effort and overtime work are unlikely to harm health if there is a clear understanding of the purpose behind it, enjoyment in the work itself, and a balance that includes quality rest and meaningful social interactions.

Sometimes it's worth thinking about the balance of effort and reward, making some adjustments to behaviour, and thereby improving the reciprocal exchange of resources with work.

High demands with no freedom in decision making

Another model of burnout includes two factors that, when added together, provide a high degree of psychological stress: high work demands with a lack of freedom in decision-making. This model has been tested in national surveys conducted in Sweden and the USA, which confirmed that it is the combination of low decision-making freedom and high work demands that is associated with overstress and job dissatisfaction. An important finding of the study suggests that increasing work decision-making capacity leads to a reduction in stress, even when job demands remain (Karasek R.A., 1979).

The results of a study conducted decades ago have proven to be remarkably relevant in the pandemic era, which has tested the resilience of many professions — particularly medical professionals, who bore the brunt of the COVID-19 pandemic. The issue of uncontrolled stress under high workloads was explored in a scientific review on burnout in doctors (Arnsten A., Shanafelt T., 2021).

Doctors, as members of the helping professions, have always been considered at higher risk for burnout, and the pandemic only amplified stressors due to increased workloads and emotional strain. Notably, burnout in healthcare professionals is strongly linked to a reduced sense of control, particularly over their workload.

Based on research into the neurobiology of uncontrollable stress, the authors suggest that preventing burnout in doctors requires increasing their sense of control. This includes enabling them to manage their workloads, take breaks and holidays, and participate in critical decisions within the clinic.

These recommendations seem applicable beyond healthcare: in any job, high demands should be balanced with empowerment, allowing employees to better manage their responsibilities and contribute meaningfully to decision-making in their areas of expertise.

When demands are not balanced with resources...

As the job demands-resources model (Demerouti E. et al., 2001) shows, demands must be balanced not only by the possibility of control and autonomy in decision making, but also by the resources that the organisation provides in the form of support from colleagues, managers, and recognition. It turns out that lack of support at work is also a way to burnout, when you are left alone with high work demands.

And this model works in the real world — in practice it is sometimes difficult to reduce work requirements, but it is possible to give more attention and support to staff. Increased support, regular feedback, and recognition of merits have a good effect: tension and the risk of burnout are reduced, engagement, loyalty, and the desire to recommend the company as a place of work grows.

Later, the resource model was expanded to include personal resources as well. And personal resources in this case include personal effectiveness, optimism, and self-esteem. (Xanthopoulou D. et al., 2009)

Thus, we once again see evidence that burnout is a multifactorial process, involving both the employee and the organisation. Schaufeli proposes using this resource model — which incorporates both organisational and personal resources — as a framework for preventing corporate burnout and enhancing employee engagement (Schaufeli W. B., 2017).

External and Internal Factors of Burnout

In summary, burnout factors can be grouped into two broad categories: internal (personal) factors and external (environmental) factors.

Internal Factors, or Personality Traits

- High expectations of oneself; ambition.
- Perfectionism.
- Need for recognition.
- Desire to please others.

- High degree of responsibility, often to the point of neglecting personal needs.
- Feelings of indispensability and an inability to delegate.
- Excessive commitment to work, leading to overload and overestimation of one's capabilities.
- Viewing work as the sole meaningful activity, substituting for a social life.
- Emotional instability.
- Conservatism and inflexible behavior patterns.

External Factors

- Increased work demands.
- Staff shortages.
- Unfavorable leadership style.
- Time pressure.
- Poor workplace atmosphere, including bullying or psychological pressure.
- Lack of freedom in decision-making.
- Problems with collaboration and teamwork; lack of cooperation.
- Poor internal communication.
- High degree of responsibility for work results.
- Poor work organisation.
- Uncertainty about or lack of career opportunities and professional development.
- Lack of clarity regarding roles.
- Lack of recognition and positive feedback.
- Lack of social support.
- Unfair remuneration or inequitable distribution of benefits.
- Conflicts over values.

Internal and external factors can act separately or in combination. If personal factors prevail, we call this active 'self-burnout' — a person himself creates conditions of tension and stress by his internal attitudes and motives. If external factors prevail, we call this the passive burnout of a 'victim of circumstances' (Kaschka W.P. et al, 2011). When both external and internal factors work together, it becomes almost impossible to avoid burnout.

Key Takeaways:

- Burnout is chronic work-related stress that manifests in three key components:

Exhaustion, experienced as feelings of powerlessness, fatigue, and emotional depletion.

Depersonalization and Cynicism, expressed as detachment, callousness, or rudeness toward others.

Reduced Personal Achievement, characterized by diminished effectiveness, lowered self-esteem, loss of purpose, and a lack of motivation to exert effort at work.

- If we experience stressors day after day, month after month, year after year, we will inevitably fall into a loop of chronic stress, where the body will give signs through fatigue, apathy, insomnia, and headaches. If we don't heed the signals, the consequences can be more serious — somatic diseases, depression, and other vital disorders.

- Burnout often occurs in those who over-identify with work and neglect other areas of life, depriving themselves of rest and activities that replenish energy reserves.

- High work demands with lack of freedom in decision-making is another predictor for burnout. Increased control in making work decisions leads to a reduction in stress, even if the work demands remain the same. Burnout will also be ensured if there is no support at work and the employee is left alone with high work demands. If more attention and support is given to the staff, it significantly increases the resilience of the team.

- Burnout is a multifactorial process in which both the employee and the organisation contribute. Thus, all burnout factors can be divided into two large groups: internal (personal) factors and external (environmental) factors. Internal and external factors can act both separately and in complex. If personal factors prevail, we call it active 'self-burnout'. If external factors prevail, we call it the passive burnout of a 'victim of circumstances'.

Six Reasons to Burnout at Work and Six Strategies to Prevent Burnout.

Michael Leiter and Christina Maslach, experts on burnout prevention in the work environment, analysed the causes of burnout at work, combined them into six categories, and developed a test for diagnosing burnout risk factors which can be used both for personal testing and for studying burnout factors at the company level (Maslach C., Leiter M.P., 2005).

I have learnt in practice that it is possible to cope with chronic stress at work only if we correctly identify the cause of the tension. Otherwise, all the recommendations — go for a rest, take care of yourself — will not work, because the cause of tension will still be active. We will be charged with energy and immediately drain it, if we do not find our energy sink. It is advisable to thoroughly analyse and clearly define the problem. "I can't cope with this amount of work," is quite a reason for burnout, but until you understand what exactly you can't cope with, it is impossible to develop a plan of action. Someone has too much work to be done by one employee, someone else lacks qualification to do it quickly and efficiently, another person is always worried about tight deadlines, and sometimes it happens that the processes in the company are poorly built. Different reasons — different ways of solving the problem.

But the most important point I want to make in this chapter is this: if you feel bad at work, it doesn't mean that the only way out is to quit. Of course, I'm not encouraging you to tolerate bad conditions, because then the tension and ill health only get worse. There is always a chance to try to change the situation to a more favourable one. It is not certain that it will work, but even an attempt will be a valuable experience of behaviour with an inner resource; we can influence rather than float along in a state of helplessness, watching injustices happen in life. Very often it seems that there is nothing we can do to counteract the situation, but this is not always the case; more often than not, there is an opportunity to achieve the desired changes.

If your relationship with work is so fulfilling that there's nothing else to improve, you can safely skip this chapter and move on to the next one. However, if you're a manager, examining the causes of workplace stress may provide valuable insights into the factors contributing to burnout among your employees. In any case, carefully analysing the sources of dissatisfaction is the first step toward developing strategies to enhance both your own work experience, and that of your team.

Sometimes, it may feel like everything at work is going wrong, but often the problem can be localized, making it easier to identify solutions. Let's try breaking the mountain into smaller pieces, to uncover the true sources of dissatisfaction by identifying our own pain points. To do this, I suggest examining six key factors that can serve as potential precursors to burnout.

Reason #1. Workload

If you feel that your workload is clearly not up to your expectations and is even ruining your life, it means that there is too much work, either too urgent or too difficult. The most common complaint about work is overload, when you feel exhausted at the end of the day and drained by the end of the week. But it's important to get to the root cause of what makes you feel overworked.

I have had to deal with situations where tension and high workload were created by overly demanding customers who filled all the employee's time, preventing him from doing other important things and sometimes creating excessive psychological pressure. If you do not help the employee to deal with the problem in time, you might get a resignation letter from him. Solutions can be different: change of the client manager, careful prescribing of service conditions for the client in the contract, and many other things that you can think of, depending on the specifics of the work. If something resonates for you in this example, think about who you could discuss your case with to find a way out.

Another example from practice involves an employee whose overload was caused by constant distractions during the day. Colleagues from different departments would email her with requests to clarify various financial issues, which consumed a huge amount of her time. As a result, she could only focus on her main tasks in the evening, once the flow of emails subsided. This situation was, of course, unsustainable; fatigue from overwork accumulated, her patience for responding kindly to everyone ran out, conflicts arose, and her health began to deteriorate. Had it not been for a thorough discussion of the problem with management, she would likely have had to resign to protect her health and wellbeing. However, following a thorough discussion with management, certain processes were successfully adjusted: communication protocols were revised, multiple team members began sharing the responsibility of answering emails, and her workload was significantly reduced.

It turns out that communicating your personal problems is very useful; it not only saves your own health, but also contributes to improving business processes.

If you are having a hard time at work, it is often a signal that you need to change work standards, optimise processes, or conduct training. Unfortunately, when we find ourselves in a difficult situation, it does not occur to us to go and discuss the problem with the management, we often sit with our pain and until the last try to show personal resilience, courageously fighting with difficulties. But the world is a different place now: it is won by those who think creatively, come up with non-standard solutions, know how to communicate and discuss problems — not by those who are destroyed by work without telling anyone what's wrong.

Young employees are especially prone to burnout. When they get their dream job, they readily take on all the tasks that are thrown at them, and then complete their projects at the cost of exorbitant effort — sacrificing their personal lives just to prove their worth at work. And it is good if such an enthusiast gets an empathic manager who is interested in the problems of employees. Then, at the early stages, it will be possible to notice the excessive workload and take the necessary measures. Some people reach a point where they feel utterly fed up with work, unable to continue, and overwhelmed by the urge to drop everything and walk away. And many people do walk away. For example, in recent years, employees have been actively moving from employment to self-employment and freelancing. I only welcome it when it is a well-considered decision. Unfortunately, if you simply run away from the problem of burnout without addressing it in employment, sometimes people repeat the same process in self-employment. It turns out that the feeling of freedom is ephemeral if you load yourself up by following a once-learnt strategy — "try harder", "hustle", or "be strong". You can find a situation for your strategy everywhere. The important thing is to try to solve the problem where it originated.

There is no point in getting discouraged, complaining about fate or the imperfections of the world, but there is a need to think about what you yourself can do in these conditions. I know from experience that if burnout has gone far, the solution is hard to find, and instead of new ideas, the employee keeps telling you why things are bad and why it is impossible to do anything. Sometimes, it's necessary to take the time to list everything that feels wrong, in order to acknowledge and process the emotions that come with it. Then you have to focus on solutions. Often, the very act of attempting change begins to shift the inner mindset, creating a sense of "I can influence and change my life."

When you outline concrete steps for change and envision the future result, your brain's reward system responds by producing dopamine. This neurotransmitter provides the mental energy and motivation needed to take action.

Just in case no ideas come to mind, I offer a few tips on what you can do if you have deep dissatisfaction with your workload.

- If there is too much work to do, you should first discuss the matter with your manager. You should prepare for the meeting and back up your assessment with figures and facts. This way you will be able to demonstrate more clearly that your workload is too much for one person. If you have ideas on how to reduce the amount of work by redistributing it or optimising processes, this is a plus, as you have already come up with possible solutions. If you don't have any ideas, however, feel free to ask the manager how the issue could be resolved. If at the meeting you come up with some decisions and steps, the implementation of these can then be monitored.
- As a result of such meetings, the manager may think about hiring additional staff or engaging freelancers. After all, as long as no one complains and everything is fine, management will not want to hire additional people. And if there is a risk of losing employees when the facts confirm a large workload, as in this case, the management may provide additional budget. Besides, the manager has more information and can suggest another solution by redistributing work among employees. And if it turns out that you are doing the same amount of work as everyone else but spending an inordinate amount of time, it's a reason to take additional training and improve some skills. Your part of the task is to analyse your workload, state the problem, and prepare for the conversation. And then work together with management to find the best solutions. Sometimes you can even optimise poorly functioning processes that are slowing you down and taking up your time.
- A common illness of young employees who have recently moved into management positions is difficulty in delegating. As a result, they do a huge amount of work themselves with a rather moderate workload of their subordinates. You must overcome this disease and learn to delegate; letting your employees develop without micromanagement, but with performance control and feedback. By investing in the development of your employees today, you save a lot of your time in the future.
- A common problem is the constant distractions of communicating, like answering emails. As a result, it is difficult to find an hour or two during the day when you can concentrate on a task that requires attention. It's a known

fact that if you're constantly distracted from a task, you'll spend time diving into that task again and again after a break and, as a result, you'll spend a lot more time on that task than if you're not distracted. It's best to block off intervals on your calendar when you're busy and ask others not to bother you. I know that some employees even shift their schedules to earlier or later hours to have an interval during the day when no one bothers them.

This is by no means a complete list of solutions to your problem, so don't be afraid to discuss possible solutions at work. In some cases you can also turn to a coach, who will be able to shine a light on those answers that you don't realise yet.

It is very important to learn to cope with difficulties where they arise. I always tell my employees that they should leave work healthy and happy, so that they can be even happier and more fulfilled in another job.

Reason #2. Sense of control and autonomy

A lack of autonomy, the inability to influence an organisation's decisions, being forced to follow directives without flexibility, and a lack of freedom in addressing issues; these factors are initially frustrating, then become increasingly annoying, and eventually sap the motivation to go to work. In the end, some may feel compelled to quit in order to preserve their wellbeing.

However, don't rush to assume that nothing can be done in such situations. It's essential to identify the root causes. Perhaps the issue lies with your manager's tendencies toward micromanagement, or the decision-making style in your department. If the problem can be localized and addressed at your level, it's worth trying to change the aspects of your work environment that you find dissatisfying.

Reflect on your relationship with work in terms of control and autonomy; your ability to influence decisions within your area of responsibility. Take a moment to honestly assess how comfortable you feel with the level of control and autonomy you currently have. If you find the current level of autonomy unsatisfactory, consider this an opportunity to take on the challenge of improving it.

For example, if you see that many decisions in your department are made by the manager alone, or by individuals who have been assigned to prepare the decision, this is an opportunity to talk to the manager about it in a one-to-one meeting or to discuss it with colleagues — they may not like the way decisions are being made either. If you have support, you can speak up at a meeting to suggest that important issues be discussed in a collegial manner. You could take the initiative to introduce brainstorming sessions to find solutions. If your manager is progressive, they are likely to appreciate your proactive approach.

In many companies, the HR department tries to listen to the opinion of employees, and for this purpose there are employee engagement and satisfaction surveys. You should also take advantage of this opportunity by noting your own areas of dissatisfaction. It is very likely that you are not the only one who is dissatisfied with some process, and there is a chance that the opinion of many employees will be taken into account by the management.

Sometimes employees feel frustrated by micromanagement from their managers. However, this behavior is not always due to malicious intent. The manager may still be learning, struggling to delegate effectively, or feeling overly concerned about achieving results.

In such cases, it may help to gently communicate that you would feel more comfortable focusing on goals and outcomes, rather than reporting on every small detail. You could also initiate a conversation about expanding your responsibilities — this demonstrates leadership qualities and is often well-received in companies with a healthy corporate culture.

It's important to approach these discussions with sensitivity and respect for the other person. Even if the situation doesn't change immediately, maintaining a respectful tone will help preserve a positive relationship with your manager.

If you see both that the team's work needs improvement and your manager's work is not perfect, you should not be annoyed; you can try to be a support for both the team and the manager. Sometimes we can do much more if we get out of the position of a bystander and become an active participant in actions.

After all, you can add to your sense of control and autonomy by going beyond the boundaries of your organisation. Active employees participate in professional communities, take part in industry competitions, and earn valuable certifications and additional education. What does this provide? External validation of value has a positive impact on self-esteem and self-confidence; you become more visible to the professional community, and there are more opportunities to move to another company; and in your own company such employees are noticed and become more valued. Sometimes, what was difficult to obtain inside the company can be achieved through external evaluation of yourself as a specialist. The most important thing is to develop an action plan and start doing something to change your position at work.

Have you ever wondered why people come to coaching and often get results?

I'll tell you a secret: it's not so much the professionalism of the coach that matters, as the fact that you get your brain working in the right direction. You build mental projections, plans, create an intention, thus giving your brain the command to execute. And then all the mental processes — conscious or unconscious — will work to realise that intention. The system of perception and processing of information will select the ones that correspond to your intention from a multitude of options. That's why it's so important to talk about and write down your plans — it significantly increases the probability of their fulfilment. So even without a coach, you will be able to get results from internal reflection, setting plans and real actions.

Still, the question remains: should we always try to salvage the situation? And when is it time to consider leaving?

I worked with a client, Catherine, an HR specialist, who had been forced to leave the company, although she had made attempts to improve her position at work. The thing is that her manager was a newcomer to management and did not always feel confident in his new role. He did not like to take responsibility for himself, and as soon as something happened, shifted his aggression on his subordinates. Catherine quickly learned not to take offence at his angry outbursts; she understood that he wasn't shouting at her, he was revealing his insecurities — he wasn't good at everything, worked under great stress, and it was easier for him to blame someone else. She was ready to perceive his behaviour as a psychologist might, but she also protected her boundaries — she taught him not to shout, but to express his thoughts in a calm tone (even if his thoughts did not change much). But she could not bear the devaluation of her labour. For two years of work Catherine raised the personnel documents, set up employee training, people began to receive bonuses for good results, but for her she heard only, "What have you done here?". When training went under the knife and bonuses started to be cut, she felt that it had all been pointless. She simply did not have enough strength to keep defending on all fronts, realising that it was impossible to influence the management's decisions. Health problems began to emerge: tachycardia, spiking blood sugar levels, and gastrointestinal issues. All interests faded away. "I could only rest passively at home to recover after work. Eventually, not only did I no longer want to go to this job, but I also wanted to leave the profession entirely and stop working altogether," she shared. At that moment the decision to quit was made, Catherine decided to go nowhere. This decision was justified — in a far-gone situation it was necessary to save herself and her health. Intuition and level of wellbeing will always be a reference point, when you can still try; when it is no longer possible, you need to run while you still have enough strength. Leaving is also a way out when there are no other alternatives.

Reason #3. Reward

What do you think of when you hear the word 'reward'? You probably think of money. Indeed, material remuneration is the monetary compensation that employees receive in the form of salary and bonuses paid for results. The attractiveness of an employer's offer is first of all evaluated by this parameter, and then everything else is taken into account. And this is normal, because most people use their earnings to pay their bills and maintain their standard of living at the desired level. So sufficient remuneration is a hygienic factor for job satisfaction.

Why are many people unhappy with their remuneration? Perhaps someone is tormented by the thought that their salary level does not cover their needs. And some people keep coming back to the annoying thought that they could earn more elsewhere. Whatever it is, dissatisfaction with the financial situation at work spoils mood and wellbeing. If this is the case, you need to deal with these issues and think of a strategy to improve your remuneration.

A colleague once shared with me the story of her experience with burnout during her time as a student. When she enrolled in the evening program at her university, she was excited to land a job as a secretary at a company. Evening classes seemed to fit well with a day job, and the secretarial position appeared ideal for someone with no prior experience or education.

However, she quickly found herself overwhelmed with countless tasks that didn't fit into regular working hours. In the evenings, she had to rush to her classes, and weekends were consumed with finishing management tasks she couldn't complete during the week. Work and study took up all her time, leaving no room for rest or personal life. At the same time, she was haunted by the thought that she was being grossly underpaid for the amount of work she was doing. This sense of unfair remuneration only grew stronger over time. She found it terrifying to approach her manager about her dissatisfaction; it felt like admitting failure, as if complaining meant she wasn't capable or good enough.

Despite her fears, she eventually gathered the courage to speak with her boss. What hurt the most was the realisation that the manager didn't even attempt to understand her concerns, showing no willingness to help and responding with indifference. This lack of empathy, combined with no prospects for a pay raise or recognition, made her see that the company's values didn't align with her own. She decided it wasn't worth continuing to pour her energy into a job that only caused frustration, paid poorly, and demanded constant overtime.

Leaving the job was bittersweet — it was her first job, after all — but she felt immense relief after making the decision. For about six months, she focused solely on her studies, as she didn't have the strength to search for another position right away. Ultimately, though, she preserved her wellbeing and values, learned valuable lessons for the future, and realised that balancing effort and rewards — both material and moral — was a top priority for her in any job.

Every experience, no matter how challenging, can be useful if we take the time to learn from it.

Not only material, but also non-material rewards are important for everyone. I think you do care how you are evaluated by your managers, how much the company recognises your merits. We are all very much in need of approval and there is nothing we can do about it. No matter how much psychotherapists work on reducing the dependence on the evaluation of others, we can only slightly adjust the settings, but we can not completely get rid of the genetic memory and formed habits of approval in society. In the old days, if an ancient man was driven out of the tribe, he had no chance to survive — it was impossible to protect himself from predators, to get food and maintain fire alone. Social death meant physical death. And even if nowadays it is difficult to equate physical survival and social status, the desire to receive approval, respect and recognition is inherent in the genes. Whether we realise it or not, the fulfilment of a social need at work will influence our wellbeing.

Another important criterion that also goes into the reward factor is the amount of time at work that we enjoy. We may not think about it, but all reward factors work together. It's hard to be happy if only the salary is satisfying but the work and recognition is not. And on the other hand, sometimes people hold on to jobs that are not ideal in terms of pay, but are satisfying and recognised.

Remuneration is a complex characteristic. Try assessing your job satisfaction on the remuneration factor; you'll probably find the reasons that keep you in your job, and you'll also find something that needs improvement. If you don't immediately come up with ideas and plans to improve the reward factor, I suggest you consider some recommendations that may be helpful to you.

If you don't like the financial remuneration, I have a question for you — have you talked to your manager about it? Have you discussed with them the conditions under which you can earn more? If not, then your manager won't know that you are unhappy with your salary, and you are looking for ways to increase it. When you share this with your manager, your financial remuneration problem will become their problem too — of course, if they value employees, and you in particular. The value of employees is high right now, and companies have a vested interest in retaining talent. Once you have identified the problem, the manager will think about how you can be rewarded — either within your job level, or maybe he or she will suggest an increase in responsibilities along with a pay rise. Even if there is no immediate solution, there may well be an opportunity for a promotion after a while — for example, the opening up of a higher position for which you may well be eligible.

If you feel that you are already getting the best you can at this company, but your expected standard of living is higher than your current earnings, you may want to consider additional income. It's a step that makes sense to consider if you like everything else about the job — the nature of the work, the recognition, and respect. In this case, you can look towards part-time work — teaching, for example, or a bit of freelance work if it's contractually permissible. Many people are now rushing into investment activities and are looking to build up a passive income. Why not? There is no rule that you must have only one source of income; you can experiment. Your task is to enjoy your work and have sufficient income, which is achieved in different ways. The main thing is that you should not consider illegal sources of income or overdo it with work, upsetting the balance of other areas of life. Everything else is within your creativity.

If you're doing well on the financial side of remuneration but lack recognition, it's a good time to ask your manager to set up meetings where you can talk about your performance. This way you will make your successes more visible to the company. In the end, you should not forget about your own assessment of your work — if you often say to yourself "I am good", if you celebrate your successes, if you report them to colleagues or in social networks, then public recognition will still catch up with you, and your self-esteem will increase. By the way, think about if you praise your colleagues. Try praising and congratulating others on their successes more often — this is how you'll start to embed a culture of recognition within your company. Over time, other employees will pick up the baton and you'll get your moment of glory too. By giving praise, supporting and recognising the results of your colleagues, you are not risking anything, but you and those you praise will enjoy it.

It is much more difficult to influence dissatisfaction with the nature of your work. If you don't like what you do, sooner or later you will want to find something to your liking. But life is more complicated than the obvious advice to find a dream job. Thousands of threads connect us with work, many of them quite strong: financial motivation, responsibility for your family, good relations with colleagues, comfortable working hours, recognition and respect. Someone can break all the other strings and go in search of self-fulfilment, while others will work for different important values in their life. Everyone has their own hierarchy of values and their own priorities. And if everything suits you except the job itself, you can try to change either the job, itself, or your attitude to it.

In any job you can find elements that bring you joy — think about how you can increase your engagement in those activities that bring you pleasure. You can work on reducing the work that causes rejection — often these are monotonous processes that are not interesting, and take a lot of time and effort. Sometimes the solution lies in changing the process, in automating it, and as a result the time for unloved operations is reduced and space is freed up for pleasant work. This is also possible, you just need to be creative and savvy; who knows what you can turn your unloved work into?

Over many years of working as a manager, I have got used to the formula: do what only you can do and delegate the rest to others. That way I can realise my best talents and at the same time develop my subordinates, giving them enough freedom and autonomy. As a result, less and less time has to be spent on mastered functions, new competences are constantly developed, and a sense of interest, involvement, and challenge is maintained.

As you can see, rewards are a multi-layered pie, and each layer will have to be dealt with separately, paying attention to detail and coming up with ideas for improvement.

Reason #4. Community.

We didn't fully realise the role of social connections at work until we were quarantined and working remotely during a pandemic. It seemed that we could survive without socialising with our colleagues, but after six months of remote working, many managers realised that employees were getting downhearted and sad, which made them urgently look for ways to maintain team spirit in the remote workplace. There are many recommendations on how to build informal ties while working remotely, and there are also initiatives and projects that unite employees around some idea, like environmental awareness, volunteering, or healthy lifestyles.

In general, we go to work not only to work, but also to socialise, make friends, and create a circle of like-minded people who share common values and interests. So, what happens when we are deprived of a significant part of social interaction? Firstly, it is frustrating, and secondly, when the balance of 'I' and 'others' is disturbed, it is more common to bury oneself in one's own thoughts — in one's narrative self — which is constantly telling stories about oneself, and these stories are not always beautiful. This is when the feeling of isolation, low self-esteem, and sometimes depression sets in.

Now we know how important it is to have a supportive and friendly environment at work. And this environment is made up not only of friendships and the ability to rely on colleagues at work, but also of transparent communications within the company, openness of people, the ability to express their point of view, and a shared purpose with the company.

It is worth thinking about how satisfied you are with the social connections at work. After all, if you are not satisfied with this parameter, you will be very reluctant to go to work because emotional ties are not strong.

The extreme degree of unfavourable social relations is situations of bullying, persecution, or insults, which is fraught with risks for mental health. Therefore, it is better to get out of such situations with professional help. Even just a lack of warmth in communication, closedness, when everyone feels on his own — such an atmosphere creates discomfort and a feeling of loneliness. Or the company has poorly built corporate communications, employees are poorly informed about what is going on, they do not feel connected to the company — this is also a rather depressing picture, which does not instil the desire to stay with the company long-term.

What can be done in these cases? Of course, if there is a conflict, it is necessary to start an open dialogue; to engage mediation consultants who help to resolve a difficult situation, taking into account all points of view. In many companies there are rules and ethics of business communication, and often an ethics committee that deals with violations. Even if a company does not have such a committee, it is always possible to bring the discussion of a conflict to the level of the HR department.

If no one offends anyone but all connections are formal, and communications are limited in the remote mode of work, then you might be concerned about expanding contacts with colleagues in the current circumstances; joint lunches, coffee, and informal conversations are no longer only practised in the office, but also remotely online. And for managers at any level, it is useful to think about communication planning, welcoming new employees, and integrating them into the team.

Unifying social projects and volunteer work are very powerful incentives for developing ties outside of work. When people work toward the common good, it fosters unity and creates a sense of purpose. It's even better when there are numerous such projects available, allowing everyone to find something that resonates with them; whether it's environmental conservation, social assistance, or improving the living environment.

And it is not always necessary to wait for a command from above; often the initiative arises from one of the employees, who reports his idea to his manager or HR, and under favourable circumstances the initiative turns into a big project.

Strengthening ties within the company has a very positive effect on people's wellbeing and engagement — it is always more pleasant to work in a community of friends, who share the same values as you.

Reason #5. Fairness.

Think back to how you felt when you experienced an injustice to yourself — for example, when you found out that someone in the same position with the same responsibilities was paid more, or you received a bonus that was lower than expected based on your performance. You may have experienced situations where you were promoted later than others, or felt work was unfairly distributed. All of these situations can kill motivation — and sometimes not just motivation. If the thought of unfair treatment is firmly lodged in the head, constantly spinning in the mind, provoking feelings of resentment, anger, or despair, then this emotional strain can affect physical and mental health. Feelings of injustice and unfairness may well lead to burnout and a desire to quit the company.

Violation of the sense of fairness can have various causes, ranging from opaque rules for the distribution of benefits and promotions, to clear favouritism. Big corporations usually have clear rules and criteria for distributing benefits to employees, which largely eliminates the issue of unfairness. In smaller companies, different situations may occur depending on the corporate culture, and the degree of progressiveness of management.

Some companies are very serious about giving equal rights to different groups of employees — young mothers, people with disabilities, any other vulnerable groups who need additional adaptations to feel good in the team — all this is done to keep employees motivated and calm. The less people are distracted by thoughts of inequality, the more energy goes into the work itself, and creativity. So, if you feel unfairly treated, you should discuss this with your manager or HR. Generally, the company is interested in a satisfied and happy employee, so the chances are that your enquiry will be considered, and changes or clarifications will follow. However, if this is not the case and you cannot find common ground with management, then this is a reason to think about where else you can put your energy and effort.

You can try to start an open dialogue in the company; talk to your colleagues — perhaps they, like you, believe that the procedures in the company are not transparent or are unclear, and perhaps together you can formulate a request for management to clarify the principles of distribution of bonuses, salary increases, or promotions.

Maybe you'll be the person in the company to start a conversation about creating a comfortable environment for different groups of employees, or to raise the issue of objective work distribution. In general, it's up to you to decide what deliberate actions you can take to resolve your discomfort. And chances are, you will benefit the entire company by doing so.

Reason #6. Values.

At first glance, it may seem that talking about values is a pretentious conversation, when we would only like to satisfy basic needs, such as adequate remuneration and a normal workload without overtime. But experience shows that violating values strongly demotivates employees and affects their psychological wellbeing.

For example: you support environmental initiatives, try to live in a way that does not harm the planet, and think about the kind of society your children will live in. With these principles, you join a company which advocates this but, as it turns out later, has a negative impact on the environment and neglects the 'green economy', because the first priority of the organisation is profit. And you become uncomfortable in your job because you do not approve of the company's strategy and values.

You may be deeply affected by the contradiction between the company's declared values and what happens in reality. For example, a company claims that it works for its customers, cares about their wellbeing and improving their lives, but in practice it forces its employees to insert unnecessary services into contracts to increase profits — sometimes explicitly and sometimes implicitly. If such dishonesty is unacceptable to you, it can significantly affect your emotional state, and eventually you will want to change your job to get away from the internal conflict. If your values are at odds with those of the company, it can be difficult to motivate yourself to work because of internal resistance.

A friend of mine left her job because she could not find meaning in her work. She felt that her work did not benefit people, and that she was helping the company to manipulate people for commercial interest, rather than for people's wellbeing. This was so at odds with her values that she was psychologically stressed about it for a long time, and after a while she changed her job to one where she saw the results of her labour as contributing more to the wellbeing of people and the environment.

Alignment of personal and corporate values contribute to wellbeing and vice versa; value conflict is a prerequisite for stress and burnout.

Influencing values is particularly difficult, but that doesn't mean you shouldn't even try. There are two possible ways to reduce value conflict. You can start discussing ethical dilemmas within the company, raise the issue of contradictions between the declaration and reality, discuss specific examples and their impact on the company's reputation. If such actions are for some reason impossible in your company, it makes sense to pay attention to your work and think, "What can I do in this situation? How can I add more meaning and value to the product of my labour? How can I bring more personal values to my work?" You can show a little more care for your clients, or find the positive aspects of your labour and increase them. Nothing in life is black or white; more often than not we deal with shades of grey, and you can figure out how to make the shades a little bit lighter if you apply creative thinking.

Why is it so important to take action and maintain a sense of control?

Over the years of working in a corporate environment, I have learnt that burnout at work is not always worth running away from, because often there is an opportunity to influence one's situation to some extent. I have had to work with employees who brought a resignation letter because of stress at work, but in fact managed to keep these people by helping them to relieve stress and remove the reason for burnout. This becomes an invaluable experience for the employee, as in the future they will feel more stable and confident knowing that they have levers to control their lives.

To understand how the feeling of control affects us, let me share a brief account of the phenomenon of **learned helplessness**, first discovered by American psychologists Martin Seligman and Steven Maier in 1967.

The foundation for this discovery was an unexpected observation during one of Seligman's experiments in 1964. In that experiment, Seligman studied the formation of a conditioned reflex in dogs in response to a sound. The sound was paired with a mild but unpleasant electric shock, serving as a form of negative reinforcement. The goal was to condition a fear response to the sound.

After several such pairings, the cages were left open, and the dogs were presented with the sound cue alone. Instead of escaping the cage, as expected, the dogs lay down on the floor and whimpered. Seligman hypothesized that their inactivity wasn't due to fear but rather a sense of helplessness they had acquired from prior exposure to inescapable shocks.

This observation led Seligman and Maier to design a more detailed study of the phenomenon in 1967. Dogs were divided into three groups:

1. The first group received electric shocks but had the ability to stop the shocks by pressing their noses against a panel.
2. The second group experienced shocks of the same intensity and duration, but their ability to stop the shock depended entirely on the actions of the first group—they had no personal control over the situation.
3. The third group was the control group, which did not receive any shocks.

For some time, the first two groups endured equal electric shocks. The only difference was that the first group could control and terminate the stimulus, while the second group had no such agency.

In the next phase, all three groups of dogs were placed in a shuttle box with a low partition that could easily be jumped over to escape the shocks. The dogs from the first group (which had control) and the control group quickly learned to jump over the partition to avoid the shocks. However, the dogs from the second group—those that had experienced uncontrollable shocks—did not attempt to escape. They panicked briefly, then lay down, whimpered, and passively endured the shocks, even though a way out was available.

The researchers concluded that helplessness arises not from the unpleasantness of a situation itself, but from the *perception* of a lack of control. Repeated exposure to situations where attempts to cope are unsuccessful, leads to **learned helplessness** — a state of passive behavior and inaction — even when circumstances change and opportunities for influence are present.

In humans, this state can manifest under chronic stress, and is particularly evident in cases of severe burnout — where individuals feel powerless to change their circumstances despite the presence of alternatives.

But further research with humans has shown that a sense of control can be cultivated under different conditions. The desire to act and influence is associated with activation of the medial prefrontal cortex, which we can consciously influence. But for this we need to find at least small areas within which we can control the situation.

A very interesting study was conducted by psychologists Ellen Jane Langer and Judith Roden at Arden House nursing home. Two floors of the institution were randomly selected for the study: the residents of the fourth floor were the experimental group, and the residents of the first floor were the control group. The residents on the first floor were very well cared for, including the cosiness of their rooms, and had nothing to worry about.

A meeting was organised for the residents where they were given a gift of an indoor plant, mentioning that the maintenance staff would look after the flowers. Residents on the fourth floor were also given a plant as a gift at the meeting, but were asked to choose their own flower from a box, should they wish to place it in their room and care for it themselves. Also, the residents of the fourth floor were given the opportunity to change the arrangement of furniture in the room to their taste. In this way, the experimental group had the opportunity to make decisions on some life issues, while the control group was decided for by the facility staff.

After three weeks, the patients were asked questions about their overall life satisfaction, and the medical staff assessed the patients' activity, sociability, tone, and nutrition. It turned out that the level of happiness, activity level, and wellbeing of patients were significantly higher in the experimental group of patients who had more choice and control. To assess the long-term effect, the measurement was repeated after another 18 months, and the results on activity and wellbeing were again confirmed. But even more interestingly, of the participants in the experimental group, 15% of the patients died during this time, while 30% of the control group died (Rodin J., Langer E. J. 1977).

Research shows that even a little control over your life improves your wellbeing and health. It is not a bad idea to keep these facts in mind when there seems to be no way out. You can always find your 'houseplant' to take care of, and thus improve your life.

Key Takeaways:

- There are six categories of factors that affect your relationship with your work which can potentially cause burnout if you are dissatisfied: workload, control and autonomy, rewards, community, fairness, values.
- To improve your relationship with work, it makes sense to identify the main stressors and create a plan to minimise them. Dealing with the problem where it arises is one of the stress management skills that helps prevent burnout, increases your sense of control, and improves your job and life satisfaction.

The Neurophysiology of Burnout

Remember the poor dogs that Martin Seligman experimented on? Trained helplessness was the result of a stressful experience that they had no control over. Later, scientists became interested in the neurobiological mechanism that underlies learned helplessness. This time, the experiments involved rats.

A wheel was installed in the cages with the animals, which they could rotate with their paws. The rats were given an electric current, which one group of animals could stop by turning the wheel, while the other group was completely dependent on the actions of the first group — they themselves did not control the electric shocks. After this experiment, when placed in the other conditions, the rats of the two groups showed differences in behaviour; the animals that earlier were able to control the stress stimulus, easily got out of the cage, avoiding electric shocks. Animals that had not controlled the electric shocks in the first experiment were not able to find their way out.

In another experiment with rats, scientists investigated the brain's response to stressors, and the role of perceived control on brain activity. Stress, as previously established, activates several brain structures, including the limbic system and brainstem. This experiment focused on the **dorsal raphe nucleus (DRN)**, located in the medulla oblongata and recognised as the largest aggregation of serotonergic neurons. The findings revealed that uncontrollable stress resulted in significantly higher activation of serotonergic neurons in the DRN compared to stress that was perceived as controllable (Maier S.F. et al., 2006).

Crucially, the control effect was not mediated by ancient brain structures but instead involved the **neocortex**, which exerts regulatory control over subcortical regions. In conditions of controllable stress, the **medial prefrontal cortex (mPFC)** was activated, inhibiting activity in the limbic system and brainstem. This inhibition reduced fear responses and allowed the animals to maintain active behaviors. To confirm the pivotal role of the mPFC, researchers manipulated its activity during the experiments using chemical agents. The results showed that when the mPFC was activated during shock stimuli, rats—regardless of their control condition—exhibited active behaviors in future stress scenarios and effectively escaped from a cage when threatened. Conversely, when the mPFC was inactivated during the experiments, rats from both groups displayed helpless behaviors and heightened fear responses under future stress.

The evidence suggests that the mPFC detects the effect of control, facilitates learning during stress, and uses this experience to regulate future behaviors. Further research demonstrated that a history of controllable stress primes the mPFC to activate in future uncontrollable stress situations. This indicates that experiencing a sense of control during stress can confer resilience to uncontrollable stressors in the future.

After the discovery of the neurobiological mechanism of helplessness, Martin Seligman revised some provisions of the theory of learned helplessness, in an article co-authored with Stephen Maier for the 50th anniversary of his first experiments (Maier S.F., Seligman M.E., 2016). The authors concluded that what is learnt is not helplessness but control. The default sense of helplessness is related to the stress response of ancient brain structures, which can be compensated for by activation of the prefrontal cortex. Learning is related to cortical function; its activation leads to a sense of control. It turns out that helplessness does not need to be taught, but the ability to detect the zone of control in any circumstances can be taught.

The importance of control becomes apparent when one considers the consequences of uncontrolled stress. Animals undergoing such experiences became inactive and more anxious, they developed ulcers, and they were prone to rapid development of dependence on narcotic drugs. All these features were not characteristic of rats from the group that received the experience of stress control (Maier S.F., Watkins L.R., 1998).

Activation of the prefrontal cortex (PFC) allows us to create a sense of control, regulate behaviour, shift attention, and see opportunities. In essence, the PFC provides adaptation to change. But it is the prefrontal cortex that is most sensitive to the damaging effects of stress. Even a small acute uncontrolled stressor can cause a dramatic loss of cognitive ability, and longer-term exposure to stressors causes structural changes in the PFC. In acute stress, the decline in PFC function is associated with high levels of neurotransmitters accompanying the stress response. Rapidly responding subcortical structures take behavioural guidance away from the slow PFC, which in critical situations can be life-saving. Once the threat is avoided, PFC function is restored. However, in a situation of chronic stress there are structural changes and neuronal atrophy occurs. Dendrites — outgrowths of neurons — lose length and branches, the number of dendritic spines decreases, and as a result, the number of synaptic connections in the PFC decreases. In addition, the connection between the PFC and the hippocampus is disrupted, which damages memory function. While in the hippocampus itself, structural disturbances occur after several weeks of stress, the dendrites of the PFC begin to undergo changes after a week. On the contrary, amygdala dendrites are able to proliferate under conditions of chronic stress (Arnsten Amy F.T., 2009). It is disorders in the prefrontal cortex that can explain many symptoms of burnout, such as loss of control over what is happening, decreased concentration, and a sense of crisis.

Fortunately, studies show partial reversibility of chronic stress-induced changes in the brain (Savic I. et al., 2018). Patients with occupational burnout syndrome were examined by magnetic resonance imaging, the results of which showed changes in brain structure. Compared to the control group, patients with burnout showed a decrease in the thickness of the grey matter layer in the right prefrontal cortex and left superior temporal gyrus, as well as an increase in the volume of the amygdala. Moreover, the changes were more pronounced in women. Then the patients underwent cognitive therapy, and after one or two years a second MRI study was performed. The results of the second examination showed that in the patient group the grey matter thickness in the right PFC was normalised, but the amygdala volume and grey matter thinning in the left superior temporal gyrus remained. Meanwhile, no changes were found in the control group, as expected. Thus, it was shown that work-related stress leads to organic changes in the brain, but these changes are partially reversible.

It seems that in burnout the process of neuronal atrophy is associated with a decrease in brain-derived neurotrophic factor, or BDNF for short. This is an important compound that the brain uses to stimulate the growth and development of neurons. With the help of neurotrophic factor, the brain maintains its ability to grow and learn. But as a result of stress, the function of the gene that is responsible for producing BDNF is reduced (Chow Y. et al., 2018).

Chronic stress also damages the reward system, reducing sensitivity to reward. And when there is no anticipation of reward, there is no desire to achieve something — the choice is increasingly shifted to habitual behaviours when making a decision (Porcelli A.J., Delgado M.R., 2017). Such changes explain why, under prolonged stress, there is a tendency to tolerate a discomforting but familiar situation.

Acute stress increases the production of neurotransmitters — noradrenaline, dopamine, serotonin — and chronic stress depletes their amount, which, together with BDNF deficiency, leads to atrophy of neurons of the prefrontal cortex and hippocampus. The reduced regulatory role of these structures leads to hyperactivity of the hypothalamic-pituitary-adrenal system (HPA), which is a key link in the stress response. The hypothalamus incessantly stimulates the pituitary gland, which in turn stimulates the adrenal glands and the production of cortisol. Cortisol penetrates the brain and affects the limbic system, where there are a large number of corticosteroid receptors. Cortisol has a damaging effect on limbic structures and leads to neuronal loss. That is, the limbic system suffers as a result of neurotransmitter imbalance, and also from the damaging effects of cortisol, while the lack of proper BDNF levels prevents neurons from recovering. Fortunately, this process is reversible, as also evidenced by a number of studies (Chow Y. et al., 2018).

So, we have to recognise that burnout leads to both functional and structural disorders in the prefrontal cortex and limbic system. The earlier we realise the problem and notice the symptoms of burnout, the easier it will be to cope with the consequences of chronic stress. And the feeling of inner control over the situation will allow us to avoid helplessness and give a good lesson of resilience for the future.

Key Takeaways:

- Feelings of helplessness and uncontrollable stress are associated with disabling the regulatory influence of the prefrontal cortex on ancient brain structures. Activation of the prefrontal cortex (PFC) allows you to create a sense of control, regulate behaviour, see possibilities and manage stress.
- The prefrontal cortex (PFC) is the most sensitive to the damaging effects of stress. Even a small acute uncontrolled stressor can cause a dramatic loss of cognitive ability, and longer-term exposure to stressors causes structural changes in the PFC. Acute stress increases the production of neurotransmitters — norepinephrine, dopamine, serotonin, and chronic stress depletes their amount, which together with BDNF deficiency leads to atrophy of neurons of the prefrontal cortex and hippocampus.

Burnout as a process

Christina Maslach's three-factor model, foundational for understanding burnout, identifies **emotional exhaustion, depersonalization (or cynicism)**, and **reduced personal accomplishment** as its core components. Rather than reiterating the definitions, it's crucial to explore how these factors interact and manifest in daily work life.

Emotional exhaustion serves as the primary signal of burnout, often emerging from prolonged stress or overwork. This fatigue erodes emotional resilience and makes people more prone to the second component, **depersonalization**. Here, detachment and cynicism act as coping mechanisms, distancing individuals from the emotional demands of their environment. However, this detachment comes at a cost, reducing empathy and connection to others. Over time, this cascade leads to the third component, **reduced personal accomplishment**. Feeling ineffective or unmotivated amplifies the negative feedback loop, reinforcing the exhaustion and detachment. These dynamics illustrate how burnout can spiral if unaddressed, underscoring the need for early intervention and systemic prevention strategies.

Burnout is closely intertwined with mental and physical health disorders; numerous studies highlight its association with conditions such as anxiety disorders, depression, and a range of somatic illnesses. Despite these connections, burnout syndrome itself is not classified as a disease in the International Classification of Diseases, but rather as a phenomenon related to employment and occupational stress.

However, the manifestations of burnout — such as anxiety or depressive symptoms — can meet the criteria for independent clinical diagnoses. This raises an important question: why diagnose burnout if its symptoms overlap with recognised disorders?

The key lies in the specificity of the treatment approach. Diagnosing burnout alongside a clinical disorder enables a dual strategy: addressing the mental or physical illness through standard therapeutic interventions, while simultaneously identifying and mitigating the stressors that contributed to burnout. Without tackling these underlying factors — such as chronic overwork, lack of autonomy, or unresolved workplace conflicts — a complete and sustained recovery remains elusive. Thus, burnout diagnoses serve as a critical tool for achieving both immediate relief and enduring wellbeing.

How can you notice burnout manifestations in different spheres of life?

Firstly, changes occur in the ***motivational sphere:*** at first there is mobilisation of forces and increased activity, but as burnout progresses there is a decrease in motivation, loss of interest, and a feeling of fatigue.

Values and attitudes change: negativity towards people, humanity in relationships disappears, the attractiveness of work falls, it loses importance and value — sometimes it concerns work in a particular company, while sometimes burned-out employees want to leave the profession entirely.

The cognitive sphere reacts: decreased concentration, along with rigidity of thought or 'tunnel' thinking — where decision-making is limited to habitual choices, beyond which no new possibilities can be seen. The situation seems threatening and uncertain, there is poor perspective, and seemingly no way out of the impasse. That is, rational thinking is poor, and non-standard solutions do not come to mind at all.

The emotional sphere: dominated by anxiety and a sense of loss of control over the situation, up to depression at some stages.

Physiological symptoms: can be manifested by sleep disorders, appetite disorders, headaches, gastrointestinal disorders, and reduced immunity, to name a few somatic reactions. Addictions can also develop, for example to alcohol or medication.

The behavioral sphere: there is a noticeable slowdown in the usual pace of activity and a reduction in overall engagement, including communicative interactions. Employees may adopt unconstructive behaviors, become prone to conflicts, and contribute to increased tension within the team. In organisations with a high number of burned-out employees, the psychological climate deteriorates, staff turnover rises, and overall performance inevitably declines.

The Maslach & Jackson Burnout Inventory (MBI), which includes scales for measuring three factors — emotional exhaustion, depersonalisation, and reduction of personal achievements — has received validity confirmation in many studies, so it is quite widely used in measuring employee burnout. Initially, the test was developed for professions that are in close contact with people — e.g. medical workers and teachers. Later it was adapted for non-customer-facing professions. It became clear that the experience of burnout is not limited only to 'helping' professions, although the risks of burnout are certainly higher there.

The original MBI test is offered by the authors on a fee basis — access to the test can be found at (https://www.mindgarden.com/312-mbi-general-survey).

Even if you only suspect burnout or aim to prevent it, it is crucial to identify the specific stressors in your life and take them seriously. Developing a plan to reduce their impact is an essential step toward maintaining wellbeing and preventing burnout from escalating.

Stages of Burnout

There are many procedural models of burnout that consider it a process, in the form of stages of increasing manifestations.

B. Perlman and E. Hartman describe burnout as a process progressing through four stages. It begins with tension arising from the need to exert additional effort to adapt, and culminates in the final stage where burnout manifests as a multifaceted experience of chronic stress. This includes physical exhaustion, emotional and motivational depletion, and an overarching sense of ill-being (Perlman B., Hartman E. A., 1982).

J. S. Greenberg outlines five stages in the burnout process. The first stage, known as the "honeymoon phase", is marked by heightened enthusiasm and energy. As the process progresses, it moves through stages of fatigue and the accumulation of chronic symptoms, ultimately reaching the fifth stage, referred to as "hitting the wall". This final stage is characterized by the onset of severe health problems that can jeopardize not only a person's career, but also their life (Greenberg J. S., 2002).

M. Burisch conceptualizes burnout as a six-stage process. It begins with the warning phase, marked by heightened activity and overexertion. As the process unfolds, individuals experience fatigue and exhaustion, followed by increasing cynicism, indifference toward work and others, and even aggression. These emotional states give way to depression and a range of psychosomatic reactions, including weakened immunity, elevated blood pressure, tachycardia, headaches, musculoskeletal pain, or gastrointestinal disturbances. There may also be a growing dependency on substances such as nicotine, caffeine, or alcohol. The final phase is defined by profound feelings of helplessness, a sense of the meaninglessness of life, and existential despair (Burisch M., 1989).

Freudenberger identified 12 stages in the burnout process (Freudenberger H.J., 1980). While the process is broken into many discrete steps, the overall progression remains similar. It begins with a stage of excessive activity, driven by high ambition and overcommitment. This is followed by the emergence of cynicism, aggression, communication difficulties, lowered self-esteem, a loss of purpose, and eventually depression. In the most severe cases, burnout can culminate in complete physical and mental collapse, requiring immediate medical intervention.

Unfortunately, it must be noted that the presented models lack accompanying diagnostic criteria, making them difficult to apply in practice.

The dynamics of the burnout process are most conveniently studied using the three-component model of Maslach and Jackson. This model can be viewed as a process that begins with fatigue and emotional exhaustion. Over time, cynicism, emotional detachment, and negative attitudes toward others develop — a protective phase aimed at conserving emotional energy or suppressing emotional responses. This is followed by a phase characterized by a negative self-image, reduced self-esteem, and, in its most extreme form, depression accompanied by a sense of "I'm not OK."

It is also valuable to incorporate an initial phase, often noted by researchers: the phase of heightened enthusiasm and overcommitment. Recognising this early stage is crucial, as it is here that burnout can most effectively be prevented by identifying signs of excessive energy expenditure without adequate replenishment of resources. With this addition, the classification of burnout stages is as follows.

1. Warning Phase — 'Omnipotence'

At the first stage, a person feels inspired, interested in work, burning with some idea, and nothing seems to foreshadow the onset of burnout on the horizon. This is that wonderful state when you give yourself to your work with abandon. This happens when you get a dream job or an interesting project, when the desire to do the best you can — and even more — is great. Or you feel a sense of responsibility and importance of your role in the work process, you value what you do. The value can be in serving the common good, but also in the value for personal success, the desire to achieve more in your professional trajectory.

It is interesting that initially burnout syndrome was described by Freidenberger for people with idealistic views who imagined their life as a service to people, for example, doctors and nurses, who chose their profession out of a desire to alleviate people's suffering. We still observe burnout among people who devote themselves to public service, but nowadays it is not only people with high goals who give themselves wholeheartedly to their work.

In today's age of meritocracy (literally "power of the worthy") — which emphasizes the advancement of the most capable individuals, regardless of their social background or financial status — anyone has the opportunity to climb high on the career ladder. Ambitious individuals often set lofty goals for themselves and may work tirelessly in pursuit of these ambitions, neglecting other aspects of life, believing they can focus on those only after reaching the top. Neoliberalism, with its emphasis on the free market and unrestricted competition as drivers of progress, further fuels personal ambition. Under this framework, ambition is no longer limited by class but is instead defined by individual abilities and desires. The drive to succeed is fuelled by famous examples: politicians who have made themselves, or famous social media personalities who have attracted huge followings and made a lot of money without help, support, or start-up capital. Such stories evoke the desire to make extra efforts to use one's own abilities to the fullest to achieve one's dreams. This path is often accompanied by excessive stress, neglect of basic needs, and will inevitably lead to burnout if the inefficient burning process is not noticed and stopped. Behind every successful example of self-made persons there is a whole army of those who burned out on the way to their dreams.

Since the process of burnout often begins with excessive dedication to work, these signs should make you think about what will happen next, if the life balance is constantly skewed towards work and other areas of life are in disrepair. Work gradually consumes your life, leaving no time for rest, communication with relatives and friends, going to the gym, or doing your favourite hobbies. And sometimes there is no time left for sleep and proper nutrition, which is replaced by fast food on the run.

Often such driven individuals do not have enough time even to organise a normal meal for themselves. How many times I have heard from victims of burnout that in their work they forgot to eat, stopped cooking, ate fast food on the run, because they simply stopped paying attention to this side of life? Often the intention to get back on track sounds like, "I'm going to start cooking and eating healthy food again." If you're experiencing something like this, I recommend that you immediately think about the fact that eating wholesome food is the foundation of health. And if you intend to achieve more, it is worth taking care of quality fuel for your burning ambition and replenish it in time — the replenishment of which includes not only nutrition, but also sleep, physical activity, socialising, and in quality rest outside of work.

The overactive stage is fuelled by strong motivation and high levels of dopamine, which creates a pleasant feeling of anticipation of victory. It seems that everything is possible, and you want to prolong and prolong this wonderful state of omnipotence. But it will end sooner or later if you forget about rest and all your other needs. In the worst case, the stage of omnipotence will turn into a phase of exhaustion.

2. Depletion phase – 'Running out of fuel'

In the second stage, the main sign is almost constant physical and emotional fatigue. Weekends are not enough to rest, and long holidays have only a short-term effect. The body starts to protect itself and reduces energy expenditure, which means that the reward system no longer provides dopamine, motivation decreases, and interest is lost; you don't want to run anywhere, and the question arises, "Why am I doing all this?"

There is not enough resource for energy-intensive cognitive processes, which leads to lack of creativity, rigidity of thinking, and difficulties in finding solutions. At this stage, there is still enough energy to drop everything and go somewhere else; some people go to rehabilitation and search for new meanings, while others, who have not yet burned out, plan to go to the next job to feel the dopamine flow again, and to be ignited by a new idea.

In my experience, it is at this stage that employees most often write a resignation letter and often state the reason for leaving as "burned out", "sick of the job", "tired", or "I need time to figure out where to go next".

If you don't listen to yourself, if you don't change the situation, then the body starts to adapt to the low energy state in a rather crooked way, and gradually there is a transition to the stage of negativism and cynicism.

3. Negativism and cynicism phase – "The world is not OK"

The third phase is much less common in the corporate environment, as people usually intuitively pick themselves out of the second phase and recover. But there are also those who fixate in the state of burnout, minimising energy expenditures. When burnout is far advanced, energy has to be seriously saved, and is no longer enough for human communications with clients and employees. When the organism exists in survival mode, there is no empathy or sympathy. Often, people become indifferent, detached, even callous. You may recall an encounter with a doctor who seemed to see you as an object rather than a person in pain, perhaps not even meeting your gaze, focused instead on writing something down, barely paying attention to you. You might have wondered how someone like that chose medicine in the first place — what motivated them? It's entirely possible that they were once driven by high ideals and a genuine desire to alleviate suffering. However, chronic stress, overwhelming workloads, and constant exposure to negativity in their profession may have led to their current state. The result you observe is most likely a far-reaching process of burnout, not a character defect. Although you can of course acquire stable personality deformations if you get stuck in stress, as a rule, such changes are caused by chronic stress that lasts for years.

In this phase, the person acquires the belief that others are to blame for his or her discomfort, that the world is not a good place, and that people around him or her are only annoying. At the same time, a low level of control over emotions leads to irritation over trifles, forming conflict behaviour and a lack of desire to establish social interactions — there is neither strength nor drive to do so.

They are often called "toxic" within the company, and cause a lot of trouble for their managers and colleagues. They are not very friendly in communications, often protest, and express negative opinions on various occasions. Organisations with a favourable corporate culture treat such employees with care — they invite coaches, conflict mediators, trying to ease the person's condition a little, and reduce the negative impact of the employee on the general atmosphere in the team.

I have noticed that so-called "toxic" employees are usually valuable employees. They have experience of long-term burnout, and it seems that negative communication style was formed as a defence reaction as a result of chronic stress — although the role of individual predisposition cannot be discounted either. One of my friends, the owner of a company, shared her sadness about the negative behaviour of one of her employees, who is always protesting, opposing management decisions, causing confusion in the team, worsening the overall climate in the company. "I don't understand why she doesn't quit if she doesn't like everything?" she asks, tired of a situation of prolonged conflict with a valuable but toxic employee. My coaching experience is that often employees at this stage have no energy to change jobs, have lost interest, and have a hard time imagining what they want. There is only enough strength to continue this discomforting situation, crookedly adapting to a state of low energy and lack of motivation. In these conditions one has to continue indifferently or aggressively shutting oneself off from the world.

It is possible to live in this state for years, if the employer allows it. But sometimes it comes to dismissal, and other times the internal defense mechanism breaks down. And then there is a realisation that "I am not OK." In this case, there is a transition to the next stage.

4. Depression stage — "I'm not OK"

This stage is the most severe manifestation of burnout — existential crisis, inner emptiness, and depression. During this period most somatic diseases often appear, according to the principle of attacking weaknesses first, i.e. all predispositions to diseases, which were previously compensated for, are realised, and manifested by symptoms which can affect the cardiovascular system, gastrointestinal tract, reproductive area, immune system, skin, and many other things. However, psychosomatic symptoms of various kinds can also occur at earlier phases of burnout.

Addictions — alcohol or drug addiction, especially — are common companions of this stage, which help to escape from the hopeless reality for a while, but in fact only destroy the organism further, worsening social adaptation and opportunities to return to normal life. It is known that addiction treatment is a labour-intensive and complicated process.

Fortunately, 'deep burnout' like this is not that common, but it does require immediate medical attention and long-term rehabilitation.

The process approach to the study of burnout is just a useful tool to identify what stage of burnout a person is in, to provide the kind of support and help that is appropriate to the severity of the case. Some people, sensitive to loss of energy and exhaustion, never get beyond stage two. Sometimes it takes years to reach the stage of depression. But sometimes, as a result of severe stress, serious burnout can occur in a short period of time.

Some people tend to burn out repeatedly. But if the experience is realised, we have a chance to learn for the future. Burnout is not a judgement; it is an episode of personal history, which is important to notice as early as possible and turn into a valuable lesson.

I want to share the story of someone I know who has faced burnout multiple times, uncovered its causes, learned important lessons, and continues to move forward — guided by her values and sense of purpose.

Clare is the founder and CEO of the Women in CX community. I met her while working on this book. Clare lives in the UK and has a wealth of life experience from several careers — and several episodes of burnout, which she shared with me in our conversation.

Her first burnout occurred after 15 years in corporate roles at large companies. As Head of Customer Experience (CX) for a multinational corporation, Clare realised she was completely burnt out. Her recovery began with a bold decision: she quit her job and embarked on a journey of rediscovery through travel. For six weeks, Clare visited Hong Kong, Malaysia, Japan, Indonesia, and New Zealand. During this time, she experienced freedom and joy that had long been absent from her life. She decided not to return to the corporate world.

Supported by a financial cushion from her years in corporate service, Clare gave herself three months to rest and rebuild. She started going to the gym, took up horse riding, and discovered the art of baking. For the first time in years, she learned to relax without a constant need to do something.

This period of rest and self-reflection healed her burnout and clarified her values. Clare chose not to return to the corporate world, and instead built a successful consulting practice and founded her own agency. Her new life was one of freedom, discovery, and financial success; she traveled the world as a consultant and speaker, exploring new places, and enjoying the life she had always dreamed of.

But in March 2020, everything changed. The pandemic brought global travel to a halt, canceled her speaking engagements, and ended her relationship. Clare found herself isolated, out of work, and struggling with severe depression. "My mental health deteriorated, and I had to seek professional help to address the chemical imbalance caused by the depression," she shared. Gradually, she began to recover, starting with therapy and a focus on reconnecting with others.

Clare turned to social media as a way to engage with women and discuss their experiences during the pandemic. Initially, these conversations focused on CX, but they soon evolved into deeper discussions about women's rights, recovery from illness, and coping with the challenges of the pandemic. Inspired by these conversations, Clare decided to create a podcast featuring women's stories to inspire and support others. "At that time, I had no job, no money, nothing," Clare recalled. "But I focused on amplifying women's voices worldwide." For six months, she consistently produced weekly episodes, which quickly gained traction. One day, a Silicon Valley investor approached her and asked, "If I gave you $10,000, what would you do with it?" Clare answered that she would create a community where women could share their experiences, find support, and feel less alone.

The investor delivered on his promise, and Clare launched her new project. Pouring all her energy and resources into this mission, she worked tirelessly, often 80 hours a week without holidays. "It was the best and worst year of my life," she admitted, "I ran out of money, sold my house, and pushed myself to the edge of burnout multiple times."

When we spoke, Clare acknowledged that she was once again close to burnout. "I wake up at 4 a.m. and work until 8 p.m. Our community spans over 50 countries, and I see how it changes lives." Yet, she also recognised the need to prioritise her health and wellbeing. "Without a strong foundation of health, I can't accomplish what I envision. I've started planning a healthier routine: waking up in the morning, meditating, exercising, and beginning work at a reasonable hour."

Clare asked her team for support in establishing boundaries, such as not contacting her before 10 a.m. She believed this shift would help her sustain her work and achieve her goals. Over time, Clare demonstrated the value of these changes. Prioritising self-care and health became the cornerstone of her wellbeing and success.

This journey stands as a testament to resilience and transformation — a powerful example of how rebuilding on the brink of burnout can lead to profound growth. By prioritising self-care and health, Clare created a foundation for personal wellbeing, which became essential for achieving her mission and driving meaningful change. Her story highlights the power of resilience and the importance of finding balance to rebuild and thrive.

Key Takeaways:

Burnout is a process best understood by examining its stages and the escalating manifestations at each step. This approach enables tailored support and interventions that align with the severity and depth of the burnout experience.

Stages of Burnout

Warning Phase	Exhaustion	Cynicism and Negativism	Depression
Inspiration and uplift	Physical and emotional fatigue	Lack of a sense of purpose	Inner emptiness, dissatisfaction
Significant energy costs	Reduced flexibility of thinking	Emotional detachment or irritability	Anxiety, dependencies
Neglect of needs other than work	Desire for change (e.g., quitting)	Toxicity, blaming others	Depression, somatic diseases

How Do You Get Out of Burnout?

Claire's story shows that a wide arsenal of tools can be used to recover from burnout: travel and relaxation, quality self-care, and seeking professional help when the need arises.

Burnout is a result of chronic stress — when stress factors persist over a long period of time. Recovering from burnout is possible by identifying the sources of stress and addressing them effectively. Therefore, the first step is to identify the root causes, which can often be complex; facing too many changes with insufficient resources to cope, or expending significant energy at work without adequate reward. Unraveling this web of causes — analysing and addressing each thread — can help mitigate the impact of stressors and create pathways to recovery.

Once the causes of burnout are identified, a plan of action can be developed. It is crucial to find a zone of control — an area where you have the power to make changes. When this zone is defined, the feeling of being a victim of circumstances diminishes, and you regain a sense of agency. This empowers you to take control and shape your life according to your plan.

Change What We Can — the Situation, the Interpretation, and Even Ourselves....

What can you do? You can change the situation or the perception of the situation, you can change yourself by developing your inner resources.

There are many ways to address burnout, from discussing your workload and compensation with your boss, to considering a job change if the balance between effort and reward is significantly skewed. You might also decide to develop new skills, such as time management, to improve your efficiency.

If you discover that much of the pressure you feel comes from your own beliefs — such as feeling solely responsible for everything, or thinking you must never make mistakes — it's important to reevaluate those attitudes. While they may have been helpful at one point, they may now be outdated and in need of adjustment.

Additionally, it's worth identifying and addressing the energy drains in your life — those factors which sap your energy and diminish your inner resources.

Finding energy holes ...

Resistance. We lose a huge amount of energy when we resist — when we do not accept something, but keep doing it. For example, you continue to go to a job you don't like, you wait for the end of the working day every day, you dream about the weekend, and on Monday morning you have a bad mood at the beginning of the working week. This relationship with work takes a lot of energy and health, and therefore requires immediate review and change.

What can be done? We can either change the situation itself (problem-focused coping) or change our perception of it (emotion-focused coping). If the job is deeply unsatisfying and no comfort zone can be found, it might be worth taking a bold step and seeking a more suitable position. However, sometimes all it takes is a shift in perspective — reflecting on what's valuable in the situation, what skills or experience you're gaining — and a new, constructive outlook can transform how you interpret events. Resistance diminishes, and tension eases.

By simply adding more value and meaning to what we do, the dreaded should can turn into want. For example, if you're resisting because you feel "I can't work this hard for this pay", it might make sense to renegotiate your terms, and that could resolve the issue. The key is to find solutions that reduce resistance.

What truly matters is not how much the circumstances change, but your subjective judgment and inner state. The goal is to create inner comfort, and this goal should guide you toward the right decision. Achieving this might require trying several strategies to find the one that reduces resistance and delivers the desired result.

Unfinished business is another significant energy drain. You may have tasks that constantly distract you, but you can't seem to gather the motivation to complete them. For example, you might need to prepare a presentation, or study for an exam by a deadline, but the task feels daunting, time-consuming, and unappealing. Instead, you find yourself prioritising smaller, seemingly urgent daily tasks, postponing the important one. Yet, in the back of your mind, the unfinished task lingers, creating stress as the deadline approaches. Sound familiar?

What can you do?

You need to learn how to plan effectively and focus your attention on completing important tasks. This includes scheduling not only urgent matters but also important, non-urgent tasks — those that help you move forward and reduce the anxiety of looming deadlines. A helpful approach is to start your day with these important tasks when your energy and focus are at their peak.

For larger tasks, break them into smaller, manageable parts. Plan to complete one section or component each day; for example, by writing a few pages of a report or preparing one section of a presentation. This method of fractional planning makes big tasks less overwhelming and easier to tackle.

If you have a habit of living with numerous unfinished tasks, it's worth setting a goal to change your behavior. Implementing a system of small, consistent steps for completing large and complex projects can significantly reduce stress, and make it easier to stay on top of your responsibilities.

Being responsible for everything is energy-consuming and tiring. Nevertheless, responsible and ambitious people like to take on too much. If this sounds like you, consider if you really have to do it all yourself? Surely there must be people who can help. What chores could you delegate?

Sometimes it's good to learn the skill of asking for help, and learn to accept help; then life becomes easier and more enjoyable. And then, when you ask others for help or accept help, they at that moment get pleasure, and realise their importance and usefulness. When we ask for help, we make other people feel better. In other words, we increase the cycle of goodness on the planet. It is worth a try!

Inadequate self-esteem is the eternal "I failed again", "I could do better", "I knew I couldn't", or even "I'm a failure". How much energy is wasted on self-doubt and self-defeat? What should you do if you notice a tendency to self-criticise? First of all, we must accept ourselves. Acceptance always starts with recognising your dark sides; without them there is no integral personality and individuality, which distinguishes each person. And we must allow ourselves to make mistakes. Do not hesitate to keep trying, and interpret failures constructively: "I'll take the lessons from my mistakes and try again", "I will definitely succeed another time". And the most important thing is to say to ourselves more often: "I am OK — the world is better with me!"

The inability to say "no" is a common trait of responsible individuals with a people-pleasing mindset. If helping others brings you joy, there's no issue — it doesn't drain your energy. However, discomfort often arises when you agree to something against your will, unable to summon the courage to refuse. This can lead to internal resistance to what you've agreed to, or even feelings of victimization.

If you frequently feel pressured and unable to push back, it may be time to learn how to assert your boundaries.

Personal boundaries are the limits we establish to protect our self-worth and safeguard ourselves from external manipulation. These boundaries can be emotional, intellectual, or physical, and it's up to you to define acceptable limits with different people. Discomfort or inner conflict is a clear sign that your boundaries are being violated, even if you feel compelled to accept the situation. Learning to recognise and enforce these boundaries is essential for maintaining your wellbeing.

It took me quite a long time to learn how to say, "No thanks". But I now accept "no" from others with respect, understanding that everyone has the right to protect their own boundaries. We learn to respect the personal rights of others just as much as we want to respect our own. And if you are always sacrificing yourself by agreeing to everything, you will unconsciously expect a symmetrical response from others. Everyone has their own personal boundaries and rights: by respecting your own, you learn to respect others'. As soon as respect for personal boundaries becomes a value, you will immediately allow yourself more and not judge others for their choices. Think about what you lack in building personal boundaries, and what you don't accept in other people. Perhaps a new way of looking at the world and respecting boundaries — your own and others' — will bring more balance and peace of mind to your life.

Learning to process difficult emotions

Stress and burnout is always an emotional strain and a whole bunch of feelings. It is important to allow yourself to get to know these emotions, recognise them, and allow yourself to have whatever feelings you have. As long as you fight with emotions, deny them or devalue them, the tension will only grow — consciously or unconsciously — but emotions will drain your strength and aggravate burnout.

Emotions need to be handled gently. Whatever you are experiencing — sadness, anxiety, fear, despair, anger — just recognise that you have these emotions. Allow them to be and accept the fact that these emotions create a less-than-pleasant experience. Say to yourself, "It's OK that I don't like it." Nothing reconciles us to disturbing emotions like admitting that they create an unpleasant experience and we don't like it. Once you admit this to yourself, the emotion loses half of its power because you are no longer fighting it, but living it.

Sometimes it is difficult to control yourself when feelings take over. In all circumstances, when a strong emotion starts to unfold, capture that moment, try to realise it by concentrating on observing the sensations. And it's definitely worth taking a pause before you start reacting. Take a moment to breathe. After all, to stop (at least for five breathing cycles) means to give yourself a chance to reflect on what is happening and not to give in to a spontaneous reaction, which can be destructive for you and for others.

If you are not immediately aware of your emotions, at the moment of anger for example, and you are carried away by emotional waves, it is useful for training to analyse your behaviour afterwards and adopt a strategy to not give in to violent reactions in the future. At first, we form an intention and think about future behaviour in a calm state, and over time we begin to remember this promise in acute moments as well.

Another recommendation in case of a strong emotional reaction is to switch to an alternative activity. In general, in a situation of stress it is useful to develop a habit of shifting to another type of activity, taking your mind off the problem for a while. You can do sports, go for a walk, watch an interesting film, or engage in other pleasant activities. Some people find it helpful to cook food and feed their family — taking care of the household allows them to distract themselves from the problem. Some people like to 'step out', that is, just walk around the room, relieving emotional stress through walking. These recommendations are just first aid for excessive emotional reactions; once the intensity is reduced, it makes sense to move on to interacting with your emotion.

After all, the emotions we experience in stress and burnout have a positive meaning — they show that what is important and valuable to us has been disturbed, and thus they provide guidance on how to act. Anxiety signals a threat and asks us to worry about safety. Anger makes us stand up to defend our values. Sadness forces us to stop or slow down, to adapt in order to find a new point of balance.

Emotions become destructive only as a result of excessive or inadequate reaction, which leads to negative consequences for health and psyche. And in order to prevent emotions from destroying your life, you need to make friends with them. To begin with, you need to learn to recognise them. And indeed, to be able to manage your inner state, it is good to first learn to feel emotions — to notice what thoughts, physical reactions, sensations accompany them. We often don't even realise that we are feeling, and find ourselves shouting or slamming doors. When we observe emotions, we can also look for the reasons behind them. And investigating the causes of emotions is the way to self-regulation, to managing our emotional state.

Let's practice recognising, accepting, and observing emotions. I want to share with you a technique that I often teach in my training and use myself. This technique guides you to identify your emotion, name it, allow it to exist, and observe it with curiosity — embracing it with kindness and compassion.

Turn your attention inward for a few minutes to explore and become aware of your emotions.

Take a comfortable posture, close your eyes or simply lower your gaze down, feel your posture, the points of contact between your body and the surface of the chair or the floor. Take three deep inhalations and exhalations. On each exhalation relax your body.

Think of an unpleasant situation that you experienced recently, or some difficulty that exists in your life right now. You don't have to recall dramatic events, but just something unpleasant that upset you, on a minus ten-point scale of experience about a -2 or a -3, something you can be with for a while. Maybe it's some unresolved issue, some dispute, a situation where you felt irritation, regret or guilt about what happened, or maybe anxiety about what might happen.

Remember the emotion you felt at that time. Try to feel it. What was that emotion? Name it. Is it one emotion, or is there another emotion behind it? Name that one too. It may be a whole bunch of emotions, and you may be able to recognise several that you were feeling at that moment.

Recognise now that this emotion is there and allow it to be as it is. Don't try to avoid the experience or fix your condition. Say to yourself, it's OK that I don't like it. I can be with it. It's OK that I am experiencing this emotion in this situation. I understand why it is there and I accept it.

Look curiously at this emotion. How do you feel it? Where do you feel it? What parts of your body respond to this emotion?

Ask yourself, "Why I am experiencing this particular emotion? What is it trying to tell me?"

And think of yourself with kindness and compassion. Anything that hurts, just heal it with your care and kindness. Whatever needs forgiveness, let it be forgiven.

You can put your hand on your heart or neck, or wherever there is sensation — as a sign of love and care. And say to yourself: "I have a lot inside; a lot of power, love, care, and I can be with this experience." Be with that feeling of caring, and then come back to reality and open your eyes.

Usually, a short practice of open and accepting observation of one's emotion reduces tension, and improves psychological wellbeing.

I recommend turning to this practice when difficult emotions arise. Once you have lowered your emotional background, you will have access to cognitive ways of dealing with stress. You will be able to recognise the thoughts that led to unpleasant emotions, question them, and perhaps adjust your view of the world.

Changing the way we look at the situation ...

If you can't change the situation, change your perception!

If something unpleasant happened, consider: if it was a valuable gift, what could it be? Could it be some important lessons that teach you something? Or are you gaining resilience by going through these difficulties?

Psychological tension and the experience of negative emotions often arise from a few common situations:

Losses. We lose something precious and it is very difficult to come to terms with. Whatever the loss, it will require a period of grieving and living with difficult emotions. That said, the loss will also bring renewal afterwards. You open up to something new; there is a vector and sense to move forward.

Failures. When our expectations aren't met and we don't achieve what we aimed for, it can feel like failure. It's natural to feel disappointed, but we can choose to approach such moments differently: by learning lessons, appreciating the experience, adjusting our actions, and moving forward.

Take inspiration from the famous inventor Thomas Edison, who conducted countless experiments in his quest to create a working electric light bulb. He once said, "Many of life's failures are people who did not realise how close they were to success when they gave up."

And let his other words inspire you with hope: "Good fortune is what happens when opportunity meets preparation."

Relationships. Social relationships are often incredibly important to people. Poor relationships at home or work can make life feel unbearable. However, much depends on how we behave and how we perceive our interactions with others. It's essential to focus on understanding a person's intentions rather than judging their behavior.

We often feel anger or frustration because we think, "This person shouldn't act this way" or "They shouldn't think like that." Psychology and coaching offer a valuable axiom to shift our perspective: Every behavior is driven by a positive intention, and there is a context in which it holds value. At first, this idea might seem counterintuitive, but when you reflect on it, it makes sense.

Every behavior stems from a positive intention, shaped by an individual's specific circumstances, experiences, and internal resources. People aim to achieve something beneficial — whether for themselves or others — even when their actions provoke anger or frustration. Responding to a person's underlying intention rather than their behavior can be more effective and constructive.

Consider what might have motivated the behavior: what positive outcome is the person seeking for themselves or for you? Everyone desires happiness and freedom from suffering. For example, a person might express anger as a way of defending their boundaries against perceived interference. Or they may simply lack a more constructive way to pursue their goals. Even misguided behavior can be understood in this context — they might not have all the information or skills needed to act differently.

Understanding the motivations behind someone's actions forms the foundation for building healthy relationships.

If you try to understand the other person's point of view, the negative emotions slowly start to fade away because we now think about it differently. For example, your teenage child has been rude to you — it's very hurtful and you don't want to put up with it at all, and you may want to respond symmetrically. But think about what motivates this behaviour — maybe he is learning to assert personal boundaries, but is still doing it ineptly? Asserting one's independence is a necessary stage of realising one's autonomy, and is definitely a positive intention. Or do you differ with your friends in your assessment of a situation — political, economic, whatever — but perhaps you use different sources of information that form an opinion? Therefore, there is no point in getting angry, but it is better to listen to each other calmly, and maybe you will find points of agreement. By understanding the appropriateness of behaviour in a certain context, we significantly reduce the degree of aggression and anger in response to any situation.

When you have a conflict situation with someone, try to imagine yourself in that person's shoes — how does he or she feel, what need is he or she defending? By putting yourself in the other person's position, you will start to react a little differently, bring other arguments, you will want to take both interests into account. You will begin to understand people and their intentions better; their behaviour will seem to you just a clumsy attempt to achieve the desired result.

So gradually one can learn to see beyond the obvious meaning of unfavourable events, to change interpretation, and find value in difficult experiences. And then stress will turn into stressful growth.

Learning to relax and take breaks

It is essential for all those facing burnout to learn how to take care of themselves. Sleep, nutrition, rest, and physical activity are elements of a supportive environment for escaping burnout. These are necessary, but not always sufficient, ways to get out of stress. Because if the stressor continues to act with the same force, rest will have only a short-term effect.

We are almost constantly faced with high information load, multitasking, and stress, and we need to have an effective antidote to these side effects of an interesting and dynamic life. Therefore, everyone should acquire self-help tools and learn relaxation techniques. It is crucial to stop and exhale regularly to slow down, release tension, and calm the mind. And the more complex the context and the more intense the rhythm of life, the more often you should do this.

For me, respite means simply stopping and observing my breathing. Once you begin to focus on your breathing, it naturally becomes steadier, deeper, and calmer, bringing a sense of peace. The breath is like an anchor in a stormy sea. When everything around you feels chaotic or incomprehensible, observing and balancing your breath can gradually bring order and clarity.

Unpleasant experiences, confusion, and surprises become fleeting when viewed against the steady rhythm of breathing. After all, the breath is always with us — both in moments of joy and in times of struggle. With this constant support, we can move from discomfort to a zone of relative comfort.

By taking short pauses to reconnect with the breath, you can weave a thread of calmness throughout your day.

It is important to note that we all know how to breathe without training. When something goes wrong, you just have to observe your breathing — a few minutes of watching the inhalation and exhalation, its natural rhythm — and then the whole external context will be organised in the appropriate order.

You can get a little fancy and use the recommendation to breathe 'square' for several breathing cycles; in this breathing we use pauses, which contribute to greater calmness. It is easy to memorise the technique by imagining a square: we look at the top left corner of the square and inhale for four counts, we look across at the top right corner and pause for four counts, then we look down at the bottom right corner and exhale for four counts, then we look across at the bottom left corner and hold our breath for four counts. Thus, we pass the square, alternating inhalation, pause, exhalation, pause, and start the cycle from the beginning.

The argument that you don't have time to stop is completely untenable — after all, can you at least find one minute to take a breather?

If you have only one minute to rest, just ten breathing cycles will work perfectly. We put one hand on our chest and the other on our abdomen, close our eyes, and start watching our breathing. We engage abdominal breathing and pay attention to how the abdominal wall rises during inhalation and falls during exhalation. The rhythm of breathing slows down and becomes deeper. At this time, our sympathetic nervous system relaxes, the parasympathetic nervous system is activated, and the body gets a little respite.

When you only have 20 seconds, just stop the flow of thoughts and think about how you are *right now:* what emotions you are feeling, what thoughts are swirling around in your head, what your body is sensing. Frequent contact with yourself is very helpful and doesn't take time. The main thing is to remember it.

And you probably drink tea or coffee once in a while — make this ritual a stop in the stormy sea of everyday life. Tell yourself: there's nothing to do right now. And just enjoy a cup of tea without any gadgets, communications, or thoughts.

The more often throughout the day we suspend our thoughts, the clearer we think, the calmer we feel, and the less tired we are from multitasking.

It is extremely helpful to offload thoughts onto paper and free up your RAM. Just try sifting through your thoughts and transfer a significant portion of them to paper. If you have written down a thought or scheduled a matter in your diary, you can safely forget about it knowing that you have it under control. This is a very simple technique that helps to reduce anxiety by removing the feeling of swarming thoughts in your head, and it frees up your energy for other things.

After a busy or difficult day, it's a good idea to do some free writing — write whatever springs to mind, unload whatever comes up, dump any stuck thoughts onto paper, and end the hard day with peace of mind by giving your notebook all the day's hustle and bustle.

We should not forget about the healing effect of music. It is known that pleasant, soothing music slows down the heart rate and breathing, and reduces cortisol levels. It integrates the activity of the two hemispheres and generally has a positive effect on wellbeing by stimulating the production of dopamine. After a busy day, try listening to soft, pleasant background music or nature sounds — anything that you enjoy and has a calming effect will do. If you like music, you may feel a reduction in stress immediately.

To relieve emotional tension, it is very good to learn additional relaxation techniques that help you relax. There are quite a lot of such techniques — progressive muscle relaxation, yoga nidra, autogenic training — you can try them, and choose what suits you best.

And I will share with you the practice of progressive muscle relaxation — it is alternate tension and relaxation of different muscle groups, which leads to deep relaxation of the whole body. By alternating states of tension and relaxation, we are able to memorise the relaxed state by contrast. And if this exercise is practised regularly, the skills of controlled relaxation through the body gradually emerge.

You only need 10 — 15 minutes to practice progressive muscle relaxation. I recommend giving it a try!

Progressive muscle relaxation techniques are a versatile way to relax the body after a busy day. Working with the body will allow you to calm down, shake off tiredness in the middle of the day, and better prepare for sleep. With this technique you learn the skills of voluntary muscular and mental relaxation.

This technique is based on the sequential tensing and relaxation of different muscle groups. You tense the muscles as much as possible, but do not overstretch them.

Position yourself comfortably lying on the floor, on a mat, on your back. Legs straightened. Arms slightly away from the body. Eyes closed.

Take a deep breath in, hold, and exhale deeply.

- *Turn your attention to the soles of your feet. Bend your toes to the soles of your feet, hold the tension (5 sec.). Take a breath and on the exhale, release. Observe how the muscles relax. Feel a state of rest in the feet (5 sec.).*

- *Pay attention to the shins. Pull the toes of your feet towards you, feel the tension in your shins, hold the tension (5 sec.). Breathe in and as you exhale, slowly relax (5 sec.). Remember the state of rest.*

- *Now stretch the toes away from you and concentrate on the sensation of this tension. Hold the tension (5 sec.). Take a deep breath in and relax as you exhale. Note the contrast between tension and relaxation (5 sec.).*

- *Pay attention to your thighs. Tense your thigh muscles and turn your legs slightly inwards, feel the tension in your thighs, hold it (5 sec.). Breathe in and slowly relax as you exhale. Remember this state of relaxation (5 sec.).*

- *Turn your attention to your feet as a whole. Lift your feet off the floor to a height of 10-20cms. Note the sensation of tension (5 sec.). Inhale and, as you exhale, slowly lower your legs. Feel calm and relaxed (5 sec.).*

- *Direct your attention to the buttocks. Tuck your pelvis towards yourself, squeeze your tailbone with your buttocks, feel the tension (5 sec.). Breathe in and release the tension as you exhale. Note the difference between tension and rest (5 sec.).*

- *Turn your attention to your hands. Clench your right fist — hold the tension (5 seconds). Inhale and, as you exhale, relax your fist. Note the sensation of rest (5 sec.). Clench your left fist — hold the tension (5 sec.). Inhale, and as you exhale, relax your fist. Note the feeling of rest (5 sec.).*

- *Pay attention to your right arm. Bend your right arm at the elbow and tense your arm and shoulder muscles. Hold the tension (5 sec.). Inhale, and on the exhale slowly relax the arm (5 sec.). Pay attention to the left arm. Bend your left arm at the elbow, and on the inhale, tense the muscles of the forearm and shoulders (5 sec.). Note the tension, and as you exhale, slowly relax the arm (5 sec.).*

- *Now bend both arms at the elbows. Tense both shoulders and forearms simultaneously. Hold the tension (5 sec.), inhale and on exhalation relax the hands, rest. Note a pleasant state of rest (5 sec.).*

- *Pay attention to your abdomen, to the movements of the abdominal wall while breathing. As you inhale, push your abdomen outwards. Hold the breath, keep the tension (5 sec.), and slowly exhale, relax the abdominal muscles (5 sec.).*

Enjoy a state of peace and relaxation.

- *Now lift your pelvis by bending your torso and resting on your heels, elbows, and shoulders. Feel the tension in your body (5 sec.) and as you exhale on a breath, relax. Feel the state of rest (5 sec.).*

- *Pay attention to the chest. As you inhale, fill your lungs with air and expand your chest, hold your breath. Hold the tension (5 sec.) and on exhalation slowly lower the chest. Rest, feel peace and relaxation (5 sec.).*

- *Now, in the supine position, lift your head by pulling your chin to your chest. Feel the tension in your neck muscles (5 sec.). Slowly exhale and lower your head. Feel relaxed (5 sec.).*

- *Pay attention to your face. Clench your jaws and pull the corners of your mouth back towards your ears, tensing the muscles of the lower third of your face. Feel the tension (5 sec.), inhale deeply and relax your jaw on the exhale. Enjoy the relaxation (5 sec.).*

- *Raise your eyebrows as high as possible and open your mouth wide, tensing your facial muscles. Hold the tension (5 sec.). Inhale deeply and relax with the exhalation. Feel a state of calm (5 sec.).*

- *Now strongly close your eyes, frown and wrinkle your nose, tensing the muscles of the middle third of your face. Hold the tension (5 sec.). Inhale, and then as you exhale, relax (5 sec.). Rest, feel the state of calm.*

- *Turn your inner gaze to the whole body. Try to tense your whole body at the same time. Start tensing from the feet, legs, abdomen, arms, facial muscles. Hold the tension (5 sec.). Take a breath in and on the exhalation slowly relax (5 sec.). Once again tense the whole body — feet, legs, abdomen, arms, face muscles. Hold the tension (5 sec.). Inhale and as you exhale, slowly relax (5 sec.).*
Rest and allow yourself to enjoy a state of calm.

Pay attention to the sensations in your body, your thoughts, your emotions. And just relax. The state of relaxation is very pleasant and very useful, both for your body and for your psyche.
And gradually return: wiggle your fingers and toes, stretch, turn on your side, open your eyes when ready.

It All Depends on the Stage of Burnout

When people ask me how to get out of burnout, I try not to give immediate advice so as not to do any harm. Because in each individual case it is important to use the means that correspond to the moment and depth of burnout.

Restoring balance to the warning phase ...

As I said before, it is easiest to interrupt the burnout process at the initial phase. It prevents the process of exhaustion when energy is still flowing. At this stage, the brain is still flexible and sputtering with ideas, so it's worth taking advantage of this to find the cause. It is important to watch out for warning signs during this phase.

If you suddenly notice that because of work you have started to miss out on enjoyable events — trips to the fitness centre, meetings with relatives and friends, less time to devote to your children, or your favourite hobby has been neglected — this is a reason to think about it and create a plan to bring back the activities that used to give you pleasure. Obviously, at that moment it seems that all this is not so important — at this stage work is more valuable for some reason — but it's an illusion that you have to devote all your time to work for high performance. We are more productive when we are juggling different activities, switching, engaging all the networks of the brain. And it is the passive brain network that serves as an incubator for generating new ideas. It is not a secret that many inventions came into the minds of scientists during their holidays. So the change of brain modes, alternating concentration and relaxation, help to find the best solutions.

Sometimes, we need to look for ingenious solutions or create works of art, or sometimes we just have a lot of things to do, and they do not fit into the narrow framework of working hours. In these cases, too, there are solutions:

— It is worth thinking about prioritising tasks and delegating. Maybe some things should be removed and others delegated? And now you have a few hours a week for fitness, normal sleep, and socialising.

— It may be worth looking into time management; look for time-absorbers, or learn to plan your work day better.

— Alternate between intensive work and adequate rest. I know the state of emergency work and extremely busy schedules. There are periods of increased workload; you can't escape them, it's part of the profession. But then you need to take quality rest after the emergency work; set yourself relatively empty days after this period, try not to plan anything, or even take a short holiday — time off to recover a little after intensive work.

It's important to schedule short breaks throughout the day; block out lunch time on your calendar, and try to get quality rest on the weekends. Quality means doing things that energise you, not wasting it on other activities that drain your energy. Observe how you spend your weekend, how you feel at the end — if awake and rested, you are energised; if tired and broken, you've been doing something unhelpful.

Perhaps you know all this, but it seems unrealistic to implement. What if you try to move from the *knowing* stage to the *implementing* stage, i.e. start creating new rules for your life. For example, plan your holidays in the same way as you plan your work — put them on a calendar and follow the schedule as if it were an important job too. You can think about personal boundaries and learn to say "no" when it hurts your wellbeing and balance. Such rules only make you more effective; it's been proven many times.

It is probably unnecessary to remind you that sleep, nutrition, and physical activity are basic needs on which professional — and any other — wellbeing is built. If you forget about them when you are thinking about great things or fighting with important projects, it is better to remember in time and pay attention to taking care of your resources.

And to add to your inspiration for a quality holiday, I recommend making a list of activities that you enjoy and energise you. It's best to take the time to do this; pour a cup of tea, sit down with a blanket on the sofa, and dream about all the things you would enjoy. Let your imagination go wild, and then your list will include not only the obvious items like *visit a museum* or *go to fitness class*, but also, for example, *go to a bookstore and hang out there for an hour, reading, and then come home with a weighty stack of books to read for the next month* or *go to a creative shop and pick out everything you like, go to a book club meeting and enjoy discussing an interesting book, getting to know people and their points of view.* The list can be hung up in a prominent place, and then your battery-charging plan will always be in sight, and you can refer to it when you have an hour or two to relax.

If all these tools don't work for you or don't fit into your life, perhaps it's time to adjust your beliefs? Maybe you strive too much for perfection, for an unattainable ideal? If it is difficult to work with your own beliefs, a psychologist will definitely help you with this.

Removing stressors in the exhaustion phase ...

If you have reached the stage of exhaustion, you should not be surprised and panic — it is not an uncommon phenomenon in our time. And during the course of life, almost everyone has found themselves in a state of emotional and physical exhaustion, when there is no energy, and more and more often the questions arise: "Why? What is it all for? What am I doing? Shouldn't I give up?"

Exhaustion indicates chronic stress, which means that some factors causing discomfort are still active. In this case, the recommendation to get more rest has a right to exist, but it does not eliminate stress if its cause is still active. Therefore, at this stage you should first think about what in your life creates stress and emotional tension.

Professional burnout often originates in the domain of work relationships, making work-related factors the logical starting point for diagnosing stressors in one's life. Each factor — whether related to rewards, workload, autonomy, relationships, feelings of injustice, or value conflicts — can be addressed by identifying a point of control and taking steps to improve the situation.

In practice, however, life turns out to be more complicated than simple schemes. I can say from experience that one can deal with problems at work, but the main cause of burnout lies, for example, in child-parent relations or relations with a partner. And you can't get out of apathy if you work only with organisational factors. But several sessions of psychotherapy to work with the main problem influence all spheres of life at once: interest and energy appear, and the profession that seemed uninteresting — because *"I've been working for a long time, I know everything, I'm bored"* — suddenly starts to play with new colours; inspiration and interest appear.

Sometimes burnout at work is influenced by the accumulation of significant life events over the past year — illnesses, relocations, completing an education course, and more. According to the social adaptation scale (or Holmes and Rahe stress scale), the higher your score, the more adaptive energy is required to cope. Since energy is a finite resource, it may become insufficient, especially for demanding and stressful work. It's no surprise that the workplace is often where we first feel the strain of this resource depletion.

In the corporate environment, burnout most often manifests at the exhaustion stage, with deeper stages occurring less frequently. The bad news for employers is that this is the stage when employees are most likely to quit, driven to escape further harm by a healthy instinct for self-preservation. The good news, however, is that recovery from this stage can happen relatively quickly — provided the key cause of stress is identified and addressed.

Let's assume the burnout factor has been identified and addressed. How can you recover from exhaustion? If you've left your job, it's important not to rush into a new career immediately. Instead, spend some time focusing on rehabilitation and restoring your energy. Interestingly, many people who quit due to burnout often find themselves stuck in limbo, without a clear understanding of what they want next. This is completely normal, and it's essential to allow yourself to be in that state without judgment.

When exhaustion is severe, your body operates in survival mode, conserving energy primarily for basic physiological functions. If your energy feels completely depleted, the first step is to place yourself in an enriched environment: ensure you get enough sleep, rest, eat nourishing meals, and incorporate regular physical movement into your routine.

Rest in the style of a spa or sanatorium — focused on relaxation and recovery — can significantly help replenish physical energy. As your energy begins to return, positive emotions will emerge, life will regain its vibrancy, and you'll gradually have the capacity to make new plans and set goals. With this renewed energy, motivation for action will naturally follow.

At the stage of rehabilitation, some people find relaxation and nature therapy very helpful, others immerse themselves in long-neglected hobbies — drawing, photography, music, travelling — anything that once brought pleasure but was abandoned because of work. And if someone likes to learn, it is advised only not to immediately start an a major educational course which requires a lot of energy, discipline and will; it is likely they will not have enough strength for it. But if you love to learn, you can always find an affordable and small-scale format of education.

Mindfulness and relaxation techniques are highly effective tools for managing stress, especially at this stage. During my studies in various mindfulness programs, I noticed that many of my fellow participants came on the recommendation of a psychologist or coach, who was supporting them in recovering from burnout. Regular meditation practice not only aids in overcoming chronic stress but also serves as a powerful tool to prevent falling into it in future.

Professional help for the negativism and cynicism phase ...

If you stay in the state of burnout for a long time (and sometimes you can stay in it for years), the organism, forced to adapt to the discomfort, acquires a lot of defense mechanisms. Detachment from the world and an indifferent attitude to people grows. Emotional reactions are either blunted or expressed in aggression, containing which is hard. Everyone around is blamed — and this is also a defence reaction to preserve the perception of one's own value.

It is quite difficult to cope with this stage on your own — rigidity of thinking, lack of motivation, and a distorted perception of reality hinder you. After all, when everyone is to blame, it is others who need to change! At this stage it helps to work with a coach or a psychologist, who can lead to changes with the help of a system of very small steps. Since it took a long time to enter this stage, it is simplistic to expect a quick exit.

The primary focus at this stage is finding meaning and purpose, though it may feel challenging to envision the future. The mind often feels stuck, unwilling to dream or imagine possibilities. However, imaginative thinking can be a valuable tool; working with visual imagery and metaphorical cards helps bypass cognitive barriers, and uncover a future worth striving for.

This approach makes sense. Logical and rational thinking relies on existing beliefs and tends to dismiss what seems unrealistic in the present. In contrast, figurative thinking and metaphors tap into a holistic inner experience, allowing individuals to visualise their desired outcomes without being constrained by limiting beliefs or rigid rules.

Images create a sense of dissociation, enabling a person to see themselves as separate from the picture, almost as an observer of their own story. This bypasses the censorship of the prefrontal cortex, which typically filters ideas to align with realistic, conventional views of oneself. When someone describes a picture or metaphor, they are, in essence, talking about themselves. This process reveals insights into their beliefs, aspirations, and dreams, offering a clearer path forward.

When an image of the desired future emerges, the intention to change the present naturally begins to take shape. However, there is often not enough energy for significant changes right away, so it's essential to start with small steps. This might involve modifying aspects of your work process, making adjustments in your personal space, or rediscovering activities that once brought you joy.

Celebrate each small step with self-affirmation: "I'm doing great!" By acknowledging these efforts, you can gradually build confidence, strengthen motivation, and gather the resources needed for further progress.

Sometimes, gaining enough energy and motivation leads to making bigger decisions, such as leaving a company. As energy levels rise and stressors are addressed, a readiness for major life changes often follows.

It's highly beneficial to navigate this journey with the support of a professional — whether a psychologist or a coach — who can guide you through the process and help you sustain your progress.

In the depression phase, treatment is essential ...

The final stage of burnout often leads to serious mental health disorders, addictions, and somatic illnesses. At this point, a coach or psychologist is no longer sufficient; qualified medical intervention is necessary. Treatment may need to be comprehensive, combining medication, psychotherapy, and rehabilitation in a restorative setting, such as a sanatorium.

At this stage, prioritising self-care and making the decision to seek treatment are critical. Recognising the need for help and taking that first step can pave the way to recovery.

Fortunately, severe stages of burnout are relatively rare. However, it's important to be mindful of these potential outcomes. This awareness can empower you to intervene early before reaching this stage, by addressing the warning signs when you first notice yourself neglecting basic needs and rushing through life at an unsustainable pace.

Key Takeaways:

- In order to get out of the state of burnout it is important to find chronic stress factors and reduce their influence, and it is necessary to develop internal resources that increase personal resilience. Self-care skills, the ability to live emotions ecologically, the ability to identify one's own non-constructive patterns of behaviour and thinking, all help to cope with stress and avoid burnout.

• A set of measures to get out of stress depends on the depth of burnout. Thus, at the first warning stage it is worth paying attention to the first signals that lead to loss of energy. This will allow you to change your lifestyle in time, restore balance, and prevent the transition to subsequent stages.

• In the exhaustion stage, the first thing to do is to think about what is causing stress and emotional strain in your life. This stage requires identifying chronic stressors in order to minimise or eliminate them. It also requires rest and rehabilitation to replenish your energy and find new meaning.

• At the stages of deep burnout, it is recommended to seek professional help — psychological and, if necessary, medical.

How Can Employers Take Care of Employees?

Fortunately, employers are increasingly recognising the impact of work on employees' health. Wellbeing programs are gaining momentum and acceptance in many companies, with HR managers now adept at demonstrating to leadership the tangible value a happy employee brings to the business.

This growing interest in wellbeing — human wellbeing in the broadest sense — is no coincidence. Before the pandemic, the world was often described as VUCA (Volatile, Uncertain, Complex, Ambiguous), reflecting its instability and unpredictability. The pandemic, however, ushered in an era characterized as BANI (Brittle, Anxious, Nonlinear, Incomprehensible) — a world more fragile, anxious, nonlinear, and incomprehensible than ever. Geopolitical tensions have only deepened this sense of fragility, while global inflation and economic challenges have fueled additional concerns about financial stability.

Paradoxically, the comfortable and progressive 21st century has suddenly shaken one of the basic human needs — the need for security. And under stress, a person is unable to work effectively; work is done by force, without attention or interest. Companies are focused on efficiency, and concern for business success is not the last reason why management votes in favour of investing in staff wellbeing. Companies that prioritise efficiency have come to realise that concern for employees' wellbeing directly contributes to business success.

However, the motivation to embrace wellbeing culture isn't purely commercial. The pandemic and other global crises have heightened awareness of humanity, prompting organisations to become more empathetic and humane. This shift is evident in the rhetoric of business events, where discussions increasingly center on people and their challenges.

Corporate culture is not static; it is changing, albeit slowly, as a result of many factors. The importance of social responsibility in business is growing, the values of managers are changing — they are thinking about self-realisation and mission, not just about the profit of the organisation and their own bonuses. Human resources are highly valued, and companies are striving to retain talent that prioritises not only profits but also a supportive corporate culture. Consequently, organisations are focusing more on fostering employee happiness and wellbeing.

Recent upheavals have demonstrated that employers can serve as islands of stability amid external chaos, whether during a pandemic or other crisis. The companies that quickly adapted to sudden changes, provided support, offered stress management training, and facilitated access to psychological assistance proved to be invaluable anchors. While not all companies have embraced this approach, a growing number are leading the way.

Yet, in the pursuit of introducing something good for staff, it is very easy to get carried away with the chaotic addition of various pleasant perks — here's yoga in the morning, fruit, a healthy habits marathon, and a spa day. These are all great activities as long as they are also combined with other basic principles of corporate culture. If, however, a company encourages a workaholic culture that disturbs the work-life balance, and perks are introduced only to ensure that employees can withstand heavy workloads, this can hardly be called a sincere approach to the topic of people's wellbeing.

To competently implement wellbeing programmes, the diagnosis of psychosocial factors — which are the causes of stress and burnout in the company — should be put in the foreground. After all, in order to deal with problems, it is necessary to identify them first. That's why many employers are now studying not only staff satisfaction and engagement, but also measuring key indicators of mental health, staff wellbeing, and psychosocial risks. The insights gained from these surveys form the foundation for developing targeted and impactful wellbeing initiatives.

A holistic approach to wellbeing: from health support to self-actualisation ...

The wellbeing of employees is rooted in the satisfaction of basic human needs. Here, it is worth recalling Abraham Maslow's famous hierarchy of needs, which is often simplified as a pyramid. According to his theory, detailed in the book Motivation and Personality (1954), the fulfillment of higher-order needs, such as self-actualisation, depends on the satisfaction of more fundamental needs and the creation of supportive external conditions.

Despite the criticism of Maslow's theory for a lack of empirical support, it is difficult to dispute the idea that when a person is in survival mode — struggling to meet basic needs such as food and shelter — there is little time or energy left for creativity and self-expression. The immediate demands of survival take precedence. However, as these basic needs are met, individuals naturally aspire to more. They begin to think about realising their potential and seek to express themselves through meaningful activity.

This transition to fulfilling higher-order needs benefits not only the individual but also the organisation they work for. At this level, employees are more likely to harness their full potential in addressing workplace challenges, contributing creatively and effectively to organisational goals.

The approach to fostering wellbeing within a company becomes clear when viewed through the lens of human needs. First and foremost, basic conditions related to physiological and safety needs must be ensured. Initiatives aimed at physical, mental, and financial wellbeing align with this priority. Providing a friendly and safe working environment, support for stress management, and resources to maintain physical and mental health all help employees feel secure and resourced.

The next level addresses the needs for belonging, respect, and recognition. Measures supporting employees' social wellbeing are essential at this stage. This includes developing emotional intelligence in both managers and employees, and fostering effective internal corporate communications. These efforts create an environment where communication is constructive, feedback is meaningful, and recognition is genuine. As a result, employees feel valued and significant within the organisation.

Once these foundational needs are fulfilled, employees can direct their energy toward creativity and self-actualisation. At this stage, they are ready to realise their potential, contributing fully to the company's success. In return, the organisation gains engaged, effective employees, enhancing the overall wellbeing of the human-company system.

It's evident that organisations with happy employees are more likely to cultivate happy customers. Such companies are also better positioned to innovate, implement groundbreaking ideas, and establish themselves as market leaders.

Creating a comfortable environment for employees has long been a cornerstone of IT companies' success. These organisations thrive, grow, and significantly increase their market capitalisation largely due to the quality of their human resources — employees whose creativity and innovative approaches drive solutions to complex problems. The key to their success lies in fostering conditions that unlock creative potential.

A notable example is Google. In 2014, the company was named "Best Company to Work For" by the Great Place to Work Institute and Fortune magazine. Google has consistently prioritised employee wellbeing, creating an environment where individuals can focus their energy on productive work and innovation. In this way, a supportive corporate culture becomes the foundation of happiness and productivity, and the company's success is a direct result of this approach.

While Google's extensive list of employee benefits is widely known, two standout examples highlight the company's commitment to fostering creativity and efficiency. First, at Google's East Coast headquarters, no workspace is more than 150 feet from a food source, and employees are offered free, high-quality meals. This arrangement serves dual purposes: it saves employees time and energy otherwise spent searching for meals, and encourages spontaneous meetings over food, where innovative ideas may spark and lead to groundbreaking projects.

Second, Google's famous '20% Time' policy allows employees to dedicate one day a week — 20% of their working hours — to projects or activities of their choosing. This freedom nurtures creativity, autonomy, and work-life balance, fostering an environment where innovation can thrive. While the specifics of how the policy is implemented have evolved over time, its impact on Google's culture of experimentation and creativity is undeniable. By giving employees space to explore their passions, the company has cultivated a workplace where new ideas and innovative solutions can emerge organically.

By focusing on creating an environment that supports employees' needs and encourages innovation, Google exemplifies how a culture of wellbeing drives both individual and organisational success.

Perhaps the example of Google is too high-profile, but there are countless other cases, including those from smaller companies, that consistently foster a corporate culture of responsibility and care for people. One notable example comes from the restaurant industry. At a business event, a manager shared how their company managed to significantly reduce staff turnover—an issue that often challenges this sector.

The secret lies in the company's genuine care for its employees and the community. This care is reflected in providing fair wages, good working conditions, and actively involving employees in meaningful initiatives, such as environmental efforts like waste sorting and charitable activities to support people in difficult circumstances. Employees see and appreciate the company's human-centered approach and its commitment to social responsibility.

Moreover, the management and staff share common values, fostering a sense of alignment and mutual respect. This creates a virtuous cycle: employees respond with loyalty, engagement, and a deeper sense of commitment in return for their employer's responsible and caring attitude. This example demonstrates that a people-first approach can lead to remarkable results for both employees and the business, regardless of the sector.

In general, fostering a corporate culture of wellbeing is about caring for people, not just about having a big budget. Many initiatives can be implemented with minimal resources and through employees' own efforts. Within any organisation, there are likely individuals passionate about sports, yoga, healthy lifestyles, or self-development. Why not encourage them to volunteer and lead classes for their colleagues in areas they care about? Why not inspire them to become health ambassadors for the company? A simple message to the HR department can help organise such activities.

I am a health volunteer in my workplace, and for several years I have been leading weekly morning practices that include exercise, meditation, and journaling. These sessions are open to everyone and can be joined online. This small initiative carries significant meaning: it allows me to share my knowledge and skills to support others' health, while participants gain energy and focus. No matter how intense the work gets, these small islands of calm provide moments of balance. They reinforce a shared corporate value: we care for ourselves and our wellbeing, and in doing so, we also care for those around us. Calmness and a friendly attitude ripple outward, positively affecting everyone we interact with.

Surely you can confirm from your own examples that caring for people and contributing to their wellbeing is the shortest way to their heart, loyalty, and engagement. So, a corporate culture of wellbeing and care is a shared value — for the individual and for the business.

Stress management in organisations ...

In times of crisis, companies have become islands of stability, providing resources and reassurance when global challenges arise. Be it a pandemic, economic uncertainty, or geopolitical conflict, timely and decisive employer actions — such as open communication, clear decisions, and practical support — help employees regain a sense of control.

To effectively manage stress within an organisation, the following measures are key:

1. *Open Communication Channels*
Transparent communication between leadership and employees fosters trust. Timely updates and feedback ensure clarity, reducing the anxiety caused by uncertainty.
2. *Effective Internal Communications*

Clear messaging during crises acts as a powerful anti-anxiety tool. Regular updates reassure employees, help them focus on work, and align the organisation during challenging times.

3. *Stress Management and Resilience Training*

Equipping employees with resilience and stress-management skills boosts their ability to navigate complexity and adapt to challenges, benefiting both their health and productivity.

4. *Emotional Intelligence and Empathy Development*

Managers must learn to understand and address employees' emotional needs, fostering supportive leadership that unlocks potential and enhances team morale.

5. *Employee Assistance Programs (EAPs)*

Professional psychological, financial, and legal support services address critical employee needs. Promoting these programs ensures their adoption and helps resolve issues efficiently.

6. *Flexible Working Arrangements*

The pandemic normalised remote and hybrid work, offering employees flexibility. Balancing in-office and remote options accommodates modern expectations and enhances work-life balance.

7. *Health and Wellness Education*

Employers can encourage healthier lifestyles through education and initiatives that reduce burnout and chronic stress. Supporting employees in managing their health benefits both individuals and organisational outcomes.

8. *Motivation and Career Development*

Transparent career tracks and constructive feedback systems address uncertainties, enhancing motivation and reducing workplace stress.

By implementing these measures, companies can not only mitigate stress but also create an environment where employees feel valued, resilient, and engaged.

Programmes to Prevent and Address Burnout

Burnout prevention and intervention programmes can significantly benefit both employees and organisations. Effective programmes often include the following components:

- **Understanding Stress and Burnout:** Providing theoretical knowledge about stress mechanisms and burnout helps employees better manage their responses to challenging situations.

- **Relaxation Techniques**: Teaching employees and managers methods for relaxation is essential in navigating high-stress environments.
- **Mindfulness Practices**: Training in mindfulness promotes non-judgmental awareness of thoughts and emotions. Numerous studies confirm its benefits in reducing anxiety, improving focus, and fostering resilience.
- **Coping Skills Development**: Educating employees in problem-focused and emotion-focused coping strategies enhances their ability to regain control and confidence during stressful periods.
- **Reframing Unhelpful Beliefs**: Shifting negative attitudes and beliefs fosters more constructive perspectives and behaviours.
- **Social Skills Training**: Developing interpersonal communication skills, empathy, and the ability to seek and offer support strengthens team cohesion and individual wellbeing.
- **Emotional Competence and Positive Emotions**: Enhancing emotional intelligence and fostering a positive emotional environment can reduce stress and improve workplace dynamics.

The effectiveness of such programmes has been widely documented in scientific literature, showing improvements in mental health, stress resistance, and burnout reduction. Crucially, these initiatives must go beyond theoretical knowledge to focus on practical application. We change our neural connections if we acquire new habits of thinking, interpreting, and acting. Therefore, it is useful to build learning situations, simulations, and role-plays into educational programmes. If stressful situations are played out in a learning environment, the level of preparedness for real stress will be significantly higher.

Key Takeaways:

- Employee wellbeing is based on the fulfilment of basic needs. First and foremost, basic conditions related to physiological needs and safety must be guaranteed. Measures aimed at physical, mental, and financial wellbeing correspond to this. The next level relates to the needs for belonging, respect and recognition; this is the focus of measures aimed at supporting the employee's social wellbeing, which involves developing emotional intelligence skills, recognising merit, and ensuring effective communication within the company.

Once the basic needs are fulfilled, energy is directed towards creativity, and the employee is ready to realise his or her potential for the benefit of the company.

- To manage stress in an organisation, an employer can use many means and tools: effective internal corporate communications, employee assistance programmes, training and educational programmes, provision of flexible working hours, involvement of employees in managing their own health, effective motivation, and incentive programmes.

- A corporate culture of wellbeing and care is a shared value for the individual and for the business. Employees are provided with the conditions for health and wellbeing, and the company receives an engaged, loyal, and motivated employee.

Stress Management Algorithm

Finishing the story about stress and burnout, I would like to emphasise once again that stress is in many senses a useful adaptive reaction of the organism, and an inevitable part of life. Whether stress is useful or harmful depends on our attitude to it and the duration of stressors. We can use stress as energy for growth and development, or we can sink into a state of passive helplessness and illness. It all depends on our perspective, on our perception, and also on the strategies we use to cope with stress. Whatever the external context, we always have the freedom to influence, rely on ourselves, and gain a sense of control.

When faced with a difficult situation, the following algorithm can help you navigate and manage stress effectively:

1. Recognise and Accept

Acknowledge the situation and identify the causes of stress. Accept your feelings without judgment, allowing yourself to process them fully.

2. Define Your Zone of Control

Ask yourself:
- Can I change the situation?
- What steps are necessary to change it?

If change is not possible, focus on reframing your attitude or perspective toward the situation.

3. Develop a Plan for Improvement

Consider key areas of your life and ask:
- How can I better care for myself (e.g., physically, mentally)?
- How can I improve my relationship with work?
- How can I strengthen my interactions with others?

Based on these reflections, create an action plan and start implementing it step by step.

4. Monitor and Adjust

Regularly evaluate the outcomes of your actions. Are things improving or worsening? Adjust your strategy as needed to stay on track.

Accepting your feelings and situation is an important first step, and I share a meditation practice for accepting emotions.

Prepare for meditation. Sit cross-legged on a mat — you can use a meditation cushion for comfort — or sit on a chair with your feet parallel to the floor. The back does not touch the back of the chair, it is straight, but not tense, you can lean slightly forward, imitating the posture of the coachman. Your hands are resting on your knees. Make sure you are sitting comfortably.

Concentrate your gaze on a point on the floor about two metres away from you, try to unfocus your gaze, then more objects fall into the area of perception, but you see them indistinctly, unfocused. You can close your eyes if it is more comfortable.

Feel the sounds around you, feel the air touching your skin.

Turn your attention inward. Notice what you are thinking about?

What emotion are you feeling at this moment? Try to name that emotion. Maybe it is interest, or boredom, or anxiety, or sadness, or calmness, serenity. Feel the sensations in your body.

Inhale deeply — hold your breath — and exhale deeply. And three more deep inhales and exhales, letting go of all feelings, thoughts, worries.

Begin to observe your breath. Feel the inhalation — how the air fills the lungs, and the exhalation — how the air leaves the lungs.

Choose a point to observe your breath; it could be the point at the base of your nose where the air enters your nasal cavity — it's cooler — and then the slightly warmer air leaves your body. So, observe the breath — just inhale and exhale. If thoughts come, you note them and let them go, returning to observing the breath at the point you chose.

For a couple of minutes continue to observe the breath; if the mind is distracted, you can add a mental counting of breathing cycles.

Gradually finish watching the breath. Now think of a situation that caused you unpleasant feelings in the recent past — not a dramatic, unpleasant situation, but about a -2 on the negative scale of -1 to -10. Think back to that situation at minus two: how did you feel at that moment? What were you thinking? What was your body feeling? Try to feel that state now. Explore it. Say to yourself — this is my body's stress response to an unpleasant situation. Stress is part of our life, it's an adaptive response. I can live with it, I can tolerate stress. I don't fight these feelings and I accept them.

I can be with these feelings, watch them change, transform. As soon as I accept my feelings, they become less intense and gradually go away on their own. I don't banish these feelings. All the things I feel — pleasant and unpleasant emotions — are part of life, its richness and diversity. I can be with it. Let me be comfortable and at ease with it.

Imagine that emotions, thoughts, feelings are clouds floating in the sky. You are the vast static sky, you let the feelings be, float across the sky, without clinging or chasing them away. And then your unpleasant feelings float by. And you remembered something good and smiled, and there are other clouds floating across the sky. You don't cling to those clouds either. They're all floating by. Even when something very unpleasant has happened, that too will pass. No matter how thick and black the clouds are, they too will pass, and behind the clouds there is always sunshine and clear blue sky. You are not equal to your feelings, you allow them to be, accept them and observe them. You are more than thoughts, feelings, and sensations. And you stay with the sky, letting the clouds float across the sky.

Talk to yourself: "Stress is a normal part of life, I can be with it, I accept these feelings. They come and go, and let me be comfortable and calm always". Think of something very good, smile, create an image of a big and beautiful sky with light clouds floating on it. "May I be comfortable and calm always."

And gradually we come back. Open your eyes when ready.

PART 3. MASTERING BALANCE: THE PATH TO A BURNOUT-FREE LIFE

Wellbeing is about finding a balance between external challenges and internal resources. Since challenges are often beyond our control — they tend to arrive uninvited — our focus must shift to training and developing inner resources. By doing so, we can better navigate the growing complexities of the world, experiencing stress-related growth rather than succumbing to burnout or depression.

In my book *Finding Serenity Amid the Chaos: How Managing Your Stress Can Enhance Your Creativity and Wellbeing*, I explore in detail how to maintain both physical and psychological resources. A positive outlook on life, optimism, constructive beliefs, confidence, and healthy self-esteem are vital prerequisites for building resilience. At the same time, a healthy diet, regular physical activity, and quality sleep help sustain the physical energy needed to handle life's challenges, frequent changes, and its fast pace.

But how do we learn to invest in ourselves and make self-care a priority? Many people understand what they need to do to stay healthy, but few succeed in integrating those practices into their daily lives. Others may view self-care as selfish. How can we reframe these attitudes and bridge the gap between knowing and doing?

Do you remember Clare's story of repeated burnout episodes? When we last spoke, she was on the verge of another burnout and promised to urgently change her life, saying that in a year she would not be recognisable. Two months later, I had the chance to talk to Clare again, and it was like meeting a different person. She radiated energy and joy, looked chic, her image more feminine, and she was eager to share her changes, which were visible even without her words.

Shortly after our last conversation, just before Christmas, Clare faced a devastating challenge. Buster, a horse she cared for and deeply loved, fell gravely ill with a disease that typically proves fatal. A veterinarian gave a grim prognosis: the horse's only chance was an expensive and risky surgery followed by intensive care. Without hesitation, Clare made the decision to proceed with the operation and personally handle the demanding post-operative care, despite her own exhaustion and heavy workload. This decision proved transformative.

After the surgery, Clare became the horse's primary caregiver, dedicating six hours a day to its recovery. Each morning, starting at sunrise, she would walk the horse and support its healing journey. During this month of care, Clare found herself changing as well. "Something healed inside me because I was caring for this animal. Every day I was in nature, and through this act of loving-kindness, I experienced a healing I hadn't felt in years."

As the horse's condition improved and required less attention, Clare maintained the morning routine she had established. She began rising at 5 a.m., meditating, and exercising on her new stationary exercise bike before starting her workday at 11. She continued to visit her horse but also turned her focus inward. She started listening to her body, eating healthier, and losing weight. Energy flowed back into her life, and new goals emerged. She planned a long-awaited trip to Central America and prioritised health, relationships, and wellbeing as the foundation of her life.

"This situation created space for something new to enter my life. Initially, it was my concern for the horse, but that care extended to myself, making me healthier, happier, and more successful than I've ever been. My business began to thrive too, with record sales and profitability," Clare shared with a radiant smile, one that only comes from genuine happiness.

When I asked Clare about the key to her transformation, she reflected, "The loving-kindness I felt for my horse changed my attitude toward myself. Taking care of Buster healed me too. I hadn't taken good care of myself for a long time, focusing only on work and forgetting how to nurture. This experience reminded me of what love truly means."

Humans are both simple and complex. We often overlook the basics while chasing unattainable goals, burning out in the process. Clare's journey brought her back to life's essence and its joys. "Every time I walked my horse at sunrise, I noticed the beauty around me; the changing colors of the sky, the stillness of nature. I had spent years traveling the world in search of beauty, only to find it right here, close to home," she said.

Each healing journey is invaluable, adding to our reservoir of wisdom. Some lessons build lasting stability. For Clare, this experience offered a profound understanding of how to recharge and channel her energy without burning out. I hope that Clare has now found her recipe for sustainable wellbeing and fulfillment.

Neuroplasticity and Epigenetics — the Key to Health and Happiness

Is it possible to achieve wellbeing and maintain balance even in difficult situations? It is hard to believe so, being trapped in the belief that wellbeing and happiness are something that happens to us, rather than something we can achieve through personal transformation. We know that human beings are capable of change because of the mechanism of neuroplasticity discovered by scientists, namely the process of making or breaking connections between neurons and neurogenesis.

I propose a brief excursion into the history of discoveries related to brain mechanisms. In the 19th century, Ivan Sechenov developed the doctrine of brain reflexes, laying the foundation for understanding the brain's role in controlling behavior. Later, in the early 20th century, Ivan Pavlov expanded on this with his groundbreaking discovery of the conditioned reflex. This is a learning process in which a previously neutral stimulus becomes associated with another stimulus because the second stimulus consistently accompanies the first.

In Pavlov's famous experiments, an animal, such as a dog, was repeatedly presented with an unconditioned stimulus, such as food, alongside a neutral stimulus, such as a sound or a light. After repeated pairings, the dog began to respond to the neutral stimulus alone by salivating, just as it would to the unconditioned stimulus.

From a neurobiological perspective, this process demonstrates that neurons that are activated together form a neural network, a phenomenon sometimes summarised as "neurons that fire together wire together." Through learning, we can create new neural networks, leading to changes in behavior and adaptation to new environments.

Following Ivan Pavlov, Peter Anokhin made significant contributions to the development of the doctrine of reflexes in the 20th century. He introduced the concepts of **'reverse afferentation'** and the **'acceptor of the result of action'**.

According to Anokhin, when an action is performed, the brain forms an expectation of its outcome. Reverse afferentation provides feedback to compare the actual result with the expected outcome. The acceptor of the result of action acts as a system that evaluates whether the outcome of an action aligns with the motivation behind the decision to act.

For example, if you plan to pick up a glass, your brain anticipates what that action will achieve. The acceptor of the result compares the expected outcome with the actual result. If the expectation matches the result — if the glass is successfully in your hand — the action is considered complete, and the next action programme begins. However, if the result does not match the expectation (e.g., you miss the glass), the discrepancy triggers the creation of a new action programme to achieve the desired outcome (Anokhin P.K., 1973).

This mechanism is especially significant in understanding the recovery of function after injury or stroke. The acceptor of the result ensures that the brain repeatedly compares expectations and outcomes, driving the process of recovery. Through repetitive attempts and training, the brain compensates for lost functions by forming new neural connections and refining motor programmes. This explains how functional restoration is achieved over time through the continuous melding of expectation and outcome.

Scientists have demonstrated that neural connections in the brain can change through growth and reorganisation, a phenomenon known as **neuroplasticity**. In 1964, Marian Diamond, an American professor of anatomy, provided anatomical evidence of neuroplasticity. She showed that the cerebral cortex could change under the influence of the environment.

In her experiments, Diamond placed rats in enriched environments from an early age, where they had opportunities to grow, explore, play, and navigate mazes. The results revealed that rats raised in enriched environments had a greater cerebral cortex weight — ranging from a 3.3% to 7.6% increase in various cortical regions — compared to a control group of rats raised in standard environments. While the weight differences were small, they were consistent across most individuals.

Importantly, these anatomical differences correlated with functional improvements: rats from enriched environments exhibited superior learning abilities compared to those raised in less stimulating conditions. This groundbreaking research (Diamond M.C. et al., 1964) confirmed that environmental factors play a crucial role in shaping brain structure and function.

Later, another scientist, Rusty Gage, demonstrated the phenomenon of neuroplasticity in the human brain. Contrary to the long-held belief that brain structure remains fixed after childhood, Gage showed that the creation of new neurons continues in the adult brain and that a favorable environment and training can accelerate this process.

Gage discovered neural stem cells in the adult hippocampus and proved that they could give rise to new active neurons, highlighting the brain's capacity for ongoing adaptation and growth (Siletty K., 2016).

As it disproved the hypothesis that new neurons do not appear in the adult brain, it means that at any age we are capable of change. It turns out that with the help of favourable conditions and training, our brain can develop in the direction we want. Agreed, this offers incredible opportunities for personal transformation.

The second mechanism that gives us hope for controlling our lives and wellbeing is the **supragenomic regulatory mechanism**, also known as **epigenetics**. While genetics focuses on the processes that directly influence genes, epigenetics studies changes in gene activity that occur without altering the primary structure of the genes themselves.

It has long been understood that genes do not play a 100% determining role in the expression of inherited traits. As Nobel laureate and English biologist Peter Medawar aptly put it: *"Genetics proposes, and epigenetics disposes."* This phrase underscores the critical role of epigenetics in regulating which genes are expressed and which remain dormant.

The term *epigenetics* was first coined by biologist Conrad Waddington in 1942. Working with *Drosophila* flies, Waddington observed changes in traits that were induced by external factors, specifically exposure to ether vapors. Remarkably, he discovered that some of these acquired changes could be inherited. He concluded that these changes were not caused by mutations in genes but by a supragenomic mechanism. Waddington's pioneering work laid the foundation for the concept of epigenetics, enabling later scientists to investigate the biological mechanisms underlying supragenomic regulation in greater detail.

Epigenetic regulation does not change DNA, but tells enzymes how to read the information written in DNA. It turns out that genes are tagged, for example, by putting methyl groups on certain sections of DNA that can switch the gene off, with the result that information is not read from that section of DNA. The gene isn't damaged, but it doesn't work either. DNA methylation is by no means the only mechanism; there are other ways of epigenetic regulation.

As it turns out, we differ from each other not only in our genome, but also in the set of switched on and switched off genes. This fact gives us incredible opportunities to consciously adjust our genome and even, as studies show, to inherit epigenetic settings. And it is environmental factors that have a particularly strong influence on gene activation. As shown in a number of studies examining differences in the manifestation of traits among identical twins, inherited regulatory mechanisms are responsible for a trait by 20-30% and environmental factors by 70-80% (Cheung P. et al., 2018; J. van Dongen et al., 2016).

So living and rearing conditions seriously influence epigenetic markings. Numerous animal experiments show how caring for the offspring influences the degree of anxiety of the young. For example, in caring mother rats, the offspring are calmer — they do not expect threats, they see the world as a safe place, they have fewer active genes responsible for anxiety and depression. And the opposite is true of neglectful mother rats — the stress response of their pups is always on alert — they themselves have to look out for their own safety and scan the world for possible threats. There is evidence that rats that were chronically stressed at an early age not only retained these traits throughout their lives, but also passed on the 'stress' epigenetic markings to their offspring.

Epigenetic regulation has been studied quite seriously in relation to the topic of stress, and it turns out that moderate stress stimulates the expression of stress resistance genes and slows down ageing. And stress tolerance, in turn, is associated with increased longevity. Moderate doses of stressors stimulate the body's adaptive capacity, thereby training its ability to cope with more powerful stressors. But prolonged or too strong exposure to stressors depletes the reserve forces of the organism, leads to physiological disorders, and accelerates ageing. It transpires that the optimal state of health is associated not with the eradication of all stress factors, but with their reduction to a normal level (Gems D., Partridge L., 2008).

The complete eradication of stress factors seems highly unlikely, and the challenges of recent years have significantly contributed to the development of stress resilience. However, it's important to remember that the line between good stress (eustress) and bad stress (distress) is quite thin. To avoid slipping into distress when confronted with increasingly intense stressors, it is wise to focus on strengthening one's adaptive capabilities.

When discussing factors of gene regulation, our consciousness and thought processes can also be considered environmental factors. The way we think, how we feel, the choices we make, and the behaviors we cultivate through skills and habits all serve as a foundation for gene regulation and the expression of traits. Most importantly, by investing in our own development, we have the potential to positively influence future generations as well.

Key Takeaways:

- Humans are able to change through the creation of new neural connections or the destruction of old ones, which has been proven through the mechanism of neuroplasticity discovered by scientists. Neural connections change in the brain through growth and reorganisation. With favourable conditions and training, it is possible to set the direction for development in the desired direction.
- Epigenetics is another mechanism to expect to consciously manage one's life and wellbeing. Epigenetic regulation influences which gene will be expressed and which will fail, as a supragenomic mechanism tells enzymes how to read the information written in DNA. Environmental factors have a particularly strong influence on gene activation. Consciousness, thinking, is also a kind of external factor in relation to gene regulation. How we think, how we feel, what choices we make, what behaviour we form through the development of skills and habits — all this is the basis for gene regulation and the manifestation of traits.

Mindfulness as the Foundation of Wellbeing

What we do, feel, or think depends on attention and awareness. We can become much more calm, wise, and accepting by developing mindfulness.

Awareness is a key that opens many doors. Firstly, the fullness and richness of life itself depends on the quality of the conscious experience that fills each moment. And secondly, through mindfulness, we better understand ourselves as individuals, others, and the world around us; we can make good decisions; we can see our purpose and know our next step.

Awareness helps us to be in touch with ourselves and the world around us — because we are well aware of what is happening outside — and at the same time we understand ourselves, our needs, feelings, and sensations. And then the choice of the right decision happens by itself, because there is clarity about what needs to be done right now, based on the external and internal context. In the film *Titanic*, Jack, the main character, delivers a poignant monologue about cherishing the present moment: *"Life is a gift, and it should be cherished. You can't guess what will happen to you tomorrow. Life should be accepted as it is. Every day is important!"* Jack's words reflect a deep understanding of the value of living in the present. By focusing on the present experience, we can savour life's beautiful moments, truly noticing and living them, rather than letting them slip by while our minds wander or operate on autopilot.

The uniqueness of each moment provides an opportunity not only for gaining invaluable experiences but also for taking actions that can only be performed in the present. Whether it's seizing opportunities, taking risks, or softening the impact of unfavorable circumstances, all of this becomes possible through mindful attention to the here and now. Jack exemplifies this mindset, living each moment with joy and clarity. His actions are decisive and rooted in an understanding of the importance of not hesitating or delaying, but instead acting with purpose and presence.

The skill of mindfulness teaches global acceptance of all that life has to offer. We are always striving for positive experiences and trying to avoid negative ones, and even neutral experiences are boring to us — we always want to improve them. And mindfulness allows us to step back and say, "As it is." Because as it is, it's good. Life is the moment you are living right now. Everything else is past or future. Everything that was yesterday is history, everything that will be tomorrow is still fantasy. But today is that moment between the past and the future called life. So every morning, when we wake up, it makes sense to say words of gratitude for today, for another day that we live.

Life is beautiful when we notice the beauty of nature, realise the pleasure of a heartfelt conversation or a lovely dinner with friends, and there are many more beautiful things in our lives that we often don't appreciate or notice. If we reflect more often on the beauty of the moments we experience, life really does blossom with many perfect still images of blue skies, a quiet river, a bird flying by, or children playing. And it is not necessary to go to the end of the world for this; it is only necessary to notice these perfect moments of life and absorb them with all senses, leaving a long aftertaste. And then the pleasure of life and resistance to troubles will increase.

The concept of happiness here and now is not just a catchphrase. Numerous studies support the idea that a wandering mind is an unhappy mind, whereas focusing on the present moment enhances wellbeing.

In one such study, scientists explored how often our minds wander and stray from the present moment. They recruited 5,000 participants from around the globe, using a mobile app to gather data at different times. Participants answered questions about their current activities (what they were doing), their thoughts (what they were thinking about), and their emotions — specifically, how happy they felt at that moment and whether their experiences were positive or negative.

The results were striking: 47% of people's waking hours were spent distracted from the present moment. In other words, people were thinking about something unrelated to the current situation almost as often as they were focused on it. Most significantly, these periods of distraction were strongly linked to decreased wellbeing (Killingsworth M.A., Gilbert D.T., 2010).

In my lectures, I sometimes ask participants to guess how much time our minds wander, distracted from the task at hand. Interestingly, I often hear estimates significantly higher than 47%. This suggests we are quite aware of our habit of letting our thoughts drift elsewhere. For many of us, it has become a way of life.

For instance, we might go out into nature, stroll through the woods, and instead of immersing ourselves in the moment — experiencing it fully with all our senses — we find ourselves planning for the future or worrying about things that may never happen. Or we meet friends at a café but spend much of the time on our phones, detached from the actual experience and connection around us.

This kind of distraction from the real context has somehow come to feel normal and even natural. Yet, in doing so, we overlook countless wonderful moments that could enrich our lives. By failing to engage with the present, we miss opportunities for joy, connection, and fulfillment that are only available in the here and now.

Another study provides further insight into this topic. In 2020, Roy F. Baumeister published an article examining how people mentally navigate the present, past, and future (Baumeister R.F. et al., 2020). The study involved American participants who were prompted several times a day via an app to answer questions about their thoughts. They reported whether they were thinking about the future, the present, the past, or something unrelated to time. Additionally, they rated how they felt at those moments.

The results revealed that happiness is most often experienced in the present. Thoughts focused on the present were more frequently associated with positive feelings, while thoughts about the future or the past were more likely to bring anxiety, worry, or other negative emotions. This finding aligns with common human tendencies: we habitually worry about the future and sometimes dwell on regrets from the past.

However, in the present moment, we have the opportunity to simply live and notice elements of pleasant experiences. The study underscores that the present is the least stressful and anxiety-inducing place to be. This insight is supported by mindfulness practices, which are widely used to treat anxiety and depressive disorders by encouraging focus on the here and now.

What is missing in the present? It's *meaning*. In Roy Baumeister's study, it was demonstrated that we find meaning when we think about the future, or integrate the past, present, and future. Reflecting on what is important and valuable to us allows us to make sense of past experiences while charting a direction for the future. While such thoughts may bring deeper meaning, they also come with greater anxiety.

This tension is not contradictory. Meaning arises from the dynamic interplay between what is and what we are striving for. It is the sense of incompleteness in our current state that drives our behavior, simultaneously serving as a source of both anxiety and energy.

We can think of the present moment as a state of serenity and self-focused happiness — an element of *hedonistic happiness*. Meanwhile, thoughts about the future often involve going beyond oneself, aiming to achieve happiness in harmony with the world — an element of *eudaimonic happiness*.

As we know, the key lies in harmony and balance. Striving for meaning and future fulfillment is important, but so is regularly returning to the present to release ourselves from the weight of concepts, worries, and plans. This balance enables us to navigate both the calm of the present and the aspirations of the future, creating a life that blends serenity and purpose.

Mindfulness as a skill is believed to have its roots in Eastern spiritual traditions, where it is cultivated primarily through meditation. This practice helps develop qualities such as clarity, wisdom, compassion, and equanimity. Over time, these practices have been successfully adapted for secular contexts and are now integral to many mental health improvement programs. Today, the concept of mindfulness has gained significant attention, supported by extensive scientific research demonstrating its effectiveness in managing stress, depression, and other mental health disorders.

The term *mindfulness* in English translates to "full awareness". It derives from the ancient Indian concept of *Sati*, which refers to a state of being fully present in one's current experience, as opposed to being distracted. This foundational principle continues to guide modern mindfulness practices, emphasizing a deep engagement with the present moment.

Mindfulness practices have gained recognition in the Western world primarily through the Mindfulness Based Stress Reduction (MBSR) programme, developed by John Kabat-Zinn in 1979. The programme is based on meditative practices that help people manage stress and chronic pain (Kabat-Zinn J., 1990). Since then, the programme has produced a great deal of evidence of its effectiveness, with studies showing that participants improved their condition and mental health after eight weeks of the programme.

Another mindfulness-based programme that has a scientific evidence base is MBCT (Mindfulness Based Cognitive Therapy), a cognitive therapy programme developed by Mark Williams and colleagues. This programme offers an evidence-based treatment for depression and is also recommended for anxiety and emotional trauma (Segal Z. V., Williams J. M. G., Teasdale J. D., 2002). The MBCT is based on the MBSR, and additionally uses a cognitive behavioural therapy approach to treat depression and anxiety.

There has been a huge amount of research in recent years which shows that the experience of meditation has a positive impact on people's health and wellbeing (studies often use eight-week MBSR programmes). Through mindfulness training there is an increase in personal effectiveness and learning, improved emotional self-regulation, lower stress levels, reduced anxiety and symptoms of depression, improved creativity, and increased levels of positive emotions (Dahl C. J. et al., 2020; Goleman D. et al., 2017; Ding X et al., 2014).

In essence, meditation is a practice through which we train the mind. So how do scientists explain the effects of meditation? In 2021, a curious article was published (Laukkonen R.E. et al., 2021) that explained how, in fact, meditation affects the brain and consciousness. According to the scientists, meditation initially has an effect on our predictive models. We perceive the external world and, at the same time, make predictions about how we will be threatened by a particular event. Our predictive models are an attempt to reduce uncertainty, and a key goal is to survive and protect our own boundaries. We make predictions based on personal experience and even ancestral experience. Of course, this ability to judge everything is a very useful human adaptive trait, but sometimes these predictions make life very difficult. As soon as one thought appears, another clings to it immediately, and so on and so on, and we easily reach catastrophisation of any event.

How does meditation help in this case? When we discipline our minds not to be distracted by thoughts but to follow our breath, we learn to cut off these multiple projections in favour of paying attention to the experience of the present moment. And the first effects of meditation, scientists believe, are precisely related to cutting off thought chains — projections that can lead to anxiety, lowered self-esteem, negative projections, and unpleasant feelings. If one continues to practice meditation, one gradually reduces the influence of the conceptual mind and increases one's focus on the present moment. Pure experience of the present, without reference to predictive models and concepts, is peace of mind and freedom from stress.

Researchers consider three types of meditation — focused attention (FA), open monitoring (OM) or open awareness, and non-duality perception (ND or Non-Dual) (Laukkonen R.E. et al., 2021). Essentially, these are all different types of Buddhist meditation practices that are sequentially mastered by practitioners. At the first level, FA reduces the influence of the narrative self, returning to a sense of the here and now. Then OM leads to a state where all experience is perceived without evaluation, and insights into the nature of reality arise. Finally, ND practice leads to the dissolution of the distinction between object and subject, when there is no distinction between 'I' and 'Not I'. However, achieving this experience is exceptionally challenging and not attainable for all practitioners, even with long-term practice.

These three types of meditation progressively guide practitioners toward a deeper engagement with the present moment, liberating them from predictive mental models and thoughts about the future. Through these practices, the conceptual mind gradually transforms, becoming less evaluative, less engaged in prediction, and fostering a profound sense of presence and awareness.

Metaphorically, we can say that meditation is like pruning the branches of the thought tree ('the imaginary tree') by focusing on the experience of the present moment. After all, the way our chain of thoughts is constructed is that the brain first constructs experience from sensory sensations, and then transforms them into increasingly abstract thoughts and concepts. The first projections more accurately reflect the sensory experience, but the further you go, the more abstract the thoughts become, and the greater the error between projection and reality. Meditation stops this process of turning sensations into concepts, returning attention to the 'pixels' of experience rather than words. In doing so, the perception of self is also changed, returning from an abstract model to a non-judgemental state of consciousness as-is. Our sentient self refers to the awareness of sensations in the body and events that are happening in the moment. Our narrative self (storyteller) exists because of the default mode of the brain, which is responsible for mind wandering and abstract thinking. The sensing self stops the default mode, thereby stopping the mind wandering and reducing the narrative self: there are fewer stories and more sensory experiences in the mind.

Research in neurobiology reveals a physiological mechanism underlying emotional regulation and stress reduction in meditation practitioners. Studies have shown that participants who completed the Mindfulness-Based Stress Reduction (MBSR) program exhibit reduced activity in the amygdala — responsible for processing emotional stimuli — when exposed to emotional images. Additionally, these participants demonstrate stronger activation of the prefrontal cortex, which plays a critical role in regulating and suppressing amygdala activity (Kral T.R.A. et al., 2018). This enhanced interaction between the prefrontal cortex and the limbic system suggests that the brain becomes more effective at managing stress responses through improved regulatory mechanisms.

The development of mindfulness as a skill requires both a formal definition of mindfulness and a tool to measure its level. Jon Kabat-Zinn defines mindfulness as "full attention to the present moment's experience, characterized by non-judgmental and accepting awareness of feelings, thoughts, and sensations".

As interest in mindfulness practice grew, researchers sought to create tools for measuring mindfulness, to track progress in developing the skill. Several scales are now available for this purpose. Notably, in 2006, Baer et al. published a study on using questionnaires to examine factors of mindfulness (Baer R. et al., 2006). The primary aim of their research was to explore the multifactorial nature of mindfulness by analysing data from existing self-report questionnaires.

The authors combined results from various questionnaires into a unified dataset, applied statistical analysis, and identified mindfulness as a construct consisting of five components. This led to the development of the *Five Facet Mindfulness Questionnaire* (FFMQ). They further investigated the validity of the FFMQ by comparing the mindfulness skills of experienced meditators with those of non-meditators, providing valuable insights into how mindfulness can be assessed and developed.

As expected, most components of mindfulness were significantly higher in the meditation group. Furthermore, mindfulness was positively associated with higher levels of psychological wellbeing (Baer R. et al., 2008). The various aspects of mindfulness measured by the questionnaire also demonstrated a positive correlation with emotional intelligence and openness to new experiences, while showing a negative correlation with mental health symptoms and difficulties in regulating emotional states. These findings suggest that mindfulness indirectly predicts mental health levels. Moreover, mindfulness can be understood as a set of skills that can be cultivated and enhanced through meditation practice.

According to the questionnaire, the following aspects (or factors) determine the quality of mindfulness:

1. **Observing** – Paying attention to sensations, feelings, and thoughts. This is the ability to notice what surrounds us — sounds, smells, and visual images — as well as what we think and feel in any given moment, including emotions and bodily sensations.
2. **Describing** – The ability to name and verbalize inner experiences. It refers to putting into words everything we feel and notice.
3. **Acting with Awareness** – The ability to be present in the here and now, engaging in activities with full attention rather than functioning on autopilot.
4. **Non-judging of Inner Experience** – The ability to accept any inner experience, even if it is uncomfortable or painful, without evaluating or attempting to suppress or eliminate it. This includes refraining from self-criticism for thoughts or feelings.
5. **Nonreactivity to Inner Experience** – The ability to observe images, thoughts, and feelings without becoming entangled in them, allowing

them to arise and dissipate without clinging to or being carried away by them.

To assess your mindfulness skills, you can take the *Five Facet Mindfulness Questionnaire (FFMQ)*, available on the author's website (https://ruthbaer.com/academics/FFMQ.pdf). Based on your results, you can evaluate various aspects of your mindfulness practice. If you actively train mindfulness, you can retake the test after some time to measure your progress and improvements.

One proven way to develop mindfulness is through meditation. The two main categories of meditation that form the basis for practice are Focused Attention (FA) and Open Monitoring (OM) meditation.

FA (Focused Attention) are techniques of concentration or focus. In this case, attention is focused on a single object (the object of concentration is most often the breath). It is a training of alert relaxation, when concentration of attention is combined with maximum relaxation of the body. Most often this type of meditation is where the practice begins. The main purpose of this type of meditation is to stabilise attention on the present moment. We make sure that attention does not run away from the object and bring it back if it does. In this way, meta-awareness develops — an observer's eye on where attention is. Focused attention reduces the depth of information processing to the level of sensation behind the breath, which stops thoughts. There is a distraction from the narrative self and an immersion into the sensory experience. This practice provides the foundation for more advanced practices, that focus on the ability to clearly see reality as it is.

When we train the skill of attention through meditation, the following happens at the level of neurobiological processes in the brain:

At first, the brain is distracted, and various thoughts and memories arise, indicating the activation of the so-called Default Mode Network, which is engaged when our mind wanders. We then become aware of this wandering phase and intentionally bring our attention back to the object of focus — for example, the breath. At this moment, the Salience Network is activated, helping to redirect attention back to the body.

This cycle of distraction and redirection is inevitable, and each time we bring our focus back to the breath, we train the Salience Network, gradually making it easier to notice distractions. Over time, this practice enhances our ability to observe and remain attentive.

When we successfully maintain focus, additional brain areas are activated, which together constitute the Executive Control Network. This network is responsible for sustaining concentration and inhibiting the perception of distracting stimuli, allowing attention to remain firmly fixed on the task at hand. In this phase, the brain's ability to focus is at its peak, further reinforcing our cognitive control and attentional stability through repeated practice.

Thus, during meditation, the brain learns to hold attention and to notice moments of distraction, returning to the object of concentration. The ability to concentrate and observe one's inner world, body sensations, emotions, and thoughts gradually increases. Meditation helps us to train the different networks of brain function, the coherence of which determines the ability to maintain attention, and the cognitive flexibility that is so important in finding out-of-the-box solutions.

Open Monitoring (OM) can be practiced as the next stage, once attention is well stabilised. At this point, attention is expanded to encompass the full range of sensations perceived through the senses. In OM, there is a shift in perception, where reality is experienced as a dynamic process rather than a collection of reflections or conceptualisations of reality.

This practice fosters equanimity — accepting all experiences without judgment. Thoughts, feelings, and sensations are observed as transient phenomena, arising and fading away, reinforcing the understanding of impermanence. OM includes techniques for passively observing the flow of thoughts, emotions, and sensations without intentionally directing the focus of attention. Instead, we allow mental phenomena to emerge and dissipate naturally, without interference or suppression.

This approach cultivates a deeper awareness of the present moment, and a non-reactive stance toward mental and emotional experiences.

Are there any side effects of meditation? In some sources I have read about negative effects like depression and discomfort. But more often it is a consequence of excessive dedication to the practice without proper preparation. For example, if you go on a multi-day retreat where you have to meditate for many hours a day without experience, you can expect to experience discomfort. It is unlikely that with a daily meditation practice of 10 to 40 minutes, any negative effects would occur. I can share my own experience of introducing a regular practice into my life when I first started meditating. In the first few days I had a temporary increase in anxiety. But apparently it was really nothing more than a realisation of the chronic anxiety I had accessed when I started paying attention to my inner state. That anxiety disappeared after a few days, and the first effect of meditation that I felt afterwards was a reduction in anxiety.

The most important thing in any practice is regularity and gradualness. Then the probability of side effects will be minimised. It is also a good idea to find a teacher you trust. This can be either a Buddhist teacher or a secular mindfulness coach. It all depends on your choice of what you prefer.

In addition to a formal meditation practice where you choose a place and time to practice, (e.g., morning 20-minute meditations), you can use short moments of inclusion in the present moment. Wherever you are — on the underground, on the street, at home — you can become an active observer of your inner experience, paying attention to what you see, hear, and feel. The technique of registering sensory flow is called *noting*.

The technique of *noting* is about observing and labeling what you are experiencing in the present moment. Rather than intentionally directing your attention, you allow it to move naturally, simply following where it goes. You mentally or verbally label elements of your experience — for example, 'see', 'hear', or 'feel'. The key is to observe and note without engaging or identifying with the experience, continuing to label what arises. Typically, this is done every 2-3 seconds, naming whatever is currently in your field of awareness.

Shinzen Young, a renowned meditation teacher and creator of the Unified Mindfulness system, offers a clear categorization to make this process easier. He divides sensory experiences into three primary categories, each encompassing internal and external experiences:

- See: External visual objects perceived through the eyes and internal imagery (mental pictures).
- Hear: External sounds and internal dialogue or thoughts perceived as auditory.
- Feel: External tactile sensations and internal bodily or emotional experiences, such as tension, pain, or warmth.

The specific labels you use are less important than the ability to smoothly navigate through your perceptual space, noting elements of experience, and moving on without clinging to any single one. You can adapt the labeling system to suit your needs.

This practice trains awareness, sharpens attentional control, and disrupts the cycle of operating on autopilot, which dominates much of our day. By engaging in *noting*, you cultivate mindfulness and a deeper connection to the present moment.

It is also good to briefly concentrate on your breathing several times a day. This exercise allows you to make a short switch and come to your senses after a long wandering mind. You can also concentrate on any household activities — washing dishes, brushing teeth, cooking — and do them with full attention, noting all the 'pixels' of experience instead of letting your mind wander with the automatic motor programme running.

A t-shirt I purchased at one retreat has the words "Short times many times" on it. It's a great motto for developing the skill of mindfulness. After all, these natural moments of inclusion are not time consuming, they don't draw attention to you, but they do instil the habit of including mindfulness. And the consequence of a developed skill of mindfulness is a conscious attitude towards your actions, and thus the ability to manage your life at a higher level.

Ask yourself more often: where is my attention? Is it in the moment or wandering through the labyrinths of the past, or in fantasies of the future? Is it in this particular activity, in attention to the interlocutor, in movement, in real sensations? Or is my attention in thoughts that swirl around, clinging to one another and unravelling a spiral of anxiety and worry?

If you have gained awareness and greater resilience, does that mean you have become an insensitive person? Not at all. It does not mean that you will stop reacting to adversity, but you will deal with setbacks more quickly, find your way out more easily, and learn to make the best of difficulties. You'll simply develop the skill of observation, and you'll be able to be on the outside of the situation, noting your feelings and thoughts, and managing them in a way that is helpful to you.

The 20s of this century are seriously testing us — too much stress, uncertainty, and loss. I am glad that by the beginning of this challenging period I had already had years of meditation practice under my belt, and the habit of grounding my mind in the present moment. The ability to be with difficult emotions, to observe them, to feel them, and at the same time not to go into rumination (constant replaying of negative thoughts in the head), the ability to see beauty and find islands of good, even in trying circumstances — these skills were honed in the daily practice of mindfulness, and it is these skills that allow you to find a resource in yourself and become a support for others in difficult moments. I am still a long way from complete calmness of mind, clarity, and equanimity — yes, it seems hardly achievable in secular practice. But there is no doubt that developing mindfulness gives support and reassurance in a variety of circumstances. The zone of wellbeing definitely expands — experientially verified.

Key Takeaways:

- Mindfulness is paying full attention to the experience we are having in the present moment; a non-judgemental and accepting awareness of feelings, thoughts, and sensations. Paying attention to the present moment makes us happier and less stressed.
- Mindfulness has its roots in Eastern spiritual practices, where this quality is refined through meditation. As a result of the practice, clarity, wisdom, compassion, and equanimity are developed. Nowadays, Eastern practices have been adapted for secular life and incorporated into mental health improvement programmes.
- Awareness enables you to connect deeply with yourself and the world around you. It enhances your understanding of your own needs, capabilities, and the demands of the external environment. This heightened awareness empowers you to make more effective decisions and take control of your life and health. Ultimately, awareness becomes the foundation for expanding your zone of wellbeing.

Empathy and Social Connections

What constitutes a 'good' life? Scientists have sought to answer this question through one of the longest-running studies of adults. The *Harvard Study of Adult Development* has tracked the lives of 724 men over 75 years, collecting data year after year on their work, family life, and health. The study included two groups: teenagers from disadvantaged neighborhoods in Boston, and Harvard students.

The most significant finding from this extensive research is clear: *good relationships are the key to happiness and health*. A fulfilling, long life is rooted in love and strong relationships (Vaillant, G. E., 2008).

At the very beginning of their adult lives, the study participants believed that wealth, fame, and achievements were what was needed for happiness. But throughout the 75 years, the study confirmed another truth: those who relied on relationships — family, friendship, connections with colleagues and like-minded people — were the happiest and most prosperous.

It turns out that people who have stronger ties with family, friends, and community are happier, healthier, and live longer than people with weaker ties. In addition, it has been found that good relationships don't just protect the body and make people happier, they also protect the brain from mental disorders.

It turns out that contributing to the development of positive relationships is the most profitable investment in wellbeing. Isolation, on the other hand, is hard on us. Neuroscientists have shown in animal experiments that isolation causes rapid degradation of neurons and the connections between them. In addition, lack of communication has an effect akin to starvation (Tomova L. et al., 2020). So communication is as important to us as food. These findings help to recognise the damage to mental health that a pandemic with multiple quarantines and restrictions on social connections caused — the isolation factor made a significant contribution to the burnout and stress we saw in the pandemic years.

Good emotional intelligence and the ability to build relationships — including in a professional environment — significantly reduce the risk of burnout. As a rule, people who communicate easily, can negotiate, and are able to find compromise solutions in conflict situations, rarely burn out — and feel confident thanks to their social skills and reliance on support, which they use very skilfully.

If good relationships are all good, why aren't our interactions with others always positive? Biologically, we are all born altruistic and co-operative. Studies show that babies as young as 14 months old are already helping: picking up objects and returning them to their owner, even interrupting an activity they find interesting. At this age, they do not differentiate by helping everyone (Warneken F. et al., 2007). In later, preschool age, children begin to divide the world into 'their own' and strangers, favouring their own more. As Robert Sapolsky writes in his book *Behave: The Biology of Humans at Our Best and Worst,* by the age of 3-4, children already begin to group people by gender and nationality. They tend to show a more negative attitude toward strangers, and perceive the faces of strangers as angrier than those of 'their own'. This is not surprising — growing up, individuals establish boundaries and prioritise their safety. Strangers, or those who seem different from us, are perceived as potentially unsafe because their behavior is unpredictable. This reaction is a form of adaptive response, rooted in our evolutionary history.

From a biological perspective, it is entirely natural for a person to feel aggression toward strangers while showing kindness and altruism toward 'their own'. Each individual has their own reasons and criteria for dividing the world into 'us' and 'them'. The specifics of these criteria matter less than the underlying mechanism: the lack of empathy for outsiders often grants an internal justification for aggression. As long as we adhere to these biological tendencies, violence and war will persist in society.

It stands to reason that we would inhabit a vastly different world if we could move beyond dividing people into 'ours' and 'others'.

As a reflection, I invite you to consider the concept introduced by Dan Siegel, an American professor of psychiatry and director of the *Mindsight Institute*. Siegel coined the term *"MWe"* — a combination of *'me'* and *'we'* — to emphasize the interconnectedness of the self with others. According to Siegel, the self is not an isolated entity but part of an interconnected system with those around us.

We are, on one hand, differentiated as unique individuals, but on the other, we are part of a unified community. This perspective does not call for the abandonment of individuality; instead, it highlights the importance of integrating the 'I' and the 'We'. By embracing the *MWe* perspective in our personal lives and society, it becomes clear that helping others is inherently helping ourselves, and that caring for the planet is also an act of self-care.

The key to developing positive social bonds is compassion, sympathy, and the ability to empathise not only with 'our own' but also with others. It may seem overly progressive to extend compassion to strangers or even 'enemies', but this truth is far from new — humanity has long been acquainted with the philosophy of mercy and love.

For instance, we can recall the central virtue of Hinduism and Buddhism: *ahimsa*, or non-harming and non-violence. Similarly, Christianity emphasizes love through its foundational precept: "Love your enemies." Jesus Christ preached unconditional love for all and introduced a new moral doctrine to replace the outdated principle of "An eye for an eye, a tooth for a tooth".

In modern times, the worldview of humanism upholds the sanctity of human life as the highest value.

Mercy, compassion, and the ability to forgive are skills that can be developed. Notably, some Buddhist heart-opening practices have been integrated into secular programs and are now widely used. Empathy and compassion training have become as popular as mindfulness programs, with many universities offering similar courses. These programs incorporate tools from psychology and meditative techniques, often including an adapted version of *metta* meditation (loving-kindness meditation) from the Buddhist tradition.

In recent years, a significant number of scientific studies have demonstrated the positive effects of *metta* meditation on mental health and stress resilience. There is also evidence suggesting that this practice transforms individuals, fostering greater kindness and a willingness to help others (Goleman D., Davidson R.J., 2017).

The purpose of *metta* meditation is to consistently cultivate and extend wishes of happiness and wellbeing, beginning with oneself, then moving to close loved ones, and gradually expanding the circle to include difficult individuals and, ultimately, all living beings on the planet. It is not a contemplative but an analytical meditation that serves to create new mental patterns and develop empathy. It is based on the idea that we identify ourselves with others, thinking that everyone wants happiness for themselves and their loved ones as much as we do. This is also what those we consider 'strangers' want, even without empathy for them. The habit of thinking about all people, finding similarities rather than differences, helps to expand the circle of those we consider 'our own'. Gradually this category will include all people. Strangely enough, once you have included all people in your circle, your ability to understand your interlocutor and find a compromise solution seriously expands, because you can put yourself in the other person's shoes and understand them. And this is the basis of empathy, without which it is difficult to communicate and negotiate.

Empathy is the conscious ability to resonate with another person's emotional state. It relies on the capacity of mirror neurons to reflect the feelings of others. This means that during empathy, the same neurons are activated as if we were experiencing those emotions ourselves. Importantly, we retain an awareness of origin, recognising that these feelings belong to the other person, not ourselves.

Inner sensitivity and attentiveness to one's own emotions naturally enhance the ability to understand the emotions of others. Additionally, empathy is rooted in the ability to interpret non-verbal communication, such as tone of voice, posture, and facial expressions, alongside the spoken word. By trusting not only what is said but also how it is expressed, we gain a deeper understanding of others.

The ability to empathise effectively is rewarded with the capacity to build strong connections: interacting successfully, negotiating, offering support, and, ultimately, fostering warm and trusting relationships — an essential aspect of human wellbeing.

It is possible to develop the ability to interact empathically through a number of techniques. Firstly, it is a good idea to develop the skill of attentive listening, when we pay full attention to our interlocutor when communicating, rather than doing other things in the meantime. When we are attentive to what a person is saying we react, and ask questions if something is unclear; by doing so we show interest, involvement, and create an atmosphere of trust and understanding.

It is essential to validate and support the feelings of the other person, demonstrating that you understand them and that it is normal to experience such emotions. People often try to dismiss negative feelings, and phrases like "Don't get upset over nothing" only reinforce the idea that these emotions should be suppressed or avoided. This approach does nothing to help process emotions effectively.

The best initial words of support are often as simple as, "I understand you". Begin by acknowledging that it is perfectly normal to feel these emotions in the given situation. Only then can you explore the problem from different perspectives and work toward finding solutions. Offering support and building mutual understanding should always start with affirming the legitimacy of the other person's feelings and emotions.

When we talk to a friend or loved one, it's often easy to offer support. But it's much harder to say "I understand" to someone with whom you are in conflict — someone who is complaining about you or expressing anger. For instance, a customer upset about a delayed delivery or an imperfect service has every right to feel the way they do. Their expectations weren't fully met, and as a result, they may feel frustrated or angry.

Even if you don't entirely agree with their complaint, their emotions are real and valid. Beginning the conversation with, "I understand you" can pave the way for finding a good solution and reconciliation. In contrast, starting with excuses or arguments about why you're right often escalates tension, and makes resolution harder to achieve.

Ultimately, the goal of communication is to reach a positive outcome, not to prove your point. Imagine how many conflicts could end peacefully if we made a habit of remembering the simple but powerful mantra: "I understand you."

A sincere desire to help, along with expressing gratitude to your interlocutor, fosters better interaction. Don't hold back in showing kindness, offering positive feedback, or acknowledging strengths — whether with employees, friends, or family members.

We often hesitate to give praise, and sometimes we withhold "social stroking" because we perceive it as a tool of social control. There is a common belief that excessive praise might lead someone to stop trying. You may hear such things from strict parents who want to keep their children on a tight rein; from bosses who are afraid that their employees will stop working, or think that everyone is self-sufficient and does not need external stimuli. But in the study of mental health, we saw that lack of feedback from the manager is one of the stress factors for employees. It turns out that with regular feedback and recognition of subordinates, one of the causes of stress could be easily managed. Consider how often do you praise your children, partners, colleagues, or friends. If you don't have this habit, try first to consciously and intentionally praise people in your circle. And even if at first it seems a bit artificial, you will quickly get involved when you feel the effect and see how it pleases others. You'll probably get more recognition in return.

It's important not only to show kindness and appreciation outwardly, but also to cultivate these feelings internally by adjusting your mindset. A simple technique to foster a positive outlook is to reflect on your encounters throughout the day. For each person you meet, consider: What is good about them? What are their strengths? What is the purpose of your meeting? And what value or kindness can you offer them?

While keeping your own goals in mind, approaching others with genuine goodwill contributes to win-win outcomes — the foundation of successful communication and sustainable relationships.

Try investing a little more in building connections with empathy and support. The reward will be strong, positive relationships, which are essential for a healthy and happy life. As the longest study of adults has proven, a life grounded in love and warm connections is a life of wellbeing and fulfillment.

Key Takeaways:

- The recipe for a good life is good relationships that make us more prosperous and healthier. People who have stronger ties with family, friends, and community are happier, physically healthier, and live longer.
- The key to developing positive social connections is charity, empathy, and the ability to empathise with everyone.
- Compassion, acceptance, and the ability to forgive are skills that can be trained through the practice of meditation. Many scientific studies confirm the positive effects of *metta* meditation on mental health and stress tolerance, and there is evidence that the practice changes a person, making them more kind and willing to help others.
- Empathy — the ability to feel well for another person — is rewarded by the ability to interact effectively with people, negotiate with them, and as a result build warm, trusting relationships.
- Active listening, validation of the interlocutor's feelings, a sincere desire to help, and the ability to stand in their position — these are the tools that help develop positive relationships between people and make us happier. By giving to others, we gain for ourselves.

Goals, Values and Meanings

Having a purpose and meaning in life is a necessary component of wellbeing, which has been proven by many studies. Martin Seligman, founder of positive psychology and author of the PERMA model of happy life[1], considers having meaning as one of the five components of a good life.

Our life experience confirms this: a person inspired by an idea, who understands their goals and knows what they live for, radiates vitality and optimism. Such individuals are more resilient in the face of challenges. Clarifying your purpose and values, and learning to integrate them into your daily life, significantly enhances psychological wellbeing.

But what does it mean to have a purpose or meaning? It means understanding why you do what you do, identifying what is truly valuable to you, and aligning your life with those values. For some, this might mean living for their family. Others find meaning in contributing to the world — working to preserve nature, helping others, or using their talents to create innovations or art. For some, meaning lies in harmonising with the world, consciously appreciating the beauty of each day.

It's important not to confuse a sense of purpose with being results-oriented. Here, purpose is understood as something deeper: a sense of meaning, intention, and direction. Purpose acts as a guiding vector, helping to organise our lives. When we have a clear direction, it becomes much easier to make daily decisions without the constant anxiety of choosing the 'wrong' path.

As it turns out, realising your purpose is not only important for living a life of pleasure; scientists have found that having a sense of purpose also has an impact on longevity! On the basis of a long-term study, it was shown that the presence of a purpose in life reduces the mortality rate of Americans in the age group 50+ by 2.43 times. And it was a reduction in mortality from any cause. In addition, a sense of purpose has a positive impact on mental and physical health, and quality of life (Alimujiang A. et al., 2019).

There are other studies supporting the positive impact of life purpose on

---

[1] P (Positive Emotions)
E (Engagement)
R (Relationship)
M (Meaning)
A (Accomplishment)

People with a strong purpose generally lead healthier lives and have a better prognosis for all sorts of illnesses — including depression, stroke, diabetes.

Scientists have been researching the physiological mechanisms of the positive effects of purpose on health, and have found some interesting facts: there appears to be a link between purpose in life and the expression of genes responsible for inflammation (Fredrickson B. L. et al., 2013). A purposeful life leads to lower levels of cortisol (stress hormone) and cytokines (inflammatory factors) (Ryff C. D. et al., 2004). Research that brings together psychology, genetics, and physiology proves that everything is connected to everything, and the body and mind are one interconnected system.

The importance of meaning in life has been deeply explored by Viktor Frankl, a psychiatrist and Holocaust survivor, in his seminal work *Man's Search for Meaning*. Reflecting on his years in Nazi concentration camps, Frankl sought to understand why some individuals endured the unimaginable horrors while others succumbed. He observed that those who survived longest were often those who held tightly to a sense of purpose — those who had a meaning to live for.

For some prisoners, it was the love they felt for their family or the hope of reuniting with their children. For others, it was the drive to complete an unfinished work or to fulfill a personal mission. Frankl concluded that meaning and purpose provide the strength to endure even the most harrowing circumstances. As Friedrich Nietzsche famously wrote: *"He who has a 'Why' to live for, can endure almost any 'How'."*

Frankl himself found meaning in several ways: by keeping the image of his wife alive in his heart, by helping fellow prisoners navigate the brutal conditions of camp life, and by resolving to later share his experiences and insights with the world. These sources of purpose sustained him through unimaginable suffering. After the war, Frankl went on to found logotherapy, a branch of existential psychology that centers on the idea that meaning is a fundamental driving force in human life.

Frankl's insights remind us that purpose is more than a goal — it is a deeply personal compass that helps us navigate life's hardships and find strength in adversity.

Having a purpose allows one to cope more successfully with failure, to be more resistant to uncertainty, to maintain motivation when external supports are lost. Conversely, when there is no meaning, it leads to a feeling of helplessness, decreased activity, and a decreased desire to live. This is why we see in studies the connection between a sense of meaning on the one hand, and health and longevity on the other.

It would seem that every person should have a good sense of what is important to them, what they want, and what they are striving for. But for some reason, more and more people come to coaching and psychotherapy with a request to find meaning and purpose, to sort themselves out, to understand what they really want. It is quite natural for a person to be tormented by meaning. Viktor Frankl reflects on the reasons for the loss of meaning: "No instinct tells him what he has to do, and no tradition tells him what he ought to do; sometimes he does not even know what he wishes to do." And then, "Instead, he either wishes to do what other people do (conformism) or he does what other people tell him to do (totalitarianism)." Evolution has taken care to give man the freedom of choice — but regarding how to dispose of this freedom, we do not have such an innate ability.

In order to know where to go, you need to understand your needs, your *what is good* and *what is bad*. It would seem that we should know ourselves best, but this is not a fact at all. We quite quickly begin to understand what people around us want from us, how to better adapt in society, what skills and education can provide this or that way of life. And just as quickly we forget what we want ourselves. There is nothing surprising in this, because from the first days of life, a child struggles for survival and learns to adapt to the world. From an early age, a young person realizes that their well-being depends on others — on adults — who provide food, safety, and care. The first conditioned reflexes of childhood are linked to the desire to please caregivers. A child notices that a smile elicits a smile in return, while misbehavior may cause disapproval. Over time, this fosters dependence on external validation and the desire to be liked.

Next comes a more difficult stage — school — and the need to follow many rules, to study well. When teachers don't complain to parents, it means more peace of mind and less discomfort. This is how adaptive behaviour is gradually formed, which helps to adapt to the environment, and others' grades are a marker of how well I am adapting. And then everyone around starts advising what profession to choose, in order to acquire average wellbeing and settle well in society. And obedient children gladly adopt conformist type of behaviour, moving further and further away from their individual inclinations and needs. Because a strong focus on external judgement dulls attention to their own wants. It seems better to displace emotions and not to feel them — they sometimes do not allow us to act coolly and rationally. This is how people live their lives; not feeling their desires, orientated on social trends and advice of other people. Existing in this way, it is quite possible to achieve success in career and material wellbeing, but this is not always the equivalent of personal happiness and self-realisation.

As a result, sometimes adults start psychotherapy or coaching from the very basics — by understanding their individual needs and their values:

What do I like and what don't I like?
What have I always been good at?
What activities inspire and energise me?

And the path to yourself — to your individual, not-average happiness — begins. It is never too late to ask these questions; not in your 20s, not in your 50s or 60s. We most often ask these questions when we finish one scenario and need to move on to the next one. And for that we first have to experience some existential vacuum, before we can move to the next stage and open ourselves to something new.

Jungian psychoanalyst James Hollis, in his book *The Middle Passage: From Misery to Meaning in Midlife,* justifies the need to change priorities at a certain stage of life, and talks about the benefits of new choices after the period of 'first adulthood'. A person who decides to make changes and take a new look at himself, having travelled some way, acquires freedom and the possibility of a more complete self-realisation. For some people this period can happen at the age of 40, for some people at 50 or later, and some people may never experience this transformative period if they resist the inner call for change, preferring instead to remain in familiar and comfortable environments.

By mid-life, many of the basic needs for which the ego fights in youth have been satisfied: a career has been achieved, living conditions have been organised, a social circle and family structure have been established. And then higher-order needs come to the fore, and questions beyond the usual roles become more audible: who am I, why am I, and what else?

There is nothing strange about it. Back in the last century, Abraham Maslow proposed the theory of needs, where the aspiration for self-actualisation is fully revealed after the satisfaction of basic needs. So, the vague anxiety in the middle of the journey, when the ego is satisfied, is quite natural — energy can now be spent on satisfying inner values, devoting oneself to serving something beyond the ego. As Viktor Frankl writes, "The more one forgets himself — by giving himself to a cause to serve or another person to love — the more human he is, and the more he actualises himself."

It turns out that this period of existential crisis has a positive value — it helps to rethink goals, to change the direction of movement, and sometimes to adjust the hierarchy of values. I am sure that we can go through such existential crises and revision of life goals in our life not once, not twice, but more often. Life expectancy is growing and the number of transitions between stages is increasing, and we need meaning at every moment of life.

I remember the American designer Iris Apfel, who remained optimistic, active, and young-at-heart into advanced age, and at 97 she was still signing contracts as a model. People who have big plans ahead of them, who are driven by curiosity and restless energy, tend to stand out for their longevity. Many long-livers are characterised by their ability to maintain a joyful sense of wonder about life — finding it endlessly fascinating and beautiful, never dull or tiresome. At any age — 20 or 100 years old — life is determined not by biological limitations, but rather by the inner state of interest, the presence of plans, the realisation of meaning. So, living to 100 is becoming more and more possible — not only due to medical advances, but also due to a more conscious life and a better understanding of oneself. It is important to learn how to cross the psychological threshold and move into the phase of second adulthood, and even third and fourth, having learned to find meanings and values for each stage; to be able to abandon successful strategies of the past, acquiring new choices and models of behaviour.

At the same time, periods of loss of meaning — and the search for new life supports — are painful. It is as if we are hovering between worlds, losing our footing, feeling anxious about uncertainty and sad about losing our comfort zone. But if a person is ready to change, after a while there is a beginner's excitement, a growing sense of freedom, tunnel-thinking disappears, and a wider horizon of possibilities opens up. This is an internal process; first we allow ourselves to look wider, to see ourselves in other roles and circumstances, and then from this state new decisions and new choices are made. Any transformation requires experiencing a crisis of loss of meanings, acceptance, and then transition to the birth of new meanings and goals.

Sometimes, meaning is lost in the wake of serious external crises. We may devote years to pursuing certain goals, structuring our entire lives around them, but when circumstances change so drastically that our familiar way of life is disrupted, it can lead to shattered hopes and a profound sense of lost identity. This is a difficult state to endure, but it can ultimately bring positive changes if we remain open to new possibilities rather than resisting them.

Crises in an ever-changing reality are nothing new, so it's essential to learn how to navigate periods of lost meaning, and rediscover new goals and sources of support.

Unfortunately, creating a new direction for one's life cannot happen overnight. The anxiety brought on by uncertainty, as well as the grief over what has been lost, are inevitable parts of the transition period. Feeling as though you are suspended between worlds, questioning the meaning of everything, is normal — especially in the turbulent times we live in, where so many people are experiencing similar emotions.

What can you rely on during such difficult times? Your values, your inner strengths — those qualities that have supported you in the past. Even when external achievements or circumstances feel devalued, your intrinsic worth remains unchanged. While you might lose your job, profession, or even your country, losing your sense of self is much harder. The challenge lies in figuring out how to manifest your identity and purpose in new and unfamiliar conditions.

In Buddhism, there is a concept called *bardo*, which refers to an intermediate state between two stages. In Tibetan Buddhism, when they speak of the *bardo of life*, they usually mean the interval between one life and the next. However, there are many other transitional states as well. The *bardo of dreaming* refers to the state between wakefulness and sleep; the *bardo of meditative concentration* represents the space between dualistic consciousness and an enlightened state; the *bardo of the dying process* bridges serious illness and death. Beyond these, there are many transitional states that occur during the *bardo of life*.

In essence, all of life can be seen as a bardo, a series of transitions between different states. One defining quality of any bardo is its transformative nature — it is a process of renewal and rebirth. However, if we resist accepting losses and hold on to what is no longer there, we close ourselves off to new opportunities. By trying to return to the past, we become stuck in the bardo, unable to open ourselves to a new stage of life.

How can you regain your footing and discover new meanings? The key lies in awareness: awareness of the context, awareness of your needs and values, and conscious decision-making. If understanding yourself feels challenging, seeking guidance from a coach or psychologist can help illuminate your personal values and strengths. These inner resources become a steady foundation, bringing you back from a state of uncertainty and restoring your sense of balance.

In reality, it is often not about inventing meanings and values but about uncovering them; understanding why we do what we do, the kind of person we aspire to become, and what we want to dedicate our lives to. Intuitively, everyone structures their life around what feels important, but a lack of conscious awareness of these goals can prevent us from fully experiencing satisfaction and joy along the chosen path.

Whether we devote most of our lives to work or raising children, we risk getting lost in the daily routine of tasks that demand our attention. To regain a sense of meaning and value in what we do, it's essential to reflect on the *why*. For instance, if much of your time is spent caring for your children, pause to ask yourself: "*Why do I cook dinner for my family? Why do I take my children to various activities?*"

When you answer these questions, you uncover the values that drive your actions. Perhaps it's your love for your family, your desire to create a happy life for your children, or your commitment to nurturing and supporting them. Answering the question *why* gives us meaning and purpose.

Purpose, however, is not a distant goal you hope to achieve someday. It is the life you are living now, expressed through the actions you take and the choices you make every day.

A good question that is periodically useful for everyone to answer is: "If today was suddenly your only day, would you do what you are doing?" And if you answer in the affirmative, it clarifies and confirms your purpose. And if the answer is negative, it's an indication that perhaps it's time to make a change, or it's simply necessary to do something other than what's no longer important. Each moment is an opportunity to connect with your purpose and values. And when the motives are realised, all those many *shoulds* are automatically replaced by *wants*; there is meaning in the daily routine and confidence that I am making the right choice, and building my life around the values that are important to me.

Goals and values are two sides of the same coin. Values are the guiding principles we follow in life as we navigate our way towards a goal. We are not always aware of or able to articulate our values, but regardless, consciously or unconsciously, they guide our choices, behaviours, and strongly influence our emotional background. In essence it is our idea of what we want, which we try to realise in reality. Living in harmony with values leads to a sense of wellbeing, and conversely, frustration of values leads to discomfort and even burnout.

Think about what irritates and frustrates you the most — there is probably an important unmet value behind your irritation. For example, you are annoyed by the clutter in your home. It may well be that order is a value for you, and you feel pleasure when it is clean and cosy. Or you find injustice difficult to endure, and you always stand up for those who have been unfairly punished or wronged. It is likely that the value of justice is important to you. Values usually reflect what kind of person you want to be, and how you want to live your life.

As Peter Kensok highlights in his book *The Art of Knowing Values*, personal values can be uncovered by reflecting on what we enjoy and what we find unpleasant in life. While the exercise is straightforward, it requires time and thoughtful introspection.

Step 1: Create Two Lists

Start by making two lists: one for things you like and another for things you dislike. Be as specific as possible, using concrete examples of positive and negative experiences. For instance:

- What I like: *I enjoy having a long and savoury cup of coffee in the morning, I love reading a book on weekends while wrapped in a blanket, I feel great satisfaction after completing a big task, I like doing yoga in the morning.*
- What I dislike: *I don't like being late for meetings, I dislike doing boring routine tasks.*

The longer your lists, the more comprehensive your understanding of yourself will be.

Step 2: Interpret the Experiences in Terms of Values

Reflect on the positive experiences and identify the values they satisfy. For example:
- Reading an interesting book might reflect the value of curiosity, pleasure, or self-development.
- Completing a task might satisfy values like achievement or responsibility.

It's your interpretation that matters—these are your experiences and your values.

Step 3: Identify Frustrated Values

Negative experiences point to values that were violated or frustrated. For instance:
- A messy house might frustrate your value for order.

- Being late might conflict with your value for punctuality or respect for others' time.

Step 4: List and Group the Values
From these reflections, write down all the values you identify. Some examples may align with the same value, while others will add to the list. Once you have a comprehensive list, you can group similar values together and identify the core or root value in each group.

Step 5: Prioritise Your Core Values
When you've narrowed the list to about 8–12 core values, take time to reflect on their relative importance. Arrange them in a hierarchical order, identifying which values are most central to your life.

By completing this exercise, you'll gain a deeper understanding of what drives you, what fulfills you, and what causes discomfort when these values are unmet. It's a powerful way to clarify your priorities and align your actions with what truly matters to you.

Next, you can work with your values by answering the questions:
Which of these values are satisfied?
What values are frustrated?
How can I add more value to my life? What areas of my life should I focus on?

If your value is creativity and you don't seem to be able to maintain it at this stage of your life, consider how you can bring more creativity into different areas of your life. It could be a little more focus on that value at work. Even if you're in a boring, routine job right now, think about how you can add more variety to it, go beyond your standard duties and offer something new. Or you can think of something outside of your work duties and become an organiser of an interesting event — a healthy habits challenge, a volunteer event, a corporate game, or a holiday. It seems that your duties have remained the same, but the value of creativity has found an application that improves your mood. Creativity can be added to different areas of your life — find an enjoyable hobby, spend the weekend creatively as a family, come up with an interesting game for the kids. If you are a creative person, you will find a use for your value regardless of the context.

I suggest another exercise to help you reflect on your values. Imagine that you are 90 years old, looking back on your life and summarizing your experiences. Complete the following sentences without overthinking your answers:

- "I spent too much time on…"
- "I paid too little attention to…"
- "If I could give advice from my future self to my present self, I would say…"

By answering these questions, you can identify the gap between your values and how you actually live. Interestingly, what you spend a lot of time on likely reflects one of your values — after all, you wouldn't dedicate your life to it otherwise. However, this value may be out of balance with others that you neglect or overlook. Reflecting on the balance of your values is essential, as it is this harmony that contributes to a fulfilling and prosperous life.

It's never too late to think about what you can do now to become the person you want to be and live the life you dream of. You don't have to make drastic changes to your life right away, start with small steps that will help you start moving in the direction of your values. For example, if you've realised that you're not paying enough attention to your family, think about what ritual you can add to feed your value of caring. Perhaps you will dedicate one day a week entirely to your children or, when you leave for work, kiss your loved ones. Small steps don't negate planning for massive, long-term changes that will take years, but small, quick changes can help you feel a little better right away. Following your values provides more confidence, peace of mind, and positive emotions.

The context may change, but your values stay with you. When there are crises, when everything seems to be falling apart and the compass hands go astray, it is at that very moment your values give you a foothold. And you can always figure out how you will apply them in a new environment. Let's say you have a high value of leadership, you've been successful in life, you're running an organisation. But an extraordinary event happens — your company has to close down and leave the market (and there are many such situations in the modern world). Everything has changed, the ground has dropped from under your feet, it seems that everything you have worked for is gone. But your value of leadership has not disappeared, and you continue to support your team even at the difficult stage of business winding down, because you know how to take responsibility, how to take care of people and be a support to them. Time will pass and a new phase will come, where you will again look for application and show your leadership skills. We can continue to live our values even when life is not kind to us. But when we don't retreat from what is important and valuable, we gain resilience and change the external environment to suit us. Living according to values is an opportunity to be yourself in all circumstances.

Key Takeaways:

- Having a purpose and meaning in life is essential for happiness, health, and longevity. A clear purpose helps one navigate failures, build resilience in the face of uncertainty, and stay motivated even when external supports are lost. Conversely, the absence of meaning often leads to feelings of helplessness, diminished activity, and a reduced desire to live.
- The process of revising life goals and confronting existential crises is something we may experience repeatedly. Despite the challenges they bring, these crises hold a positive significance: they encourage us to reassess our goals and realign our direction with the current stage of life.
- While people intuitively organise their lives around what feels important, a lack of conscious purpose can prevent them from experiencing full satisfaction and joy along the chosen path. It is crucial to periodically ask yourself: *Why do I do what I do? What do I want to dedicate my life to?*
- Values are the foundational principles that guide us as we pursue our goals. Living in alignment with your values fosters wellbeing, while frustration of these values can lead to discomfort and even burnout.
- While the context of life may change, your core values remain constant. These values can manifest in new ways under different circumstances. Living in accordance with your values provides an opportunity to stay true to yourself and offers a steady source of support in any situation.

What Truly Matters

Stress and difficulties can be befriended — this is supported by numerous scientific studies and countless life experiences. We cultivate resilience and wellbeing when we develop our inner resources: practicing mindfulness and self-care, opening ourselves to loving relationships, learning empathy and compassion, staying true to our values, and maintaining an optimistic outlook. By doing so, we expand our zone of wellbeing and build the strength needed to face challenges, while staying on course toward our goals and purposes.

No matter the circumstances of our birth — health, intelligence, or genetics — we always have the ability to shape our potential. Every small step, every tiny positive habit, adds to the foundation of a better, more fulfilling life.

However, personal wellbeing cannot exist in isolation from the wellbeing of society. Everything is interconnected. A society or environment cannot thrive if individuals within it are plagued by dissatisfaction or inner turmoil. Internal tension often drives people to compensate for their deficits, while unresolved psychological wounds activate defense mechanisms and an excessive focus on self. The result? A strategy of dominance and survival replaces a strategy of cooperation and shared prosperity.

In our social and professional activities, we express our worldview and values. If someone is fixated on their ego, seeking dominance, their actions will reflect that state, centered around 'I', 'my', and 'me'. Conversely, those who are attuned to their true values and connected to others naturally strive for the common good. Individuals who live in a state of psychological wellbeing are motivated by positive contributions that benefit the broader community.

At a time when humanity faces unprecedented shared threats — climate change, pandemics, geopolitical tensions — the psychological wellbeing of each person becomes a vital factor in shaping a better future. The world is at a critical juncture, where only cooperation, collaboration, and a shared search for common ground can create a sustainable future.

The search for win-win solutions is the domain of people who have transcended their ego, and embraced a worldview that is centered on interconnectedness rather than individualism. In this world-centered perspective, every person and every element of the system exists in relationship with others, rather than expecting the world to revolve around their personal desires. Psychological maturity and the development of wellbeing skills are, therefore, essential pathways to a brighter future for all.

Our present reality is the result of past decisions and behaviors. Yet it is in this very moment that we create our future — through the choices and decisions we make today. Let those choices be conscious, meaningful, and aligned with the greater good.

I wish you happiness in every moment of the present, and success in your journey toward building a sustainable and prosperous future!

List of references

The Mental Trauma of the 20s

1. State of the Global Workplace: 2021 Report, Gallup

2. Job Stress and Disruption. Ipsos International Survey, December 2020, 28 countries. — URL: https://www.ipsos.com/sites/default/files/ct/news/documents/2021-02/job-stress-and-disruptions-ipsos-wef.pdf

3. Employee Experience "The other COVID-19 crisis: Mental Health", Qualtrix, April, 2020. – URL: https://www.qualtrics.com/blog/confronting-mental-health/

4. Salari N., Hosseinian-Far A., Jalali R., Vaisi-Raygani A., Rasoulpoor S., Mohammadi M., Rasoulpoor S., Khaledi-Paveh B. *Prevalence of stress, anxiety, depression among the general population during the COVID-19 pandemic: a systematic review and meta-analysis* // Global Health. 2020. Vol. 16(1). P. 57.

5. World Happiness Report 2021. — URL: https://worldhappiness.report/ed/2021/

Part 1. The Many Faces of Stress

Stress and burnout vs. balance and wellbeing

6. Selye, Hans. *Stress Without Distress.* Philadelphia: J.B. Lippincott, 1974

7. Csikszentmihalyi M. *Flow: The Classic work on how to achieve happiness.* London: Rider Books, 2002.

8. Dodge R., Daly A., Huyton J., Sanders L. *The challenge of defining wellbeing* // International Journal of Wellbeing. 2012. Vol. 2(3). P. 222–235

Reward System

9. Sapolsky, Robert M. *Behave: The Biology of Humans at Our Best and Worst.* Penguin Press, 2017.

Stress is Wonderful and Terrible

10. Cannon, Walter B. *The Wisdom of the Body.* New York: W. W. Norton & Company, 1932.

The Positive Effects of Stress

11. Keller A., Litzelman K., Wisk L. E., Maddox T., Cheng E. R., Creswell P. D., Witt W. P. *Does the Perception that Stress Affects Health Matter? The Association with Health and Mortality* // Health Psychology. 2012. Vol. 31(5). P. 677–684.

12. Seery M. D., Holman E. A., Silver R. C. *Whatever Does Not Kill Us: Cumulative Lifetime Adversity, Vulnerability, and Resilience* // Journal of Personality and Social Psychology. 2010. Vol. 99(6). P. 1025–1041.

13. World Happiness Report, 2021. — URL: https://worldhappiness.report/ed/2021/

14. State of the Global Workplace: 2021, Report, Gallup.

The Damaging Effects of Stress

15. Health and Wellbeing at Work, Survey report, April 2019. — URL: https://www.cipd.co.uk/Images/health-and-wellbeing-at-work-2019.v1_tcm18-55881.pdf

16. Depression, WHO. — URL: https://www.who.int/news/item/30-03-2017--depression-let-s-talk-says-who-as-depression-tops-list-of-causes-of-ill-health

17. Gianaros P. J., Jennings J. R., Sheu L. K., Greer P. J., Kuller L. H., Matthews K. A. *Prospective reports of chronic life stress predict decreased grey matter volume in the hippocampus* // NeuroImage. 2007. Vol. 35(2). P. 795–803.

18. Magariños A. M., Verdugo J. M., McEwen B. S. *Chronic stress alters synaptic terminal structure in hippocampus* // Proceedings of the National Academy of Sciences of the United States of America. 1997. Vol. 94(25). P. 14002–14008.

19. Sapolsky, Robert M. *Why Zebras Don't Get Ulcers*. 3rd ed., Holt Paperbacks, 2004

Is It a Lot of Stress or Is It Just Right?

20. Rahe R. H., Meyer M., Smith M., Kjaer G., Holmes T. H. *Social stress and illness onset* // Journal of Psychosomatic Research. 1964. Vol. 8(1). P. 35–44.

21. Holmes T. H., Rahe R. H. *Social Readjustment Rating Scale (SRRS)* // Journal of Psychosomatic Research. 1967. Vol. 11(2). P. 213–218.

22. Scully J. A., Tosi H., Banning K. *Life Event Checklists: Revisiting the Social*

Readjustment Rating Scale after 30 Years // Educational and Psychological Measurement. 2000. Vol. 60(6). P. 864–876.

23. Noone P. A. *The Holmes-Rahe Stress Inventory* // Occupational Medicine. 2017. Vol. 67(7). P. 581–582.

24. The Holmes-Rahe Life Stress Inventory, The American Institute of Stress. — URL: https://www.stress.org/holmes-rahe-stress-inventory

Watch Out! Work!

25. Rath, Tom, & Harter, Jim. *Wellbeing: The Five Essential Elements.* Gallup Press, 2010

26. Taleb, N. N. *The Black Swan*, 2nd ed. New York: Random House, 2010

Why Aren't We Equal Before Stress?

27. Hobfoll S. E., Canetti-Nisim D., Johnson R. J. (2006) *Exposure to terrorism, stress-related mental health symptoms, and defensive coping among Jews and Arabs in Israel* //Journal of Consulting and Clinical Psychology. Vol. 74(2). P. 207–218.

28. Folkman, S., Lazarus, R. S., Dunkel-Schetter, C., DeLongis, A., and Gruen, R. J. (1986). *Dynamics of a stressful encounter: cognitive appraisal, coping, and encounter outcomes.* J. Pers. Soc. Psychol. 50, 992–1003. doi: 10.1037/0022-3514.50.5.992

29. Folkman S., Lazarus R. S., Gruen R. J., DeLongis A. *Appraisal, Coping, Health Status,and Psychological Symptoms* // Journal of Personality and Social Psychology. (1986B). Vol. 50(3). P. 571–579.

Part 2. Professional Burnout

30. Freudenberger H. J. *Staff Burn-Out* // Journal of Social Issues. 1974. Vol. 30(1). P. 159–165.

31. Maslach C., Leiter M. P. *The Truth About Burnout: How Organisations Cause Personal Stress and What to Do About It.* — Jossey-Bass, 1997.

32. Maske U.E., Riedel-Heller S.G., Seiffert I., Jacobi F., Hapke U. *Häufigkeit und psychiatrische Komorbiditäten von selbstberichtetem diagnostiziertem Burnout-Syndrom* // Psychiatrische Praxis. 2016. Vol. 43(1). P. 18–24.

33. Koutsimani P., Montgomery A., Georganta K. *The Relationship Between Burnout, Depression, and Anxiety: A Systematic Review and Meta-Analysis* // Frontiers Psychology. 2019. Vol. 10. P. 284.

34. Burn-out an «occupational phenomenon»: International Classification of Diseases, WHO. — URL: https://www.who.int/news/item/28-05-2019-burn-out- an-occupational-phenomenon-international-classification-of-diseases

Why Do We Burn Out?

35. Health and Wellbeing at Work 2021, CIPD & Simplyhealth. — URL: https://www.cipd.co.uk/Images/health-wellbeing-work-report-2021_tcm18-93541.pdf
36. Health and Wellbeing at Work 2022, CIPD & Simplyhealth. — URL: https://www.cipd.co.uk/Images/health-wellbeing-work-report-2022_tcm18-108440.pdf
37. Siegrist J. *The Effort-Reward Imbalance Model. The Handbook of Stress and Health: A Guide to Research and Practice*, 2017. P. 24–35.
38. Karasek R. A. *Job Demands, Job Decision Latitude, and Mental Strain: Implications for Job Redesign* // Administrative Science Quarterly. 1979. Vol. 24(2). P. 285–308.
39. Arnsten Amy F. T., Shanafelt T. *Physician Distress and Burnout: The Neurobiological Perspective* // Mayo Clinic Proceedings. 2021. Vol. 96(3). P. 763–769.
40. Demerouti E., Bakker A. B., Nachreiner F., Schaufeli W. B. *The Job Demands-Resources Model of Burnout* // Journal of Applied Psychology. 2001. Vol. 86(3). P. 499–512.
41. Xanthopoulou D., Bakker A. B., Demerouti E., Schaufeli W. B. *Reciprocal relationships between job resources, personal resources, and work engagement* // Journal of Vocational Behavior. 2008. Vol. 74(3). P. 235–244.
42. Schaufeli W. B. *Applying the Job Demands-Resources model: A «how to» guide to measuring and tackling work engagement and burnout* // Organisational Dynamics. 2017. Vol. 46(2). P. 120–132.
43. Kaschka W. P., Korczak D., Broich K. *Burnout: a fashionable diagnosis* // Dtsch Arztebl Int. 2011. Vol. 108(46). P. 781–787.

Six Reasons to Burn Out at Work and Six Strategies to Prevent Burnout

44. Maslach C., Leiter M. P. *Banishing Burnout. Six Strategies for Improving Your Relationship with Work.* — Jossey-Bass, 2005.
45. Seligman M. E., Maier S. F. *Failure to escape traumatic shock* // Journal of Experimental Psychology. 1967. Vol. 74(1). P. 1–9.
46. Rodin J., Langer E. J. *Long-term effects of a control-relevant intervention with the institutionalized aged* // Journal of Personality and Social Psychology. 1977. Vol. 35(12). P. 897–902.

The Neurophysiology of Burnout

47. Maier S. F., Amat J., Baratta M. V., Paul E., Watkins L. R. *Behavioral control, the medial prefrontal cortex, and resilience* // Dialogues Clin Neurosci. 2006. Vol. 8(4). P. 397–406.

48. Maier S. F., Watkins L. R. *Stressor Controllability, Anxiety, and Serotonin* // Cognitive Therapy and Research. 1998. Vol. 22. P. 595–613.

49. Maier S. F., Seligman M. E. *Learned Helplessness at Fifty: Insights from Neuroscience* // Psychological Review. 2016. Vol. 123(4). P. 349–367.

50. Arnsten Amy F. T. *Stress signalling pathways that impair prefrontal cortex structure and function* // Nat. Rev. Neuroscience. 2009. Vol. 10(6). P. 410–422.

51. Savic I., Perski A., Osika W. *MRI Shows that Exhaustion Syndrome Due to Chronic Occupational Stress is Associated with Partially Reversible Cerebral Changes* // Cerebral Cortex. 2018. Vol. 28(3). P. 894–906.

52. Porcelli A. J., Delgado M. R. *Stress and Decision Making: Effects on Valuation, Learning, and Risk-taking* // Current Opinion in Behavioral Sciences. 2017. Vol. 14. P. 33–39.

53. Chow Y., Masiak J., Mikołajewska E., Mikołajewski D., Wójcik G. M., Wallace B., Eugene A., Olajossy M. *Limbic brain structures and burnout* — A systematic review // Advances in Medical Sciences. 2018. Vol. 63(1). P. 192–198.

Burnout as a Process

54. Greenberg, Jerrold S. *Comprehensive Stress Management. 7th ed.*, McGraw Hill, 2002

55. Maslach C., Jackson S. E., Leiter M. P., Schaufeli W. B. *MBI: General Survey*, Mind Garden. — URL: https://www.mindgarden.com/312-mbi-general-survey

56. Freudenberger H. J., Richelson G. *Burnout: The High Cost of High Achievement.* — Anchor Press, 1980.

57. Kraft U. *Burned Out* // Scientific American Mind. 2006. Vol. 17(3). P. 28–33.

58. Burish M. *Das Burnout-Syndrom. Theorie der inneren Erschöpfung.* — Springer, 2006.

59. Perlman B., Hartman E. *Burnout: Summary and Future Research* // Human relations. 1982. Vol. 35(4). P. 283–305.

How Can Employers Take Care of Employees?

60. Maslow, Abraham H. *Motivation and Personality*. Harper & Row, 1954.

Part 3. Mastering Balance: The Path to a Burnout-Free Life

61. Bezuglova, Marina. *Finding Serenity Amid the Chaos: How Managing Your Stress Can Enhance Your Creativity and Wellbeing*. Amazon, 2023.

Neuroplasticity and Epigenetics – the Key to Health and Happiness

62. Anokhin, P. K. *"Philosophical Sense of the Problem of Natural and Artificial Intelligence."* Questions of Philosophy, no. 6, 1973, pp. 83–97.

63. Diamond M. C., Krech D., Rosenzweig M. R. *The effects of an enriched environment on the histology of the rat cerebral cortex* // The Journal of Comparative Neurology. 1964. Vol. 123. P. 111–120.

64. Siletty K., *Rusty Gage: A plastic approach to neuroscience* // Journal of Cell Biology. 2016. Vol. 215(6). P. 750–751.

65. Cheung P., Vallania F., Warsinske H. C., Donato M., Schaffert S., Chang S. E., Dvorak M. et al. *Single-Cell Chromatin Modification Profiling Reveals Increased Epigenetic Variations with Aging* // Cell. 2018. Vol. 173(6). P. 1385–1397.

66. J. van Dongen et al. *Genetic and environmental influences interact with age and sex in shaping the human methylome* // Nature Communications. 2016. Vol. 7. P. 11115.

67. Gems D., Partridge L. *Stress-response hormesis and aging: «That which does not kill us makes us stronger»* // Cell Metabolism. 2008. Vol. 7(3). P. 200–203.

Mindfulness as the Foundation of Wellbeing

68. Goleman, D., & Davidson, R. J. *Altered Traits: Science Reveals How Meditation Changes Your Mind, Brain, and Body*. Avery Publishing, 2017.

69. Killingsworth M. A., Gilbert D. T. *A wandering mind is an unhappy mind* // Science. 2010. Vol. 330(6006). P. 932.

70. Baumeister R. F., Hofmann W., Summerville A. et al. *Everyday Thoughts in Time: Experience Sampling Studies of Mental Time Travel* // Personality and Social Psychology Bulletin. 2020. Vol. 46(12). P. 1631–1648.

71. Kabat-Zinn J. *Full catastrophe living: Using the wisdom of your mind and body to face stress, pain, and illness.* — Random House, New York, 1990.

72. Segal Z. V., Williams J. M. G., Teasdale J. D. *Mindfulness-based cognitive therapy for depression: A new approach to preventing relapse.* — Guilford Publications, 2002.

73. Dahl C. J., Wilson-Mendenhall C. D., Davidson R. J. *The plasticity of wellbeing:*

A training-based framework for the cultivation of human flourishing // PNAS. 2020. Vol. 117(51). P. 32197–32206.

74. Ding X., Tang Y. Y., Tang R., Posner M. I. *Improving creativity performance by short-term meditation* // Behavioral and Brain Functions. 2014. Vol. 10(1).

75. Laukkonen R. E., Slagter H. A. *From many to (n)one: Meditation and the plasticity of the predictive mind* // Neuroscience & Biobehavioral Reviews. 2021. Vol. 128. P. 199–217.

76. Kral T. R. A., Schuyler B. S. et al. *Impact of short-and long-term mindfulness meditation training on amygdala reactivity to emotional stimuli* // Neuroimage. 2018. Vol. 181. P. 301–313.

77. Baer R. A., Smith G. T., Hopkins J. et al. *Using self-report assessment methods to explore facets of mindfulness* // Assessment. 2006. Vol. 13(1). P. 27–45.

78. Baer R. A., Smith G. T., Lykins E., Button D. et al. *Construct validity of the five-facet mindfulness questionnaire in meditating and nonmeditating samples* // Assessment. 2008. Vol. 15(3). P. 329–342.

Empathy and Social Connections

79. Goleman, D., Davidson, R. J. *Altered Traits: Science Reveals How Meditation Changes Your Mind, Brain, and Body.* Avery Publishing, 2017.

80. Vaillant G. E. *Aging Well: Surprising Guideposts to a Happier Life from the Landmark Harvard Study of Adult Development.* — Little, Brown and Company, 2003.

81. Tomova L., Wang K. L., Thompson T. et al. *Acute social isolation evokes midbrain craving responses similar to hunger* // Nature Neuroscience. 2020. Vol. 23(12). P. 1597–1605.

82. Warneken F., Tomasello M. *Helping and Cooperation at 14 Months of Age* // Infancy. 2007. Vol. 11(3). P. 271–294.

83. Warneken F., Hare B. et al. *Spontaneous altruism by chimpanzees and young children* // PLOS Biology. 2007. Vol. 5(7). e184.

Goals, Values, and Meanings

84. Alimujiang A., Wiensch A., Boss J., Fleischer N.L. et al. *Association Between Life Purpose and Mortality Among US Adults Older Than 50 Years* // JAMA Network Open. 2019. Vol. 2(5). e194270.

85. Musich S., Wang S. S., Kraemer S., Hawkins K., Wicker E. *Purpose in Life and*

Positive Health Outcomes Among Older Adults // Population Health Management. 2018. Vol. 21(2). P. 139–147.

86. Cohen R., Bavishi C., Rozanski A. *Purpose in Life and Its Relationship to All-Cause Mortality and Cardiovascular Events: A Meta-Analysis* // Psychosomatic Medicine. 2016. Vol. 78(2). P. 122–133.

87. Fredrickson B. L., Grewen K. M., Coffey K. A. et al. *A functional genomic perspective on human wellbeing* // Proceedings of the National Academy of Sciences. 2013. Vol. 110(33). P. 13684–13689.

88. Ryff C. D., Singer B. H., Dienberg Love G. *Positive health: connecting wellbeing with biology* // Philosophical Transactions of The Royal Society B Biological Sciences. 2004. Vol. 359(1449). P. 1383–1394.

www.ingramcontent.com/pod-product-compliance
Ingram Content Group UK Ltd.
Pitfield, Milton Keynes, MK11 3LW, UK
UKHW030645220625
459968UK00008B/175